Y0-EMC-489

# Studies in the Philosophy of History

Selected essays from
**HISTORY and THEORY**
Edited by George H. Nadel

# STUDIES IN THE
# PHILOSOPHY OF HISTORY

Selected essays from *History and Theory*

ḥaRpeR ☫ τoRchbooκs

*A reference-list of Harper Torchbooks, classified
by subjects, is printed at the end of this volume.*

# HISTORY AND THEORY
## STUDIES IN THE PHILOSOPHY OF HISTORY

### Editorial Committee

RAYMOND ARON, *Paris*

ISAIAH BERLIN, *Oxford*

CRANE BRINTON, *Harvard*

PIETER GEYL, *Utrecht*

SIDNEY HOOK, *New York*

MAURICE MANDELBAUM, *Johns Hopkins*

A. D. MOMIGLIANO, *London*

JOHN PASSMORE, *Canberra*

W. H. WALSH, *Edinburgh*

# STUDIES IN THE PHILOSOPHY OF HISTORY

Selected essays from *History and Theory*

CAREY B. JOYNT & NICHOLAS RESCHER

JOHN PASSMORE

MARVIN LEVICH

GEORGE H. NADEL

LEE BENSON & CUSHING STROUT

JOHN BROOKE

HARRY ECKSTEIN

GEORGE LICHTHEIM

GABRIEL KOLKO

OTTO B. VAN DER SPRENKEL

EDITED BY

## GEORGE H. NADEL

HARPER TORCHBOOKS ❦ *The Academy Library*
Harper & Row, Publishers, New York

The selections in this volume appeared as articles in *History and Theory: Studies in the Philosophy of History*, a journal now in its fifth year. They are reproduced in full, without alteration.

My short Introduction serves to place the selections and the way they are grouped into the context of contemporary philosophy of history, as it is pursued in English-speaking countries. The footnotes to it consist of references to other relevant articles which have been published in the journal. Any reader already familiar with current trends in philosophy of history, or interested in individual selections but not the subject as a whole, should skip the Introduction.

The three groups of selections vary widely in subject matter and how it is discussed. But the authors do not vary in their belief that theory, like history, can be presented without straining the reader's credulit

D16
.8
.H625

0651265277

GEORGE H. NADEL

Editor of the journal
*History and Theory*

The articles in this volume first appeared in the following numbers of the journal *History and Theory*:
JOYNT & RESCHER, Vol. I, No. 2 (1961), pp. 150-162.
PASSMORE, Vol. II, No. 2 (1962), pp. 105-123.
LEVICH, Vol. II, No. 1 (1962), pp. 41-51.
NADEL, Vol. III, No. 3 (1964), pp. 291-315.
BENSON & STROUT, Vol. I, No. 2 (1960), pp. 163-185.
BROOKE, Vol. III, No. 3 (1964), pp. 331-347.
ECKSTEIN, Vol. IV, No. 2 (1965), pp. 133-163.
LICHTHEIM, Vol. IV, No. 2 (1965), pp. 164-195.
KOLKO, Vol. I, No. 3 (1961), pp. 243-260.
VAN DER SPRENKEL, Vol. III, No. 3 (1964), pp. 348-370.

D16
.8
.H625

GL

Articles reprinted from "History and Theory" Journal copyright © 1960, 1961, 1962, 1964, 1965 by History and Theory. Used with permission.

STUDIES IN THE PHILOSOPHY OF HISTORY:
Selected essays from *History and Theory*
Copyright © 1965 by George H. Nadel

All rights reserved. For information address Harper & Row, Publishers, Incorporated
49 East 33rd Street
New York, N.Y. 10016

First HARPER TORCHBOOK edition published 1965 by Harper & Row, Publishers, Incorporated
New York, Evanston and London.

BOSTON PUBLIC LIBRARY

# CONTENTS

# INTRODUCTION

## TO THE TORCHBOOK EDITION

### BY GEORGE H. NADEL

As long as philosophy of history dealt with sweeping theories about the progress of the world and the fate of mankind it did not make much headway with American and English scholars. In Germany and other countries where metaphysical and religious thought has long been the badge of scholarship, the subject has always enjoyed greater attraction. With us, philosophy of history on the grand scale has appealed chiefly to those who are intrigued by hidden drama and panoramic prophecy but unconcerned with the technicalities on which professional philosophers and historians insist.

That we are now confronted with a large amount of scholarly writing on the subject does not mean that our philosophers and historians have changed their mind. What has changed is their notion of what the subject should be about. Its function is not to speculate about the pattern of world history, to identify the forces which have shaped the human condition, or to elicit the meaning of history. It is to enquire into what historians do and what the meaning is of the procedures, techniques, statements, and language which they use. Philosophy of history today is about historical knowledge, not about history itself.

This new version of the subject does not fit into any neat pigeonhole. There are always points of intersection between enquiring into what historians do and enquiring into the process of historical events themselves, between analyzing our forms of knowledge about the past and making assumptions about the past itself. There are ways of doing philosophy of history which may not involve any philosophizing at all, like studying historiography, the history of historical writing; there are others which require a grounding in logic; and others again where a writer may expect from his readers a knowledge of sociology or of some other behavioral science. It may be disorderly to put such varied approaches under the umbrella of "philosophy of history." But at present this seems preferable to confining the term to one approach only, leaving the others out in the rain, or applying the term to the old version only and adopting some reorganizing label, like "historical methodology," for the new. Covering too much is often a characteristic of developing subjects. As the history of subjects like the former political economy or philosophical psychology shows, accumulation of knowledge will create reorganization, but reorganization will not of itself create knowledge.

Further, the new version is not altogether new. Enquiry into what his-

torians do has gone on for a long time. The very change in our conception
of philosophy of history owes much to the disputes current in the German
historical profession half a century and more ago. Also, there will always
be some scholars who will continue with speculations and theories about the
order of historical events, who prefer to start at the top and not at the
bottom, who want to reveal the meaning of history without trudging the
more circuitous path of technical analysis of historical knowledge. This
minority is not represented in the selections in these pages. Its work is
usually derivative of older concepts which lack objective verifiability; that
puts it outside one of the main criteria of admission to contemporary scholarship. On the other hand, there are old problems which persist in our
contemporary concerns. When philosophers of fifty or even a hundred years
ago proposed their schemes for the ordering of history, they sooner or later
encountered the problem of the relationship of knowledge of history to
knowledge of other phenomena, a problem whose roots reach back into
antiquity. Before long, the big question came up whether history should be
studied as a science, and if so, whether as a "soft" or a "hard" science, a
*Geisteswissenschaft* (at the time translated as "moral" science) or a *Na-
turwissenschaft* (natural science); or whether, as some philosophically un-
burdened English historians tended to maintain, history should be studied
as an art, like the story-teller's art. At present, we reargue this old dispute
by asking whether historians deal with matters that are unique or sufficiently
classifiable to permit generalizations; whether historians explain loosely like
ordinary users of language or rigorously like scientists; whether or not differing interpretations of the same historical events are a sign that historical
method lacks objectivity.[1] Even these topics are not all new. But their
presentation shows us very clearly some of the distinguishing new features
of contemporary philosophy of history. The appeal is to objectively com-
municable assumptions about scientific method or common experience and
language, not to subjective insights; the method of unpretentious logical
analysis has shrunk the big questions of an earlier day to more manageable
and answerable proportions.

[1] The first group of three articles deals with these arguments. Another approach has
been to enquire into the existence and form of "laws" in history, undoubtedly the
oldest and most familiar approach. Cf. James Fitzjames Stephen, "The Study of
History," written in 1861, published in *History and Theory* I, 2 (1961), 186-201, and
Maurice Mandelbaum, "Historical Explanation: The Problem of 'Covering Laws,' *ibid.*
I, 3 (1961), 229-242. While most of the opposition to the concept of scientific history
used to come from idealist doctrines and now comes from certain analysis philosophies, there is also an example of a modern philosophic defense of the "story-teller's
art" position: W. B. Gallie, "The Historical Understanding," *ibid.* III, 2 (1963), 149-
202. For an overall view of the problem see the highly informative analysis by
Isaiah Berlin, "History and Theory: The Concept of Scientific History," *ibid.* I, 1
(1960), 1-31, also reprinted in *Generalizations in Historical Writing*, ed. Alexander V.
Riasanovsky and Barnes Riznik, (Philadelphia: University of Pennsylvania Press,
1963), 60-113, and in *Philosophy of History*, ed. William Dray (New York: Harper
and Row, 1965).

Less oriented to primarily logical, and more to substantive, procedures is that part of philosophy of history which deals with historical theories. By historical theories we mean, first of all, theories about the study of history. This is in keeping with the orientation already mentioned. We also mean "theories" in the looser sense, the hypotheses, interpretations, and conjectures relating to the order or occurrence of historical events, insofar as they are subject to the historian's evidential tests. But this second kind is not our primary interest. It comes into our studies chiefly when we wish to illustrate that an inadequate theory did in fact lead to a wrong interpretation; or when we deal with systems where it makes no sense to separate theories about how we know historical events from theories about their causes—in Marxism, for example, what causes events to happen also conditions our knowledge of them.

Three types of approaches to the study of historical theories should be mentioned, though undoubtedly there are many others of equal usefulness. There is, first, the enquiry into what was said about the study of history at any given period. We may find that the views expressed, including those of practicing historians, were deductions from philosophical or literary theories but had little to do with the way in which history was actually written at that time. Or we may find that theory and practice were very closely related. Each state of affairs may be extremely revealing, as may be the change from one to the other, of the varying presuppositions of historical thinking. A second approach may fasten on some event, like a war or a revolution, whose scale and general significance have made it a convenient starting point for analyzing the variety of historical writing it has attracted. It is here that the historians' application of causality and other theoretical concepts can be tested and, by comparison to actual and ideal practice, analyzed for deficiencies. For here we are not discussing theories in the abstract nor selecting, as has sometimes been done, a casual statement by some inoffensive historian for unwarranted close analysis. The importance of the event is likely to have led historians to explicit theorizing; its significance to historiography is a presumptive guarantee that statements made about it are representative of fundamental views; and its complexity ensures that the commensurate complexity of theoretical analysis is likely to be warranted. A third approach may be the choice not of a prominent event, but of a prominent historian (or school of historians) to discover and to assess what kinds of tools are used. In the case of an historian who has been a major influence on historical writing and who has, moreover, explained his views and why he held them, a rare opportunity exists. The components and intellectual ramifications of one kind of historical theory are overtly presented, instead of having to be inferred from often unlikely evidence. What the historian tells us and what he does not tell us, in his autobiographical statements and in his work alike, will illuminate also what he considers significant differences between his own theory and those of others. From that our understanding of historical theory in general may be enriched.[2]

Finally, contemporary philosophy of history has a frontier province, frequently traversed but only recently beginning to be permanently occupied. That is the limitless area of the contact of history with other social sciences. So far, this has meant traffic with the older social sciences: political science, economics, anthropology, sociology, and, to a lesser degree, psychology. Whether the same will be possible with the newer social sciences, like communication theory and preferential-behavior and general-systems theories, it is too early to say. Nor can one foretell from the little evidence there is, whether such contact will resemble the more formal one that history has with natural science or the dual, formal as well as substantive contact with the older social sciences.

Each of the established social sciences has to deal with historical data, even if in some of them this shows only as case "histories" of phenomena studied. Therefore, the social sciences have a long, and presumably instructive, experience with concepts whose application involves the passage of time —in short, with history and theory. It would bore the reader to list here the characteristics of that experience in each of the established social sciences. Suffice to say that the formulation of these experiences has tended to make challenging if indirect contact with the historian's work when the formal or methodological aspects of some social theory are being analyzed. More direct contact has arisen, especially recently, when history-minded social scientists and social-science minded historians have explicitly set out to throw light on what is conventionally regarded as the historian's business.

This process, which usually involves some demonstration of how social theories should be handled or have been handled in the past, can take a great variety of forms. It could take the form of examining the anarchy, or at least the mass of mutually contradictory accounts, with which historians and political scientists have presented us in the study of phenomena like revolution. By way of contrast and of remedy, the social theorist would propose to us a proper way of handling that type of study: what factors pertaining to revolution should be isolated, and for what reason, and what kind of model would be the most feasible for ordering the variables involved. Another and quite different type of study is to take a social theory

2 The three articles of the second group represent these approaches. For the third approach cf. also. Raymond Aron, "Thucydide et le récit des événements," *History and Theory* I, 2 (1961), 103-128, and Pieter Geyl, "Huizinga as Accuser of His Age," *ibid.* II, 3 (1963), 231-262. Other interesting ways of tackling the historian's theoretical equipment include concentrating on one of the procedures historians use, as in Vernon K. Dibble, "Four Types of Inference from Documents to Events," *ibid.* III, 2 (1963), 203-221; and examining not merely what an historian's procedures were but their correct or incorrect assimilation by others, as in Georg G. Iggers, "The Image of Ranke in American and German Historical Thought," *ibid.* II, 1 (1962), 17-40.

or an important component of it, like ideology, and study its theoretical status as a function of its historical development—what it has meant at different historical periods. That is similar to what philosophers of history who study historical theories do. It so happens that the subject examined may belong to social, or more narrowly, to political theory; but often such theory functions as an historical theory, for there is little about society that lacks historical dimension. Another approach is also analogous to the study of historical theory. We have noted that the study of influential historians may be particularly rewarding. The same is true of influential social scientists, and for the same reasons. It is especially true when the theorist whom we study is a giant, not only in his influence, but in the range of his interests, and may have written more about history than most historians. Of these, Marx has been studied to the point of general familiarity and continues to be studied, though less now than in the past. It is his intellectual opponent, Max Weber, who has recently come in for much attention by American sociologists, many of whom are his debtors. He and others have influenced analysis, in terms of social theory, of certain significant historical developments for which there seem to be no obvious—or only oversimplified—explanations. A critical investigation of the factors supporting or defeating Weber's own various analyses is an important contribution to the social-science aspect of philosophy of history.[3]

The attention to philosophical, primarily logical, analysis; enquiry into historical theories; and concern with social-theory oriented methods are not the only components of contemporary philosophy of history. But they seem to be forming themselves, however loosely, into the major divisions of the subject. The reader may therefore take the selections in this volume as a fair sample of the present state of the subject and of its probable course in the future.

[3] The four articles of the third group exemplify the various methods here discussed. See also the symposium issue "Uses of Theory in the Study of History," *History and Theory* III, 1 (1963), in which a sociologist, a psychology-oriented historian, and a political scientist apply their respective theories, each to a concrete historical problem. For psychology, on which not enough sustained theoretical work in relation to history has yet been done to permit inclusion in these selections, see the review essay by Donald B. Meyer on Erik II. Erikson's *Young Man Luther: A Study in Psychoanalysis and History* (New York: W. W. Norton & Co., 1958) in *History and Theory* I, 3 (1961), 291-297, also reprinted in *Psychoanalysis and History,* ed. Bruce Mazlish (Englewood Cliffs: Prentice Hall, 1963), 174-180; Mazlish's pioneering anthology is itself reviewed by Robert J. Lifton, *ibid.* IV, 3 (1965). All of this relates to the direct contact between history and other social sciences mentioned above, namely, application of social theory to substantive historical work, whether to a study of a revolution or a biography. For a sample of the indirect contact, namely, analysis of relevant social-science concepts whose applicability is kept on a general level only, see Peter Berger and Stanley Pullberg, "Reification and the Sociological Critique of Consciousness," *ibid.* IV, 2 (1965), 196-212. For discussion of an important book demonstrating both, specific application and general concept analysis, see Bernard Barber's review essay on Neil J. Smelser, *Theory of Collective Behavior* (New York: The Free Press of Glencoe, 1963), *ibid.* IV, 2 (1965), 264-271.

# I

## HISTORY AND
## PHILOSOPHICAL THEORY

# 1.

## THE PROBLEM OF UNIQUENESS IN HISTORY

CAREY B. JOYNT *and* NICHOLAS RESCHER

### I. INTRODUCTION

The claim is frequently made that the mode of explanation to be found in history differs radically and fundamentally from the types of explanation found in the natural or social sciences. This difference is said to lie in the fact that history, unlike science, must always deal with "the description of a situation or state of affairs which is unique".[1] It is argued that the exclusive objects of historical understanding are unique, particular, concrete events: the historian, it is contended, is primarily concerned with describing and analyzing the *unique* features of his data, unlike the scientist who looks to the *generic*.

It is the thesis of this paper that such a claim for history (which, when properly understood, contains a large measure of truth) cannot, without severe qualifications, survive objections which can be brought against it. Practicing historians, it is true, sometimes try to defend the claim of history to uniqueness, but as a rule these efforts are swept aside by the critics as special pleading that does not come to grips with the substantive arguments which can be marshalled against them.

In the interests of clarity and truth it should be frankly recognized, to begin with, that, in a significant sense, every particular event whatsoever is unique:

Every insignificant tick of my watch is a unique event, for no two ticks can be simultaneous with a given third event. With respect to uniqueness each tick is on a par with Lincoln's delivery of the Gettysburg address! ... Every individual is unique by virtue of being a distinctive assemblage of characteristics not precisely duplicated in any other individual.[2]

That is to say, it would seem to be an elemental fact about the universe that all events whatsoever are unique. Every concrete natural occurrence is unique, even the occurrence of a so-called "recurrent" phenomenon like a sunrise or of "repeatable" events like the melting of a lump of sugar in a teacup.

[1] W. Dray, *Laws and Explanation in History* (London, 1957), 44.
[2] A. Grünbaum, "Causality and the Science of Human Behavior," *American Scientist*, 40 (1952), 665-676; reprinted in M. Mandelbaum, F. W. Gramlich, and A. R. Anderson, *Philosophic Problems* (New York, 1957).

Events are rendered non-unique *in thought only,* by choosing to use them as examples of a type or class. We refer alike to "an appearance of a comet" or "a sea-fight with sailing ships", and our use of such terms, when examined, suggests that the occurrences of natural history (in the sense of non-human history) do not differ as regards uniqueness from the events of human history. Whether an event is selected for treatment as a unique, concrete particular, or is treated as the non-unique exemplar of a class of events, is essentially a matter of human interest and perspective. Galileo, rolling a ball down an inclined plane treated each roll as identical for it served his purposes so to do, just as an historian speaking of the Black Death could, if he wished, treat each unique death as identical in its contribution to a class of events called "a plague". Like the scientist, the historian resolves the dilemma of uniqueness by the use of a large variety of classes in his discussions: "nations", "wars", "revolutions", "assassinations", "budgets", and the like. The list is endless. It cannot be maintained that the use of such classes sets history apart in that they fail to exhaust the unique structure of a particular person or event, for exactly the same holds true of all scientific classification. Only *some* of the features of a given particular are described in such a classification, and no set of generic classifications could conceivably exhaust the structure of the particular objects or events so described.

Bearing these general but fundamental comments in mind, let us now examine in more detail the claim that history deals, in some sense, with unique events. Three particular areas can be utilized to throw considerable light upon this central problem: the relation of history to the "historical" sciences, the role of generalizations in history, and the requirements of interpretation in history.

## II. THE RELATION OF HISTORY TO THE "HISTORICAL" SCIENCES

History, it is clear, has no monopoly on the study of the past. The biologist who describes the evolution of life, the sociologist or anthropologist who delves into the development of human organizations and institutions, the philologist who analyzes the growth and change of languages, the geologist who studies the development of our planet, and the physical cosmologist who investigates the evolution of the cosmos, all deal with essentially "historical" questions, that is to say, with the events and occurrences of the past. Many diverse areas of scientific inquiry have the past as the "target" of their researches. It is therefore natural and appropriate to ask: How does history (history proper, i.e., *human* history) differ from these other "historical" sciences?

In attempting a reply to this question, we must recognize that it is simply not enough to insist that history deals with the doings of men in the context of civilized society, however true this remark may be. The bio-medical student of human ecology is also concerned with man and his social environment, and of course anthropologists and sociologists study the activities of men in the context of human institutions, past no less than present. Consequently, there can be no adequate grounds for maintaining that history is to be distinguished from the "historical" sciences on the basis of subject-matter considerations alone.

Nor can a warrant for the distinction be said to inhere in the methodology of research. For here also there is no hard-and-fast barrier of separation between history and the sciences. History conforms fully to the standard hypothetico-deductive paradigm of scientific inquiry, usually described in the following four steps:

1. Examination of the data.

2. Formulation of an explanatory hypothesis.

3. Analysis of the consequences of the hypothesis.

4. Test of these consequences against additional data.

Historical research follows just this pattern: the historian assembles his chronological data, frames an interpretative hypothesis to explain them, examines the consequences of this hypothesis and seeks out the additional data by which the adequacy of this hypothesis can be tested. The universal characteristics of scientific procedure characterize the work of the historian also. And even if the specific form which this generic process takes in history were to differ from that which it assumes in other areas of science in certain points of detail, this would be irrelevant to the matter at issue.[3] Botany has less need for the algebraic theory of matrices than does quantum-mechanics or the economics of production-processes; however, this does not mean that such differences in mathematical requirements can be used as a basis for claiming that these fields can be delimited on methodological grounds.

It thus appears that the definitive characteristics of history are to be found neither in its subject-matter nor in its methods. Does it follow that there is no essential difference between history and the "historical" sciences? Not at all! But to see the precise character of the distinction we must examine closely the relative role of datum and theory, of fact and law in various sciences.

Throughout the various sciences, including all of those sciences which we

[3] We do not mean to deny that in certain fields of scientific inquiry students can take advantage of their ability to repeat experiments, to devise so-called crucial experiments, and that this is a privilege denied to all the historical sciences. This issue is too intricate to be discussed adequately in a paper of this length. We would only remind our readers that (1) non-repeatability of experiments does characterize certain of the natural sciences also, and (2) so-called "thought experiments" are available to historians even as they are to physicists.

have here characterized as "historical", we find that the object of the science is the study of a certain range of basic "fact" with a view to the discovery of generalizations, ideally universal laws, which govern the range of phenomena constituting this factual domain. In consequence, particular facts have a strictly *instrumental* status for the sciences. The "facts" serve as data, as means to an end: the law. In the sciences, the particular events that comprise the facts studied play an indispensable but nonetheless strictly subordinate role: the focus of interest is the general law, and the particular fact is simply a means to this end.

In history, on the other hand, this means-end relationship is, in effect, reversed. Unlike the scientist, the historian's interest lies, first and foremost, in the particular facts of his domain. But of course he is not solely interested in historical facts and in describing them. For this is mere chronology, which may constitute the inevitable starting-point for history, but is by no means to be confused with history itself. The historian is not simply interested in dating events and describing them, but in *understanding them*. And "understanding" calls for interpretation, classification, and assessment, which can only be attained by grasping the relationship of causal and conceptual interrelation among the chronological particulars.

It is a failure to grasp this essential point which vitiates Dray's argument that it is of the essence of historical explanation that it deals with a "continuous series" of happenings and that this model of a continuous series best describes the offerings of historians.[4] In fact a continuous series of events is, taken by itself, simply chronology no less and no more. The following example, in the form of a continuous time series, illustrates the point at issue:

"At 10 A.M. Napoleon began his breakfast. At 10:20 he took off his night attire, called for his riding clothes and at 10:35 kissed his wife good-bye. At 11 A.M. he attended a meeting of his commanders, decided to begin the campaign in ten days, and returned to his quarters at 1 P.M. At 1:02 P.M. he scratched his head, patted his forelock, and at 1:03 P.M. he sat down reflectively before the large portrait of a former mistress."

It is just at this point that scientific generalizations and laws enter upon the scene. They provide the necessary means for understanding particular facts; they furnish the fundamental patterns of interrelationships that constitute the links through which the functional connections among particular events may be brought to view.

Now if this analysis is correct, it is clear that the historian in effect reverses the means-end relationship between fact and theory that we find in science. For the historian *is* interested in generalizations, and *does* concern himself with them. But he does so not because generalizations constitute the aim and objective of his discipline, but because they help him to illuminate the particular facts with which he deals. History seeks to provide an *understanding*

[4]  Dray, *op. cit.*, 66-72.

*of specific occurrences,* and has recourse to such laws and generalizations – largely borrowed from the sciences, but also drawn from ordinary human experience – which can be of service in this enterprise. But here the role of generalizations is strictly instrumental: they provide aids towards understanding particular events. The scientist's means-end relation of facts to laws is thus inverted by the historian.

Correspondingly, the very way in which history concerns itself with the past is quite different from that of the "historical" sciences. The historian is interested in the particular facts regarding the past *for themselves,* and not in an instrumental role as data for laws. Indeed, unlike the researcher in "historical" science, the historian is not a *producer* of general laws, but a *consumer* of them. His position *vis-à-vis* the sciences is essentially parasitic. The generalizations provided by anthropology, sociology, psychology, etc., are used by the historian in the interests of his mission of facilitating our understanding of the past.

On this analysis, the line of distinction between history and the "historical" sciences is not an obvious, but a rather subtle matter. Thus both the sociologist and the historian can take interest in precisely the same series of phenomena: say the assimilation of Greek learning into medieval Islam. And both may bring essentially the same apparatus to bear on the study of the facts. But for the sociologist this is a "case study" undertaken in the interests of a general characterization of the generic process of the cultural transplant of knowledge. The study serves solely as an "input", as data for a mind seeking to provide rules governing this range of phenomena in general. Now this line of approach will also interest the historian, and any general rules provided by the sociologist would be material which the historian will gladly put to use in his study of Islamic cultural history. But his interest in such generalizations is purely instrumental as a means for explicating what went on in the particular case under study. Generalizations he must have, if he wishes to reveal interpretative links among events and to surpass mere chronology. But his aim is a clarification of the past *per se,* and his purpose is to provide an understanding of the past for its own sake, not merely as an instrument in the search for laws. The difference, then, between history and the "historical" sciences resides neither in subject-matter nor in method, but in the objectives of the research, and the consequent perspective that is taken in looking at the past. History does not collect facts to establish laws; rather, it seeks to exploit laws to explain facts. In this lies part of history's claim to uniqueness.

To obtain a clearer view of this essentially distinctive and characteristic relationship of fact and law in history, it will be necessary to examine more closely the role played by generalizations in history.

### III. THE ROLE OF GENERALIZATIONS IN HISTORY

The question of the role of generalizations in history bears intimately upon the problem of the uniqueness of historical events. Since generalizations must, in the nature of things, deal with *types* or *classes* of events, it follows that they can have pertinence to specific, particular events only insofar as these are typical and classifiable, i.e., just insofar as they are *not* unique. Thus, determination of the extent to which generalizations can play a legitimate and useful role in history offers the best means of pin-pointing those ways in which historical events can properly be said to be "unique".

Perhaps the most famous thesis regarding the role of generalization in history is the doctrine which holds that there is one single grand law governing the fate of nations, empires, civilizations or cultures. On such a view, all of the really major and large-scale transactions of history fall inevitably into one and the same basic pattern. The principal and characteristic function of the historian is to discern and then articulate this supreme generalization which pervades the regularity inherent in the historical process, a procedure familiar to readers, in the present century, through the work of Spengler and Toynbee. On a view of this nature, uniqueness has at best a very restricted role in history, being limited to points of detail, in virtue of the predominant status of the basic pattern of regularity.

In reaction against this kind of thesis, various theorists have taken their position at the very opposite extreme, and have espoused the view that generalization has no place whatever in history. This view may be characterized as "historical nihilism". On this conception, the supreme fact of historical study is the total absence of generalizations from the historical domain. Pervasive uniqueness becomes the order of the day. The historian, it is argued, inevitably deals with non-repeatable particulars. Generalization is not only unwarranted, it drastically impedes all understanding of the data of history.

Our own view lies squarely between these two contrasting positions. The plain fact is that no grand generalization of the "pattern of history" has ever been formulated which is both (1) sufficiently specific to be susceptible to a critical test against the data and (2) sufficiently adequate to survive such a test. Thus it is not, in our judgment, to such a thesis that one can look for an acceptable account of the place of generalization in history. On the other hand, it is demonstrable that failure of the grand generalization approach to history in no way justifies ruling generalizations out of the historical pale. To see why this is so requires a closer look at the role of laws and generalizations in history.

To begin with, it is clear that the historian must make use of the general laws of the sciences. He cannot perform his job heedless of the information provided by science regarding the behavior of his human materials. The teachings of human biology, of medicine, or of psychology can be ignored by the historian only at his own peril. The facts offered by these sciences regarding the mortality and morbidity of men, their physical needs for nourishment, sleep, etc., their psychological make-up, and the like represent essentially unchanging constants in the functioning of the human materials with which history deals. Nor can the physical sciences which describe the behavior of man's environment, again by means of general laws, be ignored by the historian. History must ever be re-written if only because the progress of science leads inescapably to a deepening in our understanding of historical events. And because the general laws of the sciences deal with the fundamental constancies of nature, and not with idiosyncratic particulars, their role in historical understanding is a primary locus for *non-uniqueness* in history.

Going beyond this, it is important to recognize that the general laws of the natural sciences do not constitute the only basis of generalization in history. These sciences give us the characterization of the physical, biological and psychological boundary conditions within which man must inevitably operate. But there are also sets of boundary conditions which stem from man's *cultural* rather than his physical environment. These bring to the scene of historical explanation the general laws of the social sciences, which create further conditions of non-uniqueness.

Nor is this the whole story. We must now consider another mode of generalization that has pivotal importance in historical explanation, namely generalizations which represent not the strictly universal laws to which we are accustomed from the sciences, but *limited* generalizations. Such limited generalizations are rooted in *transitory regularities,* deriving from the existence of temporally restricted technological or institutional patterns. Some explanation regarding these is in order.

In any given state of technological development, various definite rules can be laid down regarding the performance of various functions within this particular state of technology. An example from the history of military technology may help to clarify this. Consider the statement: "In the sea-fights of sailing vessels in the period of 1653–1805, large formations were too cumbersome for effectual control as single units." On first view, this statement might seem to be a mere descriptive list of characteristics of certain particular engagements: a shorthand version of a long conjunction of statements about large-scale engagements during the century and a half from Texel (1653) to Trafalgar (1805). This view is incorrect, however, because the statement in question is more than an assertion regarding the characteristics of certain actual engagements. Unlike mere description, it is a true generalization in that it can serve to explain developments in cases to which it makes no reference. Furthermore, the statement has counterfactual force. It asserts that in literally any large-scale fleet action fought under the conditions in question (sailing vessels of certain types, with particular modes of armament, and with then extant communications methods) effectual control of a great battle line is hopeless. It is claimed, for example, that had Villeneuve issued from Cadiz some days earlier or later he would all the same have encountered difficulty in the management of the great allied battle fleet of over thirty sail of the line, and Nelson's strategem of dividing his force into two virtually independent units under prearranged plans would have facilitated effective management equally well as at Trafalgar.[5]

The statement in question is thus no mere descriptive summary of particular events; it functions on the more general plane of law-like statements in that it can serve as a basis for explanation, and exert counterfactual force. To be sure, the relevant individual descriptive statements which are known do provide a part of the appropriate evidence for the historical generalization. But the content of the statement itself lies beyond the sphere of mere description, and in taking this wider role historical generalizations become marked as genuine law-like statements.

Nevertheless, such historical generalizations are not unrestricted or universal in the manner in which the laws of the physical sciences are, i.e., they are not valid for all times and places. An historical generalization is limited, either tacitly or expressly, to applicability within specific geographic and temporal bounds. Usually, historical generalizations are formulated by explicit use of proper names: names of places, of groups of persons, of periods of time, of customs or institutions, of systems of technology, of culture, or the like. The restriction of application in such cases is overt in the formulation of the law. Sometimes, however, such limited generalizations are formulated as unconditionally universal statements. But in such cases the statement properly interpreted takes on a conditional form of such a kind that its applicability is *de facto* tightly restricted. If sailing ships and contemporary naval technology and ordnance *were* reinstated, the tactical principles developed from the time of Tromp and de Ruyter to that of Rodney and Nelson would prove valid guidance. But the applicability of these tactical principles is conditional upon the fulfillment of conditions which cannot reasonably be expected to recur. (This is not true of certain experimental situations in physics – like the Michelson-Morley experiment – which merely are rarely repeated.) It is clear that analogous examples of limited generalizations can be drawn from every field of technology: production, agriculture, communication, resource exploitation, medical practice, etc. And such technology-based generalizations will inevitably be of limited scope, being valid for only a particular period and era.

A second major source of limited generalizations is constituted by the entire sphere of institutional practices. Social customs, legal and political institutions, economic organization, and other institutional areas, all con-

---

[5] The example from naval history and its analysis is taken from O. Helmer and N. Rescher, "On the Epistemology of the Inexact Sciences," *Management Science*, 6 (1959), 25-52.

stitute sources of such limited generalizations. Thus a limited generalization can be based, for example, upon the U.S. practices of holding a presidential election every four years, and a population census every ten. Here again we have regularities which are limited, in temporal (and of course geographic) scope to an era during which certain fundamental institutional practices are relatively constant. Such institutional patterns will of course be of immense value to the historian in providing an explanation for the relevant events. He will seek to discover such institutional regularities precisely because they afford him the means to an explanation of occurrences. Events within a limited period can be understood and explained in terms of the limited generalizations which capture the particular institutional structure of this era. And the existence of institutionalized patterns of regularity again makes for a limitation upon the extent to which "uniqueness" obtains with respect to the data with which the historian deals.[6]

It should be noted, however, that the utilization in historical explanations of limited generalizations based upon reference to temporary technological and institutional eras does not provide the basis for a fundamental separation between history and the natural sciences. Such reliance upon transitory regularities does not make a place for uniqueness in history in any absolute sense. After all, the past stages of biological and cosmological evolution are also non-repetitive. And thus the "historical" departments of the natural sciences must also deal with non-recurring eras. And in these domains, limited generalizations can – and sometimes are – also formulated. But as a rule the scientist is concerned with such limited regularities only as a way-station en route to the universal laws which are the main focus of his interest, and therefore tends, by and large, to be relatively aloof to the peculiarly limited generalizations which also could be formulated for his domain. But the historian, whose interest must focus upon the understanding of particular events and not the formulation of universal generalizations, has a much larger stake in limited generalizations.

The upshot of the present analysis of the role of generalizations in history can thus be summarized as follows. History must and does use generalizations: first as a consumer of scientific laws, secondly as a producer of limited generalizations formulated in the interests of its explanatory mission and its focus upon specific particulars. The use of all of these types of generalizations in history is indispensable for the historian's discharge of his interpretative mission. Interpretation demands that he be able to spell out the linkages of causation and of influence between events, and this can only be done in the light of connecting generalizations. To see this more clearly, and to attain a fuller perspective of the place of interpretation in history, we turn now to an analysis of what is involved in historical interpretation.

[6]  This argument was set forth in C. B. Joynt and N. Rescher, "On Explanation in History," *Mind*, 68 (1959), 383-388.

## IV. THE REQUIREMENTS OF INTERPRETATION IN HISTORY

The considerations so far brought forward do not, however, fully meet the hard core of the claim so clearly and forcefully stated by Dray that "historical events and conditions are often unique simply in the sense of being different from others with *which it would be natural to group them under a classification term*" so that the historian is "almost invariably concerned with [an event] as *different* from other members of its class".[7] Thus the thesis claiming a characteristic role for uniqueness in history is based in the final analysis upon the assertion that historical events are "unique" in the sense that *all* classifications used will fail at a critical juncture to illuminate adequately the event in question, since the event differs in its essential characteristics from its associates in these classes.[8]

This claim of Dray's contains a vital element of truth, but it would be an error to press this thesis too far. The sad fact is that a history composed of strictly non-repeatable occurrences would be mere chronicle. Any efforts to establish connections among events, and to exhibit their mutual relevance and significance would be excluded by a strict application of Dray's dictum. But, of course, history deals not only with what has happened, but with the assessment of the significance of what has occurred. The historian is interested in Napoleon not only as a person with a unique assemblage of characteristics, but as the leader of a national group in a crucial period of its history. The moment one leaves the bare statement of brute fact and occurrence, and turns to interpretation, stark and atomic uniqueness is necessarily left behind. Interpretation and explanation forces the historian to become involved in the problem of causation, and hence to abandon uniqueness.

The inescapable fact is that the mere *record* of what happened does not suffice to *explain* anything, as Randall has so clearly pointed out.[9] On the contrary, it presents us with a series of problems, the understanding of which can be attempted only by introducing common-sense generalizations of how people act and why events happen the way they do, or by the application of knowledge derived from the sciences.

It is undeniably true that history deals with "events that are related by their position in time ... ".[10] But this surely explains very little. All events whatsoever occur within the temporal pattern, and the occurrences of history

[7]  Dray, *op. cit.*, 47.

[8]  Compare the discussion by N. Rescher, "On the Probability of Non-Recurring Events," appearing in the *Proceedings* of the December 1959 Chicago Symposium of Section L of the American Association for the Advancement of Science.

[9]  J. H. Randall, Jr., *Nature and Historical Experience* (New York, 1958), 61-64.

[10]  *The Social Sciences in Historical Study. A Report of the Committee on Historiography*, Bulletin 64 (New York, 1954), 24.

in this respect present no facets which set them apart from the events studied by the sciences. What is important for the study of history is not that its events are related by their position in time, which is at best merely a statement to the effect that events happened at a particular moment and not at another, but that it is possible to delineate time periods within which human events have a *structure* which differs in certain respects from their structure at earlier or later periods in the temporal process. The way in which men act changes over time in a way which is not true of the behavior of carbon atoms.

This thesis in no way implies that a particular structure of events thereby acquires a set of characteristics which are explicable simply by virtue of its having occurred at a particular moment in time. Rather it asserts that a particular structure of events, obtaining as it did in a particular stretch of time, must be carefully examined in order to determine the set of boundary conditions under which those events occurred. The result is to produce a series of temporally limited generalizations, which represent the central contribution of the historian. It is in this sense of a concern with temporally limited *patterns* that history deals with the "unique", and this is not a uniqueness encompassed by mere chronology. To argue otherwise is to debase history, and to confine it to the mere chronological description of brute facts. History takes its unique character not from chronology as such, but from the connection which exists between the temporal process and the existence of the limited generalizations which give a specific character to a particular historical epoch or set of historical conditions.

The wide divide separating a mere narrative chronicle from an historical account proper can best be illustrated by an example. Consider the following narrative: "On July 28, 1914 Austria-Hungary declared war on Serbia. On July 30 the Russians ordered general mobilization. On August 1 Germany declared war on Russia and on August 3 on France. The British declaration of war occurred on August 14, 1914."

As it stands this is mere narrative, in that it confines itself to a bare recital of events. In its stark nakedness it deals only with brute fact. It is a mere skeleton, lifeless, and by itself possessed of only small meaning and significance. Yet it presents within its few lines the beginnings of a tragedy which, before its end, shook the civilized world to its very foundations.

For such a passage to acquire meaning and significance – in order for it to become history – the events described must be interpreted and explained. A perusal of adequate historical accounts based on these events, whatever final form they assume, will be found to deal with a wide variety of patterns involving both generalizations and general notions in the explanation they seek to provide. Thus in our example, the events will be portrayed in terms of the balance of power, rival alliance systems, the impact of military men upon civilian leaders, the problems of cohesion in a nation-state, and the problems of decision-making under conditions of radical uncertainty, to name but a few.[11] If one examines a detailed account of how the government of one state alone viewed the decision to act or to stand aside, a fascinating picture emerges of men weighing anxiously the news arriving in the diplomatic telegrams, deeply divided as to their best course of action on grounds both practical and moral, and finally when the invasion of Belgium had begun, presenting its decisions for ratification or rejection before the institution of Parliament to which it was responsible.[12]

An examination of any satisfactory historical account of a series of events shows clearly the indispensable role played by categories, classifications and generalizations (whether universal or limited in range). Such concepts will contribute in two main ways to the reconstruction of events by the historian.

In the first place, the concepts enable the historian to *select* important and relevant facts from the infinite number of facts which are available to him. It often occurs that the body of pertinent fact is overwhelming in scope, and that the task of the historian requires judicious selection. No practicing historian has stated this proposition with greater clarity than Lord Macaulay in his *Essay on History*:

Perfectly and absolutely true it [history] cannot be; for to be perfectly and absolutely true, it ought to record *all* the slightest particulars of the slightest transactions – all the things done and all the words uttered during the time of which it treats. The omission of any circumstance, however insignificant, would be a defect. If history were written thus, the Bodleian library would not contain the occurrences of a week. What is told in the fullest and most accurate annals bears an infinitely small proportion to what is suppressed. The difference between the copious work of Clarendon and the account of the civil wars in the abridgement of Goldsmith vanishes when compared with the immense mass of fact respecting which both are equally silent. No picture, then, and no history, can present us with the whole truth: but those are the best pictures and the best histories which exhibit such parts of the truth as most nearly to produce the effect of the whole. He who is deficient in the art of selection may, by showing nothing but the truth, produce all the effect of the grossest falsehood.

Without the guidance of generalizations and general concepts, the historian would be trapped and bogged down – drowned if you will – in the welter of concrete particulars. A general concept, such as that of a "General Staff" and its corporate role in military decisions, enables historians to ignore a multitude of details which have little or no bearing upon the choices eventually made. The concept of "an alliance" in turn permits a writer to select a whole series of events directly relevant to the eventual decisions which were taken, and to erect a structure of explanation based upon it.

Secondly, such generic concepts have particular importance for the *expla-

---

[11]  See for instance A. J. P. Taylor, *The Struggle for Mastery in Europe: 1848–1918* (Oxford, 1954), 511-531.
[12]  The British Government's decision is traced in graphic detail by G. M. Trevelyan, *Grey of Fallodon* (Boston, 1937), 276-306.

*nation* of the events in question. Their use essentially determines the meaning and significance of the account which finally emerges from the historian's efforts. They are, in short, absolutely crucial to the attempt of the historian to interpret his material, to raise it above the level of narrative and chronology to the status of true history. By utilizing, in the example cited above, the concepts of alliance systems, and of the organizational role of the military in their impact upon civilian statesmen, the historian can demonstrate that France believed the Triple Entente was necessary to her survival as a Great Power, and that Germany's policy decisions were heavily influenced by the general strategy of the Schlieffen plan. In this way, definite causal patterns are erected through the use of general concepts. Similarly, it can be demonstrated that the existing technology of the period played a vital part in the eventual decisions of the various powers to order general mobilization, or to issue an ultimatum to their opponents to cease such a procedure lest war follow. Here then we find limited generalizations serving to delineate the institutional boundary conditions under which men operated, enabling the historian to set up a general pattern into which particular events can be fitted and from which certain definite conclusions can justifiably be derived.

There can be little doubt that the use of categories, classes, and generalizations are absolutely essential to, and perform a vital function for, the adequate discharge of the historian's task. Indeed, taken together, they constitute the framework and structure of history, the setting in which the recital of particulars unfolds. They constitute the hard core of explanation and interpretation and, by their presence and the vital nature of the role they play, go a very long way indeed towards qualifying the claim that history deals solely or even primarily with the unique features of particular events.

*Lehigh University*

# 2.

## EXPLANATION IN EVERYDAY LIFE, IN SCIENCE, AND IN HISTORY *

### JOHN PASSMORE

The philosophy of history, like any other "philosophy of", suffers at least as much from the impatience of the specialist as it does from the philosopher's passion for generalizing. The philosopher, often enough, is interested in history only because it presents some sort of *prima facie* exception to his general logical theories. He wants to say, for example, that enquiry always issues in generalizations, and yet must admit that history seems not to do so; or he wishes to maintain that explanations always proceed by applying general laws, but finds it hard to point to the laws employed in historical explanations. So he begins with a certain sense of irritation toward the historian, as toward someone who seems serious enough but whose conduct yet bears the unmistakable marks of frivolity. He is scarcely likely, under these circumstances, to look at the historian's actual procedures in detail and with sympathy; his concern, rather, is to show that history could be, and ought to be, no real exception to his general thesis.

On the other side, the specialist wants to begin from history. If his general interests were in explanation, causality and the like, he would be a philosopher, not a historian; nothing in his training prepares him to talk about explanation or to listen to other people talking about it. Often enough, he does not even understand that a theoretical analysis naturally begins from very elementary or simplified examples, even if the analysis ought then to be applicable to the more complicated cases which normally confront us. Socrates' opponents thought it ridiculous that, even when his theme was the highest questions of morality and politics, he should choose his examples from the trivialities of everyday life; and the philosopher ever since has had to meet that same form of misunderstanding.

My own view is that the peculiarities of history have been exaggerated. It no doubt looks peculiar when it is contrasted with mathematical physics, but it would be absurd to take mathematical physics as the typical example of

* A shorter version of this paper was read at a symposium held at Brandeis University, March 30, 1960. A paper delivered at this symposium by Professor Maurice Mandelbaum is printed in *History and Theory* I, No. 3 (1961), 229-242.

enquiry; it could scarcely be more atypical. If we understand how explanation functions in everyday life, we shall have few difficulties with the procedures of the historian. To compare historical explanation with explanation in physics is useful only as a way of bringing out, once and for all, to how slight a degree history is scientific. If I discuss trivial everyday examples, it is not because I have any fondness for them, or any belief that philosophy should restrict itself to the elucidation of ordinary, or any other, usage; it is with the special purpose of emphasizing just how ordinary history is. Yet history is not for this reason any less important, or any less interesting, except to those who find the procedures of everyday life unimportant and uninteresting.

In everyday life there is a wide variety of circumstances under which we may offer, or be offered, what we should describe as "an explanation" of an occurrence. Consider the following:

(1) "As I got into the street-car, I noticed a large brown cylinder which was emitting a continuous clicking noise. The driver explained that I was to put my fare into it."

In this instance, I am confronted by an object which I do not know how to use. The explanation tells me how to use it, "what it is for".

(2) "On the menu, there was something called 'scrod'. The waitress explained that this is young cod."

As in case (1), I am being taught how to use something – a word. But the explanation now takes the form of a definition.

(3) "I asked him why I had to submit a report on a student at mid-term. He explained that this is the common custom in American universities."

My puzzlement in this case revolved about what I took to be an unusual procedure; the explanation consists in telling me that it is not unusual, that there is nothing to be puzzled about.

(4) "One of my students did not hand in his mid-term paper. I asked him to explain."

Here what I seek as an explanation is an excuse, a justification.

(5) "I found one passage in his essay very obscure. I asked him about it, and he explained what he was getting at."

To explain is, in this case, to elucidate, to paraphrase, to make clear how something fits into a general context.

(6) "I asked him how he had got home, and he explained that he first caught a subway, then a street-car, then a taxi."

The explanation fills in detail. I already know that he got home; the explanation tells me by what stages he did so.

(7) "I thought Mary was winking at me, but they explained that she had a tic."

In this case, to explain is to re-classify, or re-interpret.

(8) "I had always been told that all Americans were hearty hail-fellow

well-met sort of people, but he explained that this is only true of the Mid-Western."

"Explained to me" because I am puzzled about the discrepancy between what I had been told and what I have experienced; the explanation tells me that I have wrongly taken to be a universal characteristic of Americans what is, in fact, characteristic only of a special class of American.

(9) "I asked him why he wrote badly, and he explained that his school course laid very little stress on English composition."

The explanation, in this case, refers to precedent conditions – this is a typical causal explanation.

These types of cases, no doubt, flow into one another; on the other hand, there may be, almost certainly are, other distinguishable instances. Enough has been said, however, to indicate under what a variety of circumstances a piece of information can be offered as an explanation. The only common factor, so far as I can see, is that in each instance I am puzzled; the explanation sets out to resolve my puzzlement. It is not just that there is something I do not know; there is something I do not know when I ask: "At what time does the train leave for New York?", but that is not a request for an explanation. Being puzzled is a special sort of not knowing, not knowing "what to make of" a situation. The puzzling situation presents characteristics which are, from our point of view, unexpected; it interrupts the smoothness of our dealings with the world. The explanation, if we accept it, gets us moving again.

An explanation need not even be a reply to a question; we may offer an explanation to somebody who is standing before a turnstile and obviously does not know what to do next, or to a child whose voice sounds puzzled as he reads aloud. In such an instance, although we are not puzzled ourselves, we recognize what there is about the situation which, in some sense, "calls for" an explanation. This is a matter of experience; we have to know that the turnstile is an unusual one, or that the child has never met the kind of behavior about which he is now reading. For, of course, no situation is intrinsically puzzling. It is puzzling only to somebody who has not yet developed particular habits, particular forms of expectation. The turnstile is not puzzling to a daily commuter, although it may be quite baffling to a visitor from abroad. The Boston-bred will, no doubt, have learned the meaning of "scrod", or acquired the habit of putting his fare into a cylinder, not by asking for explanations but simply by imitation; he will not be puzzled by the withdrawn behavior of New Englanders because he will not expect anything else of his neighbors.

Before we start asking for explanations we have already acquired a multitude of such routine, habitual expectations. We know the English language, we know how menus are constructed; when we ask the waitress what scrod is, we expect an answer which will define it, in English, as a kind of food.

She knows this, too; she will not answer, except in a pert mood: "a mono-syllable", or even: "a kind of food"; although, in a different social context, just such an answer would be the appropriate one. If, indeed, pointing to the word "with" on the menu, or even "dinner", we ask the waitress, in English: "What does that mean?", she will be wholly bewildered. In this sort of context, this relationship between ourselves and the waitress, the question makes no sense.

More generally, an assumption of unfamiliarity is written into every request for an explanation; only those who realize what is unfamiliar to us will have any idea what question we are asking. Suppose I came home on a cold winter's night. The heating system is on; the house is warm; the front door is wide open. Then if I were to ask my wife: "Why is the heating system on?", "Why is the house warm?", she would think I was disturbed in mind. "Why is the front door open?", on the other hand, is a perfectly natural question – here is the break in routine. (In mid-summer, on the contrary, the first two questions would be quite natural; the last, quite likely, would be incomprehensible.)

That is why cases where I can be said to offer an explanation fade into cases where I say that no explanation is necessary. Suppose, asked why I am travelling by jeep to some point in Central Australia, I reply: "There is no alternative." The question presupposed that there was an alternative, that I could have gone by aeroplane, for example. What I have done is to reject that presupposed alternative; in one sense, my reply consists in asserting that my action needs no explanation, that there is nothing puzzling in my choosing a jeep. Yet, reporting this, is would be quite natural to say: "He explained that he had no alternative."

Similarly, when I ask why I have to submit a mid-term report on a student and receive the answer that this is an American custom, I am being told not to be puzzled. It is presumed that I have supposed this to be a demand made upon me in particular, or uniquely by my university; now this supposition is destroyed. Again, it would be natural to report this reply as: "He explained that this was the American custom." But one might also say: "I thought the behavior of this university needed some special explanation, but I found that it was just conforming to custom."

Everything depends, then, on what I know and what I want to know. If I am asked by an adult human being why Jones died, it will be no explanation to reply: "All men are mortal", for so much, it can be presumed, he knows already; that is not the unfamiliar feature of the situation that is bothering him. To a child, on the other hand, who is quite unfamiliar with the fact of death, such an answer can be an explanation, and all the explanation he needs. Similarly, when a stranger to America asks: "Why does the drugstore sell cigars?", it will normally be safe to presume that he is, wrongly, sup-posing that the drugstore is unique; the answer: "In America, drugstores do" will perfectly suffice as an explanation. He can go on to ask: "Why do they?", but he need not do so, and usually will not do so. In any case, this is a different question, one that is always permissible but never obligatory.

It follows from all this that there can be no purely formal definition of an explanation. The schema:

"All X are Y, P is an X, ∴ P is a Y"

can sometimes be used to explain why P is a Y, but it can also be used to test the hypothesis that all X are Y, to prove that P is Y, to calculate that it is Y, to predict that it will be Y. How the schema is used will depend on what we know and what we want to know; and these are not formal considerations. To revert to my previous example, we cannot say *a priori* that: "All American drugstores sell cigars, this is an American drugstore, therefore this drugstore sells cigars", is or is not an explanation. Addressed to a stranger, it can serve to explain why the drugstore sells cigars; addressed to a travelled American, who is really wondering why any American drugstore sells cigars but may express his puzzle by a reference to a particular case, it is no explanation at all. Sometimes it will be used to convince a doubter that he ought to enter the drugstore; it will be meant as a proof that this is where cigars are to be found. Sometimes it will be a formal prediction. Explaining, in short, is a particular way of using a form of argument; it has no logical form peculiar to it.

For each type of explanation, however, there is a way of deciding whether the explanation is a good one. A student who, when asked: "Why didn't you hand in your essay?", replies that he felt lazy, has not given a good explanation; for, in the context, a good explanation has to be an acceptable excuse. A "filling-out" explanation must leave no gaps; if I live ten miles from the university, it will not do to reply to the question: "How did you get home in the snow-storm?" with the answer: "Three miles by bus and then a mile walk." A good explanation of a passage by Shakespeare stands in a special sort of interpretative relation to the original text.

Few scientists would accept such a liberal interpretation of "explanation". In the *Phaedo*, Plato represents Socrates as protesting against the already-apparent tendency of Greek scientists to assimilate all explanations to explanation by precedent conditions. Aristotle's doctrine of the "four causes" – more accurately, the "four types of explanation" – temporarily stemmed the tide; but, by the end of the seventeenth century, the battle was substantially over. Hume does not for a moment doubt that an adequate explanation of any phenomenon must refer to precedent conditions. Definition, classification, interpretation, instructions for using, all came to be regarded as auxiliaries to explanation rather than as modes of explanation; justification and excuse-making were wholly excluded from enquiry; the mere removal of misconceptions was not dignified with the name of explanation. Physicists, indeed, came to suggest that their concern lies with functional relations rather than with causal relations; such an equation as $P_1 V_2 = P_2 V_2$, they pointed out, makes no reference to precedent conditions. But by itself it does not explain, either; and when it is used as an ingredient in an explanation – to explain why, for example, the volume of gas in a pump diminishes – the explanation is of a causal character. At the very least, one can say, the scientific assumption has been that explanation always consists in using a general law as a means of explaining the behavior of a particular case or kind of case.

Historians have not been so restricted or restrictive. They regard themselves as "explaining" *how* Rome was supplied with water, *what* a phrase in mediaeval law means, *that* Socrates' attitude to his wife was "common form" in Athens, as well as *why* Luther's revolt against the Roman Catholic Church was supported by the German Princes. Often enough, they count justifying as explaining; and if they detail the route taken by the British detachment from Boston to Lexington, consider themselves as "explaining" how it got there.

Indeed, although Polybius maintained that history is a mere panorama unless the historian uncovers causes, the fact is that causal analysis is only rarely the historian's concern. Consider even such an essay as Lord Acton's *The Political Causes of the American Revolution*, which certainly gives promise in its title of being a causal analysis. For the most part, it turns out to be a defense of the general thesis that "the dispute between absolute and limited power, between centralization and self-government, has been the substance of the constitutional history of the United States". In other words, it sets out to show that controversies which appear to turn around quite other issues (e.g. slavery) should be reclassified as disputes about State rights.

So much must be conceded to those who, like Professor Dray in his well-known *Laws and Explanation in History* and other works, have criticized the common assumption that whenever the historian professes to explain he must be offering a causal explanation; the historian's way of using the word "explanation" is, indeed, almost as liberal as that of the man in the street – certainly, it lies closer to his usage than to the physicist's. Yet it ought not to be concluded that the historian *never* offers causal explanations; or, more generally, that he *never* tries to show that the events with which he is concerned can be understood as instances of some general proposition. The historian, I should say, uses whatever generally acceptable type of explanation lies nearest to his hands; and causal explanation certainly plays a large part in everyday thinking. Thus, when Acton, in the same essay, writes that: "The war with England and the long suspension of commerce which preceded it, laid the foundations of a manufacturing interest in the United States", this explanation is causal, not reclassificatory.

I propose in what follows to concentrate my attention on causal explanation, because it illustrates with special clarity my principal theme: that the standards of a good explanation in history stand closer to those of everyday life than they do to those of physical science. But I am convinced that a similar tale could be told of explanation by reclassification or of explanation by definition.

By a causal explanation I mean one which explains a difference between two phenomena by pointing to some kind of circumstance which, under certain conditions, gives rise to that sort of difference. The "two phenomena" may be earlier and later stages in the development of the same thing – for example, the pre-manufacturing and the manufacturing stages in the development of the United States. The causal circumstance in this case, if Acton is right, is the cessation of imports. If Acton's is a good explanation, it must satisfy three requirements; it must be intelligible, adequate and correct. The difference between everyday, historical, and scientific explanation lies in the degree of severity with which these criteria are applied.

Consider, first, intelligibility. Suppose I ask: "Why did Jones die?" and get the answer: "Because there was a low-pressure system over Cape Cod." Then I shall be completely bewildered; I can "see no connection" between Jones' death and the presence or absence of a low-pressure system. In contrast, the answer "He died of influenza" is at least an intelligible answer, even if I judge it to be inadequate or incorrect. What makes the difference?

The low-pressure explanation could be expanded to make it intelligible. It might then run: "The low-pressure system gave rise to a heavy rainstorm, Jones was soaked and chilled, caught influenza and so died." We might then properly object that the reference to a low-pressure system was quite unnecessary (a macabre sort of joke), but the connections are at least intelligible. This example might suggest that, as Professor Dray seems to think, an intelligible explanation is one in which "all the gaps are filled in", just as they are filled in when I explain that I completed my ten-mile trip home by travelling five miles by bus and five by taxi. But in this latter instance, the gap reveals itself as soon as we substitute "three miles" for "five miles"; and it can be defined as a gap in purely arithmetical terms. In the low-pressure case, on the contrary, there is no objective test for there being, or not being, a gap to be filled in.

Is there a gap, for example, between the existence of a low-pressure system over Cape Cod and its raining in Boston? Certainly there could be. One can easily imagine a person who would be quite bewildered by an explanation of rainfall in terms of changes in pressure. Equally, however, he might *in principle* be bewildered by any explanation we care to offer; if at some stage he is not bewildered, this will be only because we light on a kind of connection with which he is familiar, not because there is some type of connection about which it is in principle impossible for him to be bewildered. This, more than anything else, is what Hume was concerned to point out in his analysis of causality. Cause and effect are always "distinct", in the sense that it is in principle always possible to be surprised by the fact that a particular cause has a particular effect. So, in this sense, there is always a gap which can never be filled – no explanation is *intrinsically* intelligible. But we can reverse this by saying that there is no gap, unless we feel there to be one.

At the everyday level, then, any explanation is intelligible provided that it relies upon a familiar sort of connection. It follows, of course, that an explanation may be intelligible at one time to one person and yet quite unintelligible at another time or to another person. Not long ago, we should all have rejected with incomprehension the explanation that somebody had acquired a gastric ulcer because he was "too conscientious". Nowadays, that sort of explanation would be widely accepted as intelligible. What has happened meanwhile? Are we now in a position to "fill in the gap" between conscientiousness and gastric ulcers? Not at all. Rather – I am speaking at the everyday level – we no longer feel that there is a gap. We have just "got used to" this sort of explanation, as we have "got used to" explanations of weather in terms of pressure systems, of diseases in terms of virus invasions, of mental disorders in terms of childhood patterns of behavior. At the same time, we have got unused to – so now reject as unintelligible – explanations of death in terms of witchcraft, cures in terms of touchings by royalty, mental diseases in terms of demonaic possessions. An explanation is intelligible, then, if and only if it refers to modes of connection which have come to be familiar to us.

To turn now to adequacy. Adequate explanations are a sub-species of intelligible explanations. Every adequate explanation is intelligible but not every intelligible explanation is adequate. An explanation is unintelligible if we "see no connection at all" between explanation and explicandum; it is inadequate if the connection is not "strong" enough. Told that a man died because he liked novels, we shall complain that the explanation is unintelligible; told that he died because he had influenza, we might criticize the adequacy of the explanation but not its intelligibility. An intelligible explanation points to conditions which *sometimes,* so we believe, cause death; to be strictly adequate it must point to conditions sufficient to produce death *in these particular circumstances.*

In fact, of course, our everyday requests for explanations are often polite rather than searching; the answer does not concern us greatly. Provided only that the explanation is intelligible we shall in most cases presume that it is both adequate and correct. We know quite well that influenza produces death only under certain circumstances, but we take it for granted that the special conditions were fulfilled. Only if we had some special reason for believing otherwise should we protest in the manner of Eliza Doolittle: "What call would a woman of that strength have to die from influenza?" Then the reply might come: "She had a weak heart", and that would almost certainly satisfy our everyday qualms, even if we are well aware that not everybody who has a weak heart and contracts influenza dies from it. In general, we accept an explanation as adequate if it refers to conditions of which we know that they wil in many circumstances produce the given effect, *unless we have some positive reason for believing that the circumstances were peculiar.*

This does not imply that we know what the circumstances are; in most cases, perhaps, we could not specify them. Sometimes nobody knows – nobody might be able to detail the special conditions under which influenza kills. If we have had considerable experience, however, we may develop a "feel" for the conditions, the experienced doctor might call for a post-mortem even if he could not say quite what made him suspicious. But, at the everyday level, if we refuse to regard an explanation as adequate unless it points to con- ditions which are strictly sufficient to produce the effect in question, we shall be obliged to regard almost any everyday explanation, in the form in which we accept it, as inadequate. Such strict sufficiency clearly is not required for adequacy in everyday life.

Sometimes our complaint that an explanation is not, even by these accom- modating standards, an adequate one, is met by a prolonged narrative rather than by some such simple statement as "she had a weak heart". Indeed, there are people who always cast their explanations in narrative form, with a meticulous concern for detail. "He came home from the office in a snow- storm; it was that sudden November storm; the snow was very wet; he had said he felt quite warm before he left home – it must have been the fever coming on – and he hadn't taken a coat . . ." etc., until we feel that the explanation is indeed an adequate one. Under these circumstances – and perhaps, we might add, with this woman as nurse – it is no wonder the man died.

Yet, if the story is coldly examined, we might be forced to admit that even in these elaborated circumstances the man could have survived, that such cases are not unknown. "Corroborative detail", as Pooh-Bah knew, often has a psychological effect not wholly justified by its logical force. So many factors have been particularized that we feel they must add up to a situation in which influenza would be a sufficient condition of death; but, of course, this need not be so. Once more, however, it would be cavilling to complain that the man's death might have been brought about by some factor other than influenza if we have no alternative explanation to offer and do not even know what additional conditions would have to be mentioned in order to satisfy us. A rough and ready test of adequacy, in these circumstances, is the reasonable one to employ.

Now for correctness. In judging an explanation to be correct, we at the same time take it to be adequate and intelligible. But it can be adequate and intelligible without being correct. We arrive home, perhaps, to find that a vase, dear to our sentimental heart, lies shattered on the floor; we ask our daughter for an explanation. "The wind", she tells us, "blew the curtain against the vase and knocked it off the table." This is certainly an intelligible and, by ordinary standards, an adequate explanation. Yet it may not be correct. Consider the following possibilities:

1. She has made a mistake. She thought the curtain knocked it over; in fact, it was the cat, concealed by the curtain.

2. She is lying, to save the cat from our wrath. There was no wind; the cat knocked the vase off the table.

3. Everything happened exactly as she says it did; but the vase did not break. She had always hated it and when she saw it lying on the floor unharmed she was so annoyed that she smashed it with a hammer.

4. The vase would certainly have broken, but she caught it as it fell. Then, regretting that she had saved it, she lifted it high in the air and let it fall.

Possibilities (1) and (2) depend on the unreliability of testimony; possibilities (3) and (4) on the fact that the explanation, although adequate by ordinary standards, has not pointed to a condition which is strictly *sufficient* to produce the effect. Vases fall without breaking. All four possibilities lie open only because, under the conditions as we know them, the action of the wind is not *necessary* to break the vase. So there is room for lying, or for an honest mistake, or for misleading silences, even when the vase lies there before us, smashed.

Just as in everyday life we usually accept an explanation as being adequate if it is intelligible, so too we generally presume that an adequate explanation is correct. We rely upon testimony unless we have special reason to be suspicious of it; and if we refused to accept an explanation as a good one unless it referred to necessary conditions, explanation would play a very small part indeed in everyday life.

Consider now the situation in science. Science, of course, developed out of our everyday activities. There were explanations, as there was proof, long before there was science. Nor has the connection with everyday procedures been entirely lost; the scientist, too, looks for an explanation when he is puzzled and tries, in his explanations, to remove that puzzlement. In important respects, however, he sets out to realize what, in everyday experience, only appears as an ideal limit.

Take first the case of intelligibility. The scientist has a great deal to do with changing our standards of intelligibility; he educates us into accepting explanations of weather-changes which refer to pressure systems, or explanations of disease which refer to viruses and bacteria. But he begins, as often as not, by taking as unintelligible, as being in need of an explanation, what seems to us already to be satisfactorily clear. In this sense, Karl Popper is right when, in opposition to the view (strongly supported by what we have so far said) that explanation derives the unfamiliar from the familiar, he argues that scientific explanation proceeds from the familiar to the un-familiar.

Thus we are not ordinarily puzzled in the slightest degree by the fact that if a porcelain vase is dropped from a height on to a hard floor it will break. That is just a familiar brute fact, which we use in explaining why a particular ornament has broken, but do not feel under any obligation to explain. The scientist, on the other hand, may begin to wonder why the vase breaks; not in the sense of wondering how this particular vase comes to get broken, but, rather, why porcelain vases break when dropped and metal vases do not. Very soon, indeed, he completely loses interest in the fate of our favourite vase – although its mishap might happen to be the stimulus which led him to reflect about fragility. The vase is transformed into a particular structure of molecules; our dropping it and the solid floor are expressed as forces. So, when the physical scientist explains why the vase breaks when we drop it, he no longer refers to familiar forms of connection between everyday objects – propositions like "the floor is hard" do not appear in his explanations – but to unfamiliar relations between unfamiliar objects. Indeed, unless we have been specially trained, the scientist's explanation will mean nothing to us. We understand a man who tells us a picture appears on the television screen because he pushed a button, but all this talk about ionized particles . . .

The scientist often works with quite special conceptions of intelligibility. Very often he presumes, in the fashion traditional to rationalistic philoso-phies, that some form of connection is intrinsically intelligible and that all explanations ought to exhibit one of these intrinsically-intelligible forms. For example, in everyday life explanations very often refer to ends or pur-poses; over considerable periods of human history this, indeed, has been the "normal form" of intelligible explanations. The Platonic-Aristotelian re-action against Milesian science tried to establish the teleological form of explanation as the truly intelligible pattern for science. The general tendency of science, however – although with powerful resistance from within biology – has been to argue that this sort of connection is not really intelligible; that a thing's "purpose" consists in certain of the effects which its activities produce (or, in the case of human action, which they set out to produce), and that it is unintelligible to suggest that these effects, or attempted effects, explain the activities themselves. Thus, whereas in everyday life it is quite natural to reply to the question: "Why did Jane go to town?" with the answer: "To buy a new hat", a "really intelligible" explanation, on this view, will refer to the stimulus of an advertisement, or of the sight of her neighbor's new hat, operating upon a Jane conceived of either as a mechanism of response or as a field of forces. Jane's going to town and her buying a hat will now be considered as stages in the response to a stimulus; they will not be related as explicandum to explanation.

There are very good reasons for taking this view: it is, indeed, unintelligible to suggest that something that might not exist at all (for the hat might not be bought) can be an explanation of something that does happen (the trip to town). Of course, in everyday life, when the psychologist is asked why his wife has gone to town, he will continue to reply: "To buy a hat", and will expect to be understood; just as the biologist might, when asked by his children why men have two eyes, explain that it enables them to tell more precisely where objects are; or the physicist, asked why the vase breaks, and the saucepan does not, might reply that the vase is fragile. In each case, however, he would think that he had not given the "real" explanation, but only a rough-and-ready clue to the real explanation.

As I have already suggested, this is in part because he accepts certain general metaphysical principles which we, too, may accept, e.g. the principle that only what is actual, not what is possible, can explain the occurrence of an act. But, as well, he may work with principles which are less defensible; for example, the principle that in some ill-defined sense an intelligible explanation must be "like" what it explains. This is why, as Hume pointed out, scientists were attracted by what we might call "billiard-ball" explanations. When a billiard ball moves as the result of the impact of another billiard ball, both the cause and the effect are moving billiard balls and the relation between them is the very familiar (and therefore "intelligible") relation of pushing.

In this deeper sense, the scientist does, after all, try to explain the unfamiliar in terms of the familiar – a special mode of connection as a variant of a very general, very familiar, mode of connection. Thus, for example, the behavior of gases is in many respects unique, quite unlike the behavior of solids; to explain it in terms of the movement of minute objects like tiny billiard balls rather than as a system of relationship between three distinct properties – pressure, motion and temperature – is to see in its behavior an exemplification of a familiar mode of connection.

Of course, "familiar" is a relative conception. What is familiar to the scientist might not at all be familiar to the man in the street. At first it was "natural" to explain electrical phenomena in terms of the more familiar behavior of fluids, as a "current" flowing through a wire just as a fluid flows through a pipe; but now the scientist may rather describe the behavior of fluids in terms of what have come to be familiar phenomena of electricity. The "normal form" of explanation, the form which to the scientist is peculiarly intelligible, has varied greatly as science has developed. At any given time, however, he is tempted to regard that "normal form" as being *intrinsically* intelligible, whereas, or so I have wanted to suggest, it is only a form of connection which happens to be, for some reason, particularly familiar to him. It is always possible, in principle, to seek an explanation of it, but at a given time it may not be fruitful to do so. (As it was once not fruitful to ask questions about what, in their internal structure, explained the behavior of cells.) The scientist looks for such a "normal form" of explanation because he is always seeking to develop a theory of the most general kind, one that will enable him to predict, as well as to explain; and the best hope of doing that is to seize upon some form of connection which is already known to be present in a diversity of cases and to try to extend it to other cases. However, as Hume also argued, a form of explanation in which both explicandum and explanation can be represented as different values of the same variable – as, for example, as different masses and accelerations – has no advantage in point of "rationality" over any other sort of explanation. That one body can move another by impact, for example, is no more "intrinsically" intelligible than that I can influence another human being by persuasion; the gain, if the second can be expressed in terms of the first, is in generality, not in intelligibility. But it can easily come to seem less intelligible to us, if our attention is almost wholly devoted to the study of impacts. Insofar as he believes that he can work towards a situation in which everything can be so displayed that its connections are *intrinsically* intelligible – a situation in which there are no "brute" facts – the scientist, I should say, is suffering under a particular kind of metaphysical illusion. But, undoubtedly, he can often persuade us to change our mind about what we take to be the form of an intelligible explanation.

As for adequacy, the scientist – again in part because he wishes to predict – will be dissatisfied with explanations which are less than strictly sufficient. Indeed, science in large part has consisted in looking for strictly sufficient and strictly necessary conditions where, at the everyday level, we can point only to sufficiency under unspecified conditions. This comes out in the special emphasis the scientist places on exceptions. At the everyday level, people were quite happy to say, for example, that swamps produced malaria, ignoring as unimportant exceptions the case in which swamp-dwellers did not get malaria or non-swamp dwellers contracted the disease. The discovery that the true cause is a bite from an infected anopheles mosquito arose out of the search for conditions which were truly sufficient and necessary. As in the malaria example, this may involve identifying a previously unknown agent; in other instances, it may rather proceed by way of a re-examination of the effect, so as to determine precisely the kind of effect for which the everyday "cause" is actually sufficient and necessary. Thus, for example, it was discovered that infection by a small-pox virus is necessary and sufficient to produce small-pox in *all* persons who *have not already had contact with cow-pox*.

For the scientist, the "adequate" explanations of everyday life are at best tentative hypotheses, to be explored critically in the search for conditions which are necessary and sufficient. For the most part, indeed, he is not to be fobbed off with an "adequate" explanation; he is looking for a *correct* explanation. But he has often to work for long periods of time with merely adequate hypotheses, hypotheses, for example, about hypothetical entities of which he can only say that if they possess such-and-such characteristics their existence would be sufficient to account for a particular range of effects. For example, the invasion of the body by minute imperceptible organisms would explain the mode of development of certain types of disease, or the existence of particles of such-and-such dimensions and such-and-such a charge would account for certain types of chemical relationship. (Of course, he can suport his "would account for" by his actual experience of organisms and of electrically-charged bodies, but the organisms and particles of his theory may not be discernible.) Some philosophers of science, conventionalist in their general outlook, have drawn attention to the use of such "fictional entities" in science in order to suggest that the physical scientist is really concerned only with *adequate* explanations, that in the higher reaches of science the notion of correctness has no place. But in fact the attempt – sometimes successful – to determine whether there *really are* such entities (to isolate a virus, to detect the presence of genes) has played a vital role in scientific enquiry. Only in contemplating the more abstract branches of physical science (which are certainly not typical of science in general) do we sometimes feel that there is no possibility of determining whether the alleged entities actually exist, and hence of transforming explanations believed to be adequate into explanations known to be correct or, what comes to the same thing, of showing that sufficient conditions are also necessary.

Now, at last, for history. In an article mainly addressed to the historian, the delay in reaching my proper purpose may seem to be both interminable and unjustifiable. It is deliberate; for, as I began by suggesting, very many of the difficulties and controversies which have recently emerged in the discussions of explanation in history flow from underlying misconceptions about the nature of explanation in general. The historian who is genuinely interested in the philosophy of history will have to widen his interests to consider many of the traditional problems of philosophy.

Unlike the scientist, the historian cannot presume that his audience, even when he is writing only for fellow-historians, is acquainted with any general principles which are usable as explanations, except such as are familiar to every educated man. Studying history does not consist in learning novel general propositions, but rather in becoming acquainted in depth with a particular historical period. The historian may know, as other people do not know, just what was the state of the English monasteries at the time of the Reformation or just what changes occurred during the composition of the Declaration of Independence; he would be delighted to know "what song the sirens sang, and what name Achilles took when he hid amongst the women"; but he is seldom a great reader of theoretical works. It is true that there are certain sorts of generalization of which the historian is master; but they are generalizations with a very limited range, propositions like: "In the Edinburgh of the early eighteenth century, it was still unsafe publicly to express unorthodox views on theology", which may be used to explain the cautious behavior of some particular critic of Christianity. But as for general propositions not thus limited in time and space, he has none of his own to deploy. Thus his standards of intelligibility are precisely those of the ordinary man; he presumes only such general modes of connection as are already familiar in everyday life. The general reader, attempting to read a major contribution to history, may find himself bored by the detail, but the explanatory principles involved, the arguments employed, the transitions from point to point, will certainly not bewilder him, as he will almost certainly be bewildered by any major contribution to science.

The historian's explanations, again, are couched in wholly familiar terms. The physicist transforms the wind, the curtain, the vase, the wooden floor into masses, velocities, accelerations; for the traditional historian, as for the ordinary man, they are the wind, the curtain, the vase, the wooden floor. The Marxists, indeed, set out to transform history in this respect; social and personal actions were to be transformed into productive forces, social institutions into productive relations. Tolstoy, I suppose, anticipated a similar transformation when, in *War and Peace*, he suggested that the historian should explain historical occurrences by referring to "the common, infinitesimally small elements by which the masses are moved". But no "scientific history", in this sense of the phrase, has yet recommended itself to the general body of historians. They still talk in terms of people, of parties, of States; neither explanation nor explicandum is represented as a complex of unfamiliar concepts.

Nowadays, no doubt, the historian may use economic or psychological explanations. He may write, for example, that "as a result of the sharp rise in interest rates, there was considerable unemployment"; but this is only because he thinks he can now presume that this mode of connection is familiar to his readers. (As, on the other side, even the most devout of historians do not now explain historical events in terms of the intervention of supernatural forces.) It is not the historian's job to defend an economic theory, in the sense in which it certainly is his concern to show that on some particular occasion there was in fact a rise in interest rates, or that there was in fact unemployment. Whether he be a narrative historian like Wedgwood or Runciman, or a cross-sectional historian like Huizinga, he will not wish to pause in his historical exposition in order to justify the use of a particular mode of connection in his explanations.

On the side of adequacy much the same is true; the historian will not, in general, be fussier than his fellow-men. He will explain the Duke of Guise's death as being the result of an assassin's stab, although he knows that not all stab wounds kill. The man certainly was stabbed, he certainly died, and it is natural to presume, unless there is some special reason for believing to the contrary, that the wound was of the kind that kills. Perhaps his associates took advantage of his helpless state to kill him off in some other way; but such abstract possibilities do not generally disturb the sleep of historians.

The fact that the historian is not in general predicting, or retrodicting, but already knows the facts and is simply connecting them in familiar ways, makes it possible for him to be somewhat casual. However, if he knows that the Duke of Guise was stabbed, but can only deduce that he died; or knows he died, but not from what cause, much more caution and detail will be necessary, and he will feel the need for stricter general principles. For example, economics, in theory, can be of particular usefulness to the historian because, with its help, he can sometimes infer the existence of economic phenomena which were not, in times less conscious of economic questions, specifically recorded; and then use them in explanation of other, recorded, phenomena. But few historians, in practice, happily engage in reasoning of this sort, unless they are what, perhaps significantly, are ordinarily described as "pre-historians"; they generally do not care to infer that, say, popular discontent was increased by a rise in prices if that rise in prices cannot be actually documented.

Suppose a historian is faced by some such puzzle as why the belief in witchcraft declined so rapidly in the latter half of the seventeenth century. How does he set about explaining it? If he is writing a summarized text, he may content himself with such a near-tautology as the explanation that men lost their belief in witchcraft "because they became more enlightened". But in general he prefers to present a picture, in considerable detail, of the way in which this man or that (generally described as "typical") came to change his beliefs. By looking carefully at such an instance, or a few such instances, we are to "see" what happened. In part, the historian prefers this mode of presentation because – and this fact must be kept firmly in mind – the historian *likes* detail, otherwise he could never endure to be an historian. His readers like it, too, otherwise they would not be reading history. Listen to an historian's conversation, or his contributions to a faculty meeting; it will soon be apparent that the anecdotal development of a particular case rather than the enunciation of a general principle is his natural mode of communicating his thoughts, especially when he is thinking at his best. Like a novelist, he helps us to see how a change occurred, by showing it in process; in so doing he appeals to our sense of what connections are "natural", not to unfamiliar principles. He relies upon our agreeing, for example, that men will prefer courses of action which make them more powerful, or wealthier, or which bring preferment for their family, unless they have peculiarities of character which the historian will then have to bring out descriptively. That matters could not have happened otherwise, he could rarely show us, and does not need to. Generally speaking, he knows what happened and has only the task of emphasizing the moments in its development which, we shall agree, were particularly significant.

Which moments were significant, only our experience can tell us; we believe that it "matters", in understanding Burke's political career, how his speeches were received in the House of Commons, but not what he ordinarily ate for breakfast.

Disputes about adequacy, however, can, and do, arise; these are the fundamental disputes which sometimes disturb the peaceful researches of historians. Is it ever enough in explaining a large-scale social change to refer to the actions of great men? Is it important to refer to the platforms of intellectuals? In discussions of changes in belief, can any explanation be adequate which does not refer to economic transformations?

Look at successive accounts of the French Revolution and it will at once be apparent how conceptions of adequacy can be modified over periods of time. But, in general, changes of this kind have their origins outside history rather than within it; they arise from general modifications in the attitude of educated men, rather than from internal dissatisfactions among historians themselves. Not the historians but the economists, the sociologists, the psychologists, have drawn attention to the inadequacy of traditional modes of explaining individual and social actions; and thus have affected – usually after a decent interval and a considerable show of reluctance – the procedures of historians. Very many social scientists look with considerable disfavor on the historical work of our times; they think of it as being superficial in its modes of explanation, as ignoring the "true causes" of action. This superficiality, however – if their claims are justified – arises inevitably out of the character of history. A generalization is of no use to an historian, as an explanatory principle, until it no longer needs to be defended; until, that is, it is woven into everyday conceptions of what is a sufficient mode of explanation, of what is "natural" and "intelligible". The nineteenth-century historian could write: "Forced to campaign throughout the summer in a region notorious for its swamps, the army was sorely stricken by malaria"; now he would be obliged to substitute: "infested by mosquitoes" for "notorious for its swamps". But obviously it is no part of his province to change the popular view about malaria, nor to be in advance of general educated opinion in accepting the new doctrines. The modern historian cannot, unlike a mediaeval chronicler, ascribe the success of an army to the support of the Virgin Mary; but he may refer to their belief that they had this support as a factor in their success; he is not obliged to ascribe their success to the superiority of their diet, as some nineteenth-century materialists would have wished him to do. He will no longer arouse surprise by introducing a discussion of economic changes into his account of the Reformation, or of religious beliefs into his account of the economic development of the United States. Indeed, such references will be demanded of him; his explanation will be regarded as insufficient if he ignores the interplay of economic and religious beliefs. But he cannot *defend* the view that a certain type of explanation is adequate without venturing beyond history into general theory. He can be slightly, but only slightly, in advance of the ordinary educated man, who must be prepared by more theoretical discussions to accept modifications in the explanatory methods of historians, as in the explanations of everyday life. Like the ordinary man, the historian accepts, as adequate, explanations which refer to conditions which are not strictly necessary and sufficient; like such ordinary men as incline to narration, he hopes, by describing the situation in sufficient detail, to persuade us that his explanations are in these circumstances sufficient, even when he cannot specify the peculiarity of the situation in general terms.

Correctness is in a different category; here the historian is much less easily satisfied than the ordinary man. It is not enough for him that some occurrence would, had it happened, have been sufficient to produce a given effect; he wants to be sure that it did happen. So far he is like the scientist. The scientist, however, when he rejects an explanation as incorrect, usually does so on the ground that the conditions referred to are not sufficient or necessary to produce the given effect; the historian sometimes does this – as when he questions Turner's frontier hypothesis – but, more typically, he challenges testimony. He does not doubt that had Hitler thought he would win an easy victory in Russia, this would explain why he invaded it; he doubts whether Hitler did so believe, for all that his intimates ascribe this belief to him. His general attitude to testimony is considerably more suspicious than that of the ordinary man; in this respect, he resembles the lawyer. He is more alert to inconsistencies, to faked documents, to doctored minutes, to published explanations which conceal rather than reveal the true facts. Here, again, he is remote from the scientist. The scientist's only documents are the experimental records of other scientists; he knows that his fellow-scientists will sometimes make mistakes, but deliberate deception is not, for him, a commonplace. If the historian can describe himself as "scientific" this is only because he has special techniques for testing the reliability of documents; his courses on "historical method" teach him how to do this, but not how to test general hypotheses.

For the most part, then, there is nothing much to say about historical explanation; nothing that cannot be said about explanation in everyday life. Scientific explanation is the peculiar thing – the odd-man-out – in the general use of explanation; peculiar in its overriding concern with what is only, from the historian's as from the everyday point of view, one type of explanation; in its search for strictly necessary and sufficient conditions which can be formulated as equations; in its transformation of its subject matter; in its setting up of certain patterns of explanation as peculiarly intelligible. Most of the time, of course, the historian is not even attempting to explain, as the scientist understands explanation. He is telling us what happened on some interesting occasion, as we might describe our adventures on a trip abroad –

except that the occasion will be an important moment in the development of a society. Or he is picturing for us the state of society at a given time, trying to portray what Huizinga calls "the picture of an age". Occasionally something he says will be puzzling, or he thinks it might puzzle us, and so he suggests an explanation which will have that sort of adequacy and intelligibility we expect in everyday life.

Very often an explanation will have already been offered by contemporary witnesses; these may disagree or, perhaps, their explanation will be of the sort we do not now regard as intelligible or adequate. Then the historian may suggest an alternative explanation, based on a careful discussion of the detail in the original document. Only in this respect, in his skill in handling documents, does he differ notably from the ordinary narrator. Even that skill is more often directed towards finding out what actually happened than towards an explanation of it. It is all very casual and informal; no wonder historians are often puzzled to know what philosophers of history are fussing about! In fact, however, it often becomes too casual, too informal, too uninformed about, say, the discoveries of anthropologists, economists, or psychologists (all of whom the historian, in England especially, often regards with the darkest suspicion). The historian can at least be expected to consider how far new theoretical work bears on his habits of explanation; and he does not always live up to that level. What we cannot expect of him is that he should adopt the standards of the physicist or of the physiologist. For his task has no relation to theirs; he is not attempting to develop a body of theory, but to show us something about the way in which a particular course of events developed.

*Australian National University*

# 3.

## DISAGREEMENT AND CONTROVERSY IN HISTORY

MARVIN LEVICH

Historians and philosophers have argued that historical inquiries are different in kind from the inquiries of the natural sciences, because the subject-matter of human behavior demands a method irreducibly sensitive to elements of whim or personal preference. I think that the standard line of argument which leads to this conclusion has been turned effectively by Ernest Nagel, who has shown that it rests upon a radical misunderstanding of the methods of the natural sciences and of the obligations which must be accepted by any discipline which claims intellectual respectability.[1]

Nonetheless, the power of Nagel's objections has not swept the detractors of history from the field and, moreover, raises substantial questions about the objective adequacy of historical accounts. For the critic of history can point to the manifest controversies about matters of fact which appear to divide competent investigators in the field and suggest, as a result, that practicing historians have not adopted the methodological safeguards which are in theory available to them and which would preserve them, if adopted, from irresponsible or idiosyncratic judgments. The critic of history can suggest that no mere recitation of facts appears sufficient to resolve controversies about the truth of propositions which purportedly describe or explain them and conclude, therefore, that such propositions are maintained because they appeal to the whims or prejudices of the historians who advocate them.

W. H. Walsh has suggested, for example, that any adequate defense of history must blunt the point of the charge that the spectacle of interminable disagreements among historians is fatal for any claims which that discipline can have upon intellectual respectability.

... Do historians aim at objectivity in anything like the scientific sense? Is it their hope to produce results which any enquirer, who started from the same evidence, might be expected to accept?

It is not easy to give a straightforward answer to these questions, for the facts are not simple. Certainly it is true that reputable historians are united in demanding a species of impartiality and impersonality in historical work: historical writing

[1] Ernest Nagel, "Some Issues in the Logic of Historical Analysis", *Scientific Monthly*, LXXIV (1952), 162-169.

in which arguments and conclusions are twisted to suit the personal prejudices or propagandist aims of the writers is universally condemned as bad. Whatever it is, genuine history is thought by historians to be distinguished from propaganda, and would be said to have objective validity just because of that. But there is another side to the matter. One of the things which strikes the outsider most when he looks at history is the plurality of divergent accounts of the same subject which he finds. Not only is it true that each generation finds it necessary to rewrite the histories written by its predecessors; at any given point of time and place there are available differing and apparently inconsistent versions of the same set of events, each of them claiming to give, if not the whole truth about it, at any rate as much of the truth as can now be come by. The interpretations of one historian are indignantly repudiated by another, and how to reconcile them is not apparent, since the disputes are not merely technical (over the correct interpretation of evidence), but rather depend on ultimate preconceptions which in this case are emphatically not universally shared.[2]

And, he remarks later:

... there is without doubt some *prima facie* case for an ultimate historical scepticism, *a case which the spectacle of actual differences* [3] among historians greatly strengthens. To ignore this case altogether is to bury one's head in the sand.[4]

The purpose of this paper is not to inquire whether the objectives of historical inquiry *require* a method different in kind from the methods of the positive sciences, but whether the incidence of seemingly interminable disagreements among historians suggests that historians *are* using a method more "subjective" and less responsible than the methods of the positive sciences. I shall argue that, in the main, disagreements among historians are not genuine disagreements and that their apparent disagreements do not warrant the charge of intellectual irresponsibility. But I shall argue also that, while the apparent disagreements need not impugn the factual integrity of the propositions which express them, they are not silly disagreements. They reflect substantial differences among historians about the nature and objectives of historical inquiries.

The task of the first part of this discussion is to show that some historical controversies are not factual disagreements and that, therefore, the critic of the objective adequacy of history has not completed his case by reciting and then deploring such controversies. He must establish, in addition, that the controversies reflect a serious debility in the canons of inquiry which have permitted them to arise. My case in point will be a particularly instructive example of controversy among historians – the controversy about the Renaissance.

Consider first a hypothetical case of agreement between historians. It is perfectly obvious that two historians could both say that the *Quattrocento*

[2]  W. H. Walsh, *An Introduction to Philosophy of History* (New York, 1960), 97-98.
[3]  The italics are mine.
[4]  *Ibid.*, 108.

was a Renaissance period and yet mean by it quite different things. One historian might mean that the *Quattrocento* was remarkably productive in the natural sciences and the other that it converted the natural economy of the Middle Ages into an economy primarily dependent upon international trade. Since the two historians are using the same sentence to express different views about the *Quattrocento*, the evidence which would sanction one view would be different in kind from the evidence which would sanction the other. The second historian would have to reply, for example, to the objection of R. S. Lopez[5] that fifteenth-century Italy suffered a noticeable lag in economic development while the first historian would be unaffected by the objection unless *ad hoc* assumptions were introduced about the relation of economic development, to scientific activity. It is unnecessary to labor the point that the occurrence of factual agreement does not turn upon the identity of sentences. Agreement hinges instead upon the sentences expresing propositions which affirm the same states of affairs. It is unnecessary also to labor the corollary point that factual dissent from a proposition turns upon something more than affixing "not" to the sentence which expresses it. The obvious moral is that sentences do not proclaim on their face their asserted content and that both cases of agreement and disagreement can be incorrectly identified if attention is paid only to their syntactical character.

An obvious rejoinder to this moral is that its truth is so transparent that no one in a sophisticated branch of inquiry such as history would make the mistake it describes. But the rejoinder overlooks less obvious cases of seeming agreement and disagreement where such misunderstanding could arise. Hans Baron has argued, for example, that the *Quattrocento* was a Renaissance and adduces evidence from different fields of scientific inquiry to defend his position.[6] The interested student of the *Quattrocento* might conclude that Baron agreed with our hypothetical historian (call him A) who had described the *Quattrocento* as a Renaissance because of its scientific productivity. But while Baron insists that the *Quattrocento* deserves to be called a Renaissance because it effected a recrudescence in scientific activity, he admits that the century was not especially noteworthy for its interest in or successful practice of the natural sciences. Baron maintains instead that certain economic, political, and cultural phenomena in that century introduced the conditions which spurred the developments in science in the sixteenth and seventeenth century.

Our interested student would be clearly misled if he concluded that Baron had agreed with historian A. Historian A would be mistaken if, in fact, the scientific activity of the *Quattrocento* was slight and unproductive. But Baron would not be mistaken for the same reason unless it were assumed

[5] R. S. Lopez, "Communication", *The American Historical Review*, LXI (1956), 1087-89.
[6] See note 7 below.

that whatever events contribute to the development of a discipline must iterate the features of that discipline. The application of the assumption in this case would demand that if an event were not designated as distinctively scientific it could not contribute to the development of some other event which was so designated. And it would suggest further that Baron had agreed with Historian A since the adequacy of his claim would assume the presence of substantial scientific activity in the fifteenth century.

The assumption is of course a gross blunder. It would be as foolhardy to claim that the invention of the printing press could not contribute to the development of mathematics because it is not a mathematical locution as it would be to claim that oxygen cannot contribute to the growth of intelligence because it lacks the manifest traits of intelligence.

Accordingly Historian A and Hans Baron have used the same sentence to describe identifiably different features of the *Quattrocento*. But what is interesting is that the propriety of this conclusion depended upon showing that an assumption which would have compelled their agreement is, in fact, spurious. The obvious point for introducing the assumption was not to demonstrate for the reader its transparent deficiencies. It was rather to suggest that the evidential force of propositions and therefore their agreement or disagreement cannot be adequately assessed in a given branch of inquiry without consulting the preconceptions about the relationship of events which in that branch of inquiry partially decide the sector of subject-matter which the propositions describe. As a result, the degree of agreement or disagreement between propositions is not an easy matter to assess and the text-book moral which distinguishes sentences from propositions could be accepted while the results of its application in a particular case might be mistaken.

I have tried so far to establish that mistakes about the agreement or disagreement of historical propositions are, in principle, possible. I want now to describe a particular case where such mistakes have arisen. I shall consider a symposium on the Renaissance in the *Journal of the History of Ideas* where the chief contributors are Dana B. Durand and Hans Baron and where they themselves are responsible for the mistakes.[7]

Durand introduces his essay by saying:

The immediate purpose of this symposium is, I take it, to weigh the elements of tradition against those of innovation in fifteenth-century Italian science and scientific thought. The ultimate purpose is to test in a single instance the validity of the opinion, commonly held since Burckhardt, that the *Quattrocento* marks a radical break with the Middle Ages and institutes the era of Modern Europe. The instance is crucial since by general consent science is fundamental to the modern

---

[7] Dana B. Durand, "Tradition and Innovation in Fifteenth-Century Italy", *Journal of the History of Ideas*, IV (1943), 1-20; and Hans Baron, "Towards a More Positive Evaluation of the Fifteenth-Century Renaissance", *ibid.*, 21-49.

world, and yet Burckhardt in his *Culture of the Renaissance in Italy* ignored it almost completely.

What I shall examine may be described in the phrase, 'Il Primato Dell' Italia', the primacy claimed for Italy in the field of science, more narrowly in the fields of scientific methodology, cosmology, mathematics and physics.[8]

Durand concludes:

The diversity of social life, the wide basis of economic prosperity in her cities, permitted Italy to cultivate a greater variety of disciplines and arts than could have been found during the same period in the north. Nevertheless, it does not appear that she was uncontestedly supreme in any of those fields examined in this paper. Antecedents in scholastic tradition have been found for nearly all her scientific achievements... The increments of classical knowledge through translation and discovery appear to have been slender in the fields of cosmology, mathematics, and physics...

The chief increments of knowledge – or units of innovation – must be classed as internal elaboration of traditional material rather than as mutations... The evidence, as I see it, points to a qualified estimate, an estimate which satisfies the two cardinal articles of the historian's faith: continuity and spontaneity in historical process. That estimate in this case may be put as follows: the balance of tradition and innovation in fifteenth-century Italy was not so decisively favorable as to distinguish that century radically from those that preceded it, nor to constitute the *Quattrocento* a unique and unrivalled moment in the history of western thought.[9]

Baron accepts Durand's assessment of scientific achievement: "... to the humanist Renaissance of the fourteenth and fifteenth centuries, interest in natural science, however fundamental to the modern world, was as unfamiliar as the institutions of the modern nation-state. Natural science was the one great sector of intellectual activity that was almost wholly excluded from the humanistic program for almost a century and a half, in favor of the new study of man and history".[10]

But he then qualifies the assent by suggesting that if there is "any fallacy in the argument propounded by Dr. Durand, knowledge gained in other areas of Renaissance research will help to avoid possible pitfalls resulting from limitations to a single field".[11] The fallacy is described later in the following way:

... the story of the birth of modern science cannot be fully told before inquiry into the *causes* of the rising tendency to see life as a 'dynamic' vision; before it is explained how the belief in a universe as an immovable, God-given order was overcome by the idea of a decentralized, infinite universe, a world in evolution, and *so paved the way for the later readiness* to reduce all physical phenomena to a successive flux, and for the evolutionary views characteristic of modern thought.[12]

[8]   Durand, 1.
[9]   Durand, 19-20.
[10]  Baron, 28.
[11]  Baron, 21.
[12]  Baron, 36.The italics are mine.

. . . If these considerations are sound, fifteenth-century Italy contributed one of the most decisive 'innovations' to the development of modern science. The contribution, it is true, had little immediate effect on science, but, in the broader intellectual life, it *caused* the rise of those very problems and attitudes of mind that were to provide the indispensable frame of thought for the transition from 'medieval' to 'modern' science, a hundred years later.[13]

Durand argues that the contributions to physics, mathematics and related disciplines in the fifteenth-century were, for the most, nugatory. Baron accepts the estimate but thinks he makes a point against Durand by describing the extra-scientific innovations in that century which created the conditions which were conducive to the resurgence of scientific productivity in the sixteenth and seventeenth centuries. And it seems clear that Baron and Durand have not disagreed unless one or both of them is willing to maintain the spurious assumption that whatever events contribute to the growth of a discipline must iterate the distinctive features of that discipline. Only the mistaken assumption could warrant the claim that Durand has declared also that events in the fifteenth century made no contributions to subsequent developments in science because the events *themselves* cannot be described as a scientific Renaissance. Consequently Baron and Durand have formulated different and compatible theses about the *Quattrocento*. The proposition that the *Quattrocento* initiated the conditions which made Galileo and Newton possible is entirely compatible with the proposition that it produced little that was worthwhile in the natural sciences. It is perhaps appropriate to add that the descriptions of the careers of persons, disciplines, and institutions frequently invoke the distinction which would dissolve the purported disagreement between Baron and Durand. No one would contend that a biographer of Newton who mentions his lack of scientific learning at the age of two has thereby committed himself to denying that anything which happened to him at that age could have contributed to his remarkable successes in discovering the laws of motion.

And it seems to me that the remarks of Lynn Thorndike in the same symposium to the effect that he disagrees with both Durand and Baron are equally unwarranted.[14] He argues in his little polemic, "Renaissance or Prenaissance?" that the *Quattrocento* did not revive the classical learning of antiquity, that the Middle Ages anticipated every significant novelty of the *Quattrocento,* that, more particularly, the Middle Ages and not the *Quattrocento* anticipated the rise of science in the seventeenth century. I am not competent to assess the merits of these three claims, but I am confident that the results of a competent assessment would be innocent of damaging implications for the views of either Durand or Baron.

---

[13]   Baron, 37. The italics are mine.
[14]   Lynn Thorndike, "Renaissance or Prenaissance?", *Journal of the History of Ideas,* IV (1943), 65-74.

In the first place, the relation of the *Quattrocento* to antiquity has no bearing on the relation of the *Quattrocento* to the seventeenth century. Durand and Baron do not really try to reject the second claim, and the third disagrees with Baron's position only if we suppose that if one event anticipates another event then any other event is thereby excluded from playing a causal role in the production of the second event. What I shall assume is that one event anticipates another event in the career of a discipline when it adumbrates the distinctive features of the second event and when it occurs before it. On the other hand, the proposition that one event is the cause of another does not presume that the events resemble each other in any significant way. The act of striking a match clearly does not resemble the flame which it produces. But Thorndike's polemic against the views of Baron seems to suppose that he can discredit a causal proposition by demonstrating that the cause does not resemble the effect.

I conclude, therefore, that the controversy among Durand, Baron, and Thorndike is not a disagreement about the facts of the *Quattrocento*. But I think a perceptive critic of history could now reply that while a historical controversy may sometimes not reflect a factual disagreement, any discipline which allows such controversies to masquerade as factual disagreements is perforce using dubious canons of inquiry, which render suspect the evidential worth of its propositions. And he could reply further that historians are negligent if they do not extirpate the equivocations which have created the facade of disagreement. I propose now to show that the controversies do not arise from simple equivocations and that they do not discredit the factual authority of the propositions which precipitate them.

The discussion so far is misleading if it suggests that the "problem" of the Renaissance is, to use the phrase of Paul Oskar Kristeller, a "pseudo-problem" which is created by an irresponsible use of language.[15] The previous discussion might suggest that the apparent disagreements are products of verbal lapses or methodological mistakes and could be remedied by some minor linguistic repairs and a course for historians in the elementary proprieties of scientific method. But it does not follow that the phenomenon of controversy necessarily demeans the discipline in which it occurs or that it would be resolved in this case for any historians who recognized the easy distinction between controversy and disagreement.

Suppose that two biographers of John Stuart Mill disagreed about something they called the "crucial turning-point" in his career as a political philosopher. One biographer might say that the "crucial turning-point" occurred when he read De Tocqueville's *Democracy in America*. And he

---

[15]   Paul Oskar Kristeller, "The Place of Classical Humanism in Renaissance Thought", *Journal of the History of Ideas*, IV (1943), 59.

might adduce evidence to show that Mill, at this time, first entertained the views which later became a distinctive component of his mature political reflections. And suppose that another biographer says instead that the "crucial turning-point" occurred when Mill married the then Mrs. Taylor. And he then adduces evidence to show that Mill would have given up political philosophy without the relentless promptings of his wife.

My earlier remarks would suggest that "crucial-turning point" is used equivocally by the two biographers. In one case it is used to identify the point when Mill first considered and therefore *anticipated* the theory of government which is described in his mature writings. In the other case it is used to identify a personal relationship which partially *caused* or induced Mill to continue writing about the nature of government. I have already suggested in another connection that the two uses of "crucial turning-point" are not incompatible; they parallel the two uses of "Renaissance". The obvious solution would be to eradicate the apparent disagreement by bestowing the phrase "crucial turning-point" on one of the biographers and allotting a phrase to the other which reflects a difference in use – "indirect influence", perhaps. But I do not think that the biographers would accept the compromise because the phrase "crucial turning-point" has a certain intellectual prestige and each biographer reserves it for the conditions which each feels provides the *best* explanation of Mill's political philosophy. The biographers argue for the phrase because it not only designates identifiable events in Mill's life, but also tacitly pronounces upon their explanatory power. As a result, the biographer who surrenders the phrase would surrender also the aura of significance which it attached to the allegedly anticipatory or causal events in the life of Mill. The apparent disagreement between the biographers is not simply verbal, therefore, if a verbal disagreement is one that disappears after suitable re-definition, for the biographers are divided by differing estimates of the respective power of (what I term) anticipatory and causal explanations.

I have said already that a necessary condition for an anticipatory explanation is that it invoke properties which resemble and occur before whatever it explains. Causal explanations can invoke properties which resemble not at all whatever they purport to explain. Thus, a history of mathematics which was anticipatory in character would explain the discipline by tracing the successive modifications of its vocabulary and results. A history of mathematics which was causal in character would refer also to the cultural and political attributes which contributed to mathematical innovations, e.g., the impact of the flooding of the Nile on Euclidian geometry or of formally organized scientific societies upon developments in seventeenth-century mathematics. The difference in the histories arises from different views of whether the career of a person or discipline is more adequately explained by a recitation of the anticipatory or of the causal events which play a part in the development of the person or discipline. And as long as historians disagree about the respective merits of different types of explanation they will not relinquish the terms or phrases which tacitly commend the explanation they prefer.

The status, therefore, which some words transfer to the explanatory events they designate precludes resolving apparent controversies about the Renaissance through purely verbal devices. The name "Renaissance" has considerable intellectual prestige also, and I think historians wish to preserve it to appreciate the properties which in their views best explain or account for an important event such as the rise of science in the seventeenth century. Historians will sometimes accept only anticipatory explanations of later events, e.g., Thorndike in the essay already discussed, and other historians sometimes insist upon finding the political or cultural or economic conditions which precipitated the events, e.g., Baron. Thorndike's proposal, therefore, to call the *Quattrocento* the "Prenaissance" rather than the "Renaissance" is at bottom a refusal to pay an age the methodological compliment which goes with the honorific title when it lacks a significant number of anticipatory novelties. On the other hand, Baron's insistence that the *Quattrocento* is the Renaissance is at bottom an insistence that the compliment is deserved if the age played a substantial causal role in the production of seventeenth-century science.

In addition, controversies among historians can arise because they disagree about the historical subject-matters that deserve prime attention and reserve the honorific terms to baptize the privileged subject-matter. Thus some historians seem to hold that the first business of history is to identify eras which reveal a kind of cultural synthesis or distinctive "style". The historians who hold this view will allocate a term such as "Renaissance" only to an era which exhibits the desired synthesis and withhold it if the synthesis is not demonstrated. They would therefore refuse its loan to other historians who would use it instead to identify the features of an era which explain or account for significant and subsequent developments in ideas or institutions. As a result the absence of an ascertainable cultural style in the *Quattrocento* would be sufficient to disqualify the era as the Renaissance.

Other historians, the advocates of the "new history", for example, argue that the office of history is explanation of "existing conditions and opinion ... by following more or less carefully the processes that produced them".[16] Such historians would use a term like "Renaissance" to designate whatever processes satisfy this different objective. Of course, historians frequently engage in both tasks. But in those cases where apparent disagreement arises about the appropriateness of designating a period by a coveted title, one matter which may be at stake is this: the unwillingness of the stylistic historian

---

[16]  James Harvey Robinson, *The New History* (New York, 1912), 24.

to give the title to another historian who would use it to identify the explanatory function of a century rather than to appreciate its "spirit" or style.

Historians disagree about the merits of alternative explanations and about the kinds of problems which deserve explanation, and these disagreements can lead to the apparent disagreements which create the spectacle of intellectual anarchy. If I am right, verbal clarification will not subsequently resolve the disagreement, since the clarification requires the surrender of a value-laden label by one participant which otherwise endows the desired solution or privileged subject-matter with an appropriate sense of importance.

I have not, of course, answered the most difficult question of all. Why should historians differ in their estimates of the effectiveness of different kinds of explanation? I shall try an answer which is at best a guess. I suspect that the differences can be traced to different views about the kinds of problems which deserve attention in the society contemporary with the historian, and to different views about the most effective strategies for solving them. I suspect that the historian who wishes to effect changes in present institutions is concerned with discovering the causes of comparable changes in the past. If he feels that the desired modifications can be produced by cultural changes he will search for causal explanations; if he feels that the desired modifications can be produced by changes indigenous to the institutions he will search for anticipatory explanations. And it is a commonplace of historical inquiry that historians frequently provide detailed stylistic interpretations of periods which they think their contemporaries should emulate. Of course, these suggestions do not reckon with the extent to which the study of past institutions may themselves decide for the historian the moral commitments which affect his estimate of different explanatory strategies.

But while it is a legitimate intellectual exercise to inquire into the grounds for dispute among historians and to adjudicate between the merits of different kinds of explanations, it does not follow that the evidential worth of historical propositions remains at issue until the disputes are settled to the mutual satisfaction of the concerned parties. In each of the cases discussed the reason for casting a proposition in a form which appears to dispute another proposition is not identical with the reason or reasons which would be adduced to defend its factual accuracy. No respectable historian would defend the truth of a disputed proposition simply because it referred to a preferred subject-matter or because the form of the explanation which it provided was anticipatory, causal or stylistic. He would refer instead to the appropriate facts which support the proposition in question. And he would withdraw the proposition if the appropriate facts were demonstrably misconstrued. It would be alarming and damaging to the intellectual status of history if a professional historian continued to maintain, for example, that the *Quattrocento* did not anticipate the scientific discoveries of the seventeenth century after he discovered signal contributions to physics and astronomy in the earlier century. But I am not familiar with any cogent evidence to the effect that in such cases historians continue to fly in the face of the facts. As a result, the case for discrediting the objectivity of history turns upon confounding the conditions which attest to the truth of a historical proposition with the conditions which account for the special features of such propositions when disagreements arise, and converting accordingly *each* case of historical controversy into a case of genuine disagreement. Consequently, the kind of disagreement which would certify a wholesale scepticism about the factual worth of the propositions of history is not the kind of disagreement which produces the spectacle of conflict so frequently deplored by critics of history.

If these remarks have merit, the manifest controversies among historians should not suggest the conclusion that their disputes are factual only. And if their disagreements are sometimes apparent rather than genuine, it should not lead to the conclusion that their disagreements are simply verbal and that the propositions which express them are empty. And if their disagreements are sometimes unresolved, it should not lead to the conclusion that the propositions which provoke them are immune to the checks and controls of responsible inquiry.

*Reed College*

# II

## HISTORY AND
## HISTORICAL THEORY

# 4.

## PHILOSOPHY OF HISTORY BEFORE HISTORICISM *

### GEORGE H. NADEL

The dominant philosophy of history of the nineteenth century is so familiar to scholars nowadays that a few summary remarks will suffice to say what it was. Basic to it was the recognition that historical events should be studied not, as heretofore, as data for a moral or political science, but as historical phenomena. In practice, this was manifested by the emergence of history as an independent academic discipline, in fact as well as name. In theory, it found expression in two propositions: that what happened must be explained in terms of when it happened, and that there exists a science with logical procedures peculiar to itself, the science of history. Neither proposition was new except in the insistence that was placed on it, and this insistence is seen in the doctrinal exaggeration of both. The converse of the first was held to be that the history of anything constitutes a sufficient explanation of it; and those who imputed a logical order to the chronological order of events saw the science of history as a science capable of predicting the future of society. That the term for the first of these doctrines, historism, has tended to become absorbed, in English usage, by the term properly applicable to the second alone, historicism, may merely illustrate the difficulty of assimilating to other languages what were German terms for predominantly German schools of thought.[1] Or it may attest to a realization that these two doctrines are related, as indeed they were in Hegel's thought. In any case, it shows, as simplification often does, how widespread interest in historicism in all its aspects has become.

By contrast, we know very little about philosophy of history in the cen-

---

* Reprinted in *History and Theory,* by permission of the publishers, from *The Critical Approach: Essays in Honor of Karl R. Popper,* ed. Mario Bunge (New York: The Free Press of Glencoe; London: Collier-Macmillan, 1964).

[1] Dwight E. Lee and Robert N. Beck, "The Meaning of 'Historicism'", *American Historical Review* LIX (April 1954), 568 n. 1, suggest that the English "historicism", which displaced the earlier, correct rendering of *Historismus* as "historism", may have come from the Italian *storicismo* familiar through Croce's writings. That even the principal German historians of historicism, Troeltsch, Heussi, and Meinecke, seem to have been greatly mistaken about the history of the term has recently been shown by Erich Rothacker, "Das Wort 'Historismus'", *Zeitschrift für deutsche Wortforschung* N.S. I (1960), 4.

turies preceding the nineteenth. This is especially true of the sense to which it will be necessary to confine the term here: questions about the purpose of the study of history and the theories advanced to validate the answers given. For it is in this sense that philosophizing about history was principally pursued in the period I shall survey – approximately 1550 to 1750. My concern is primarily descriptive, to say what the dominant conception of history was, where it came from, how it was propagated, and why it declined. To say merely this much is to approach philosophy of history critically, if only by establishing some facts which theories about its development can no longer ignore. To attempt more does not seem to me warranted by our present state of knowledge of the subject.

In part the scantiness of dependable knowledge is due to specialization. Historians who have illuminated the Renaissance humanists' ideas on history have generally not gone beyond the fifteenth and sixteenth centuries, and thus the classical humanist influences on the later centuries have been left unexamined except by scholars of art or letters. In part, it is attributable to the general historian of ideas to whom the most attractive topic in the philosophy of history has been the ideas of Voltaire and other *philosophes* of the later eigtheenth century and the alleged sources of their ideas. What came before Voltaire has often been studied by way of projection backwards, and topics like providential history or the idea of progress have been made more of than contemporary sources warrant. The concentration on the *philosophes* and their pyrrhonistic predecessors has also led to an over-valuation of their originality. Even scholars like Ernst Cassirer and Friedrich Meinecke cited as new and revolutionary certain ideas put forward by men like Bayle and Hume which, in fact, were merely paraphrases or quotations from the classics, drearily familiar to any educated person living between the Renaissance and the nineteenth century.[2] In short, the study of philosophy of history in the period between the age of Machiavelli and the age of Voltaire lies thinly cultivated between two well-tilled fields.

## I. THE ORIGINS OF THE EXEMPLAR THEORY OF HISTORY

The first thing to bear in mind in an analysis of the historical thought of this period is that it was derived from the classics; and the second, that these were the writings of the Romans (and their Hellenistic subjects) and not those of the classical Greeks. Latin was the universal language of the educated, and in the perennial sparring between the gentleman of learning and the pedantic or paid scholar, a knowledge of Greek was sometimes reckoned as an un-

---

[2]   Ernst Cassirer, *The Philosophy of the Enlightenment* [1932] (Boston, 1961), 208-9; 226. Friedrich Meinecke, *Die Entstehung des Historismus* 2 vols. (Munich and Berlin, 1936), I, 213.

pleasant distinguishing characteristic of the latter. The translators of Greek authors into Latin declared that their purpose was to make these authors accessible to the modern world. Any major work of the sixteenth and seventeenth centuries written in the vernacular was likely to be translated into Latin, as Bacon said of his translation of the *Advancement of Learning*, "to have it read everywhere". The Romans not only provided posterity with a language for scholarship and virtually all genres of literature in prose and verse. They had also, so it seemed, come to grips with the problems of the modern state: legislation, political parties, the function of political offices and the training suitable to their discharge. Political reformers went to historians for information on Roman precedents. A commentary on Tacitus could lose a scholar his academic position or put an historian on trial for treason. In the absence of an academic establishment – the universities were auxiliary rather than principal suppliers of learning – the chief evidence of his scholarly soundness which a writer could offer to his reading public was the massive employment of classical citations and the demonstration that these supported, or authorized, his views. Literature and education were given over to classical didacticism and moralistic purpose: to instilling virtue – not merely Christian virtue, but the Roman concept of virtuous action.

Greek philosophy, however influential later, did not influence historical thought in this period. This was not merely a matter, though it was that too, of the concern with Roman thinkers rather than Greek. As indicated, and in keeping with contemporary ideas, I employ the term "philosophy of history" about history as *disciplina* and not as *res gestae*. And that was a matter of little interest to the Greek philosopher.[3] To Plato, for example, the subject of history never occurred in his plan for studies in the *Republic*. Even the Stoicism that appears is not the Old Stoicism of the Greek metaphysicians, with its pantheism and periodic world conflagrations, but that of the later schools, of the Romans and their Greek advisers. Similarly, the concept which I discuss below, the "man of action" who makes and writes history, is not Plato's philosopher-king, though it would not be difficult to establish the connection between the two. But such connections were not of particular concern to the historical theorizers of our period, nor did they bother with sociological interpretations. To inflict on them even such plausible notions as the interpretation of Thucydides as a Hippocratic clinician would be anachronistic and would miss the characteristic method of their verbal treatment of sources and authorities. Aristotle's remarks about history, it is true, influenced certain issues; but it was also complained, rightly I think, that he never theorized about history.[4] Speculation about the task and function of

---

[3]   Werner Jaeger, *Paideia: The Ideals of Greek Culture* 3 vols. (New York, 1944), III, 101-2.
[4]   Karl Popper, *The Open Society and Its Enemies* 2 vols. (3rd ed., London, 1957) II, 7-8, has shown, however, how Aristotle's theory of change, which is not an historical

the historian, and thus philosophy of history in the more limited sense of the term, belonged to the later, Hellenistic Greeks and to the Romans. It was a development of the lines laid down, not by the Greek philosophers but the Greek rhetoricians, especially by Isocrates, himself under the influence of Thucydides. It formed part of the general concern with education, in which the Isocratean antithesis of learning from the experience of the past to learning, as with Plato, from philosophy was elaborated. These elaborations were to determine the conception of history of our period – exemplar history, didactic in purpose, inductive in method, and authorized by the stereotyped dicta of the Roman Stoics, rhetoricians, and historians. I shall sketch these elaborations in turn: political education; the idea of example; and the function of the historian. To know them is to know the later conception of exemplar history in almost all its details, since it was entirely derivative and faithful to the Romans to the letter.

(i) *Political education.* Since the heyday of classical Greek philosophy the role of the philosopher, of whatever school, had come to be identified as that of a guide to life. To the Romans this meant in practice guidance to political life as well as consolidation for its not unlikely results, banishment or death. In the two principal Greek influences on Roman thought, rhetoric and Stoic philosophy, practical aims were given more importance than theorizing. The subtleties of Greek rhetoric were, as Quintilian put it, made easy. Stoicism in its five centuries from Zeno to Marcus Aurelius was changing from a more or less formally articulated philosophy to a set of attitudes; Seneca and others insisted that philosophy was useless apart from its practical results. In this process, two Greek Stoics of the second century B.C., active in Roman circles, the philosopher Panaetius and his pupil, the historian Posidonius, were most important. The former became the counselor and friend of Scipio, the latter of Pompey. Their achievement may be summed up by saying that they identified the Stoic ideal with the Roman ideal of public virtue and service to the state, and connected with this, that they

---

theory but follows from his doctrine of essences, developed into Hegelian philosophy of history. No such developments could be found before the nineteenth century. Aristotle's famous statements about the contrast between poetry and history (*Poet.* 9. 1451a, 36-38, 1451b, 1-10; 23, 1459a, 22-29), affected in the main only discussions on how the two differed. This is understandable, since Aristotle there was concerned only with defending poetry and not with saying anything significant about history. Occasionally, later theorists would quote the opinions of earlier Italian humanists on Plato or Aristotle, or repeat Aristotle's characterization of history as dealing with singulars. If we dig very hard, we might even find an otherwise unknown English philosopher superficially arguing historical knowledge in terms of Aristotle's account (*Analyt. post.*, II, xix, 100a, 4-6, 16) of how sense perception gives rise to memory and repeated memories to general ideas: [John Petvin] *Letters Concerning the Use and Method of Studying History* (London, 1753), 1-2. But intermittent concern with Aristotelian epistemology, or even metaphysics, led to no philosophy of history.

imparted to historiography its principal didactic message: moral instruction, which meant training for public service. This message may have been spread indirectly by Posidonius, whose no longer surviving historical work influenced Sallust, Tacitus, Plutarch, and others. Directly, it was spread by the historian Polybius, a member of the Scipionic circle and Stoic sympathizer. In the opening sentences of his *Histories* he nailed down the didactic purpose of history for centuries to come. Everyone, he writes with deliberate exaggeration, is agreed that the beginning and end of all historical labor is to impress on us that "the soundest education and training for a life of active politics is the study of history, and that the surest and indeed the only method of learning how to bear the vicissitudes of fortune is to recall the calamities of others" (I, 2).

It is no exaggeration to say that in the period with which I shall be concerned, few, if any, arguments appeared, which were not based on one or the other of the two propositions contained in Polybius' sentence. In that period Polybius enjoyed considerable popularity, which was increased by Casaubon's Latin translation (1609), a translation famous for a lengthy preface in which royalty were reminded of the value of history for education in virtue and politics. Moreover, the Polybean propositions were congruent with what all the Roman historians were known to have asserted or implied and with the teachings of the most authoritative of all classical authors, Cicero, who taught that virtue is practical and society its proper sphere. Already in antiquity each of Polybius' propositions was turned into a stereotype. History became the education of rulers, with the corollary, sometimes challenged, that only "men of action", that is, rulers, statesmen, or generals, were capable of writing instructive history; and that history, by presenting the experience of others, was philosophy teaching by examples.

The concept of the man of action began with the image of the statesman being taught by the Stoic philosopher – Sphaerus taught the Spartan king Cleomenes, Blossius taught a Gracchus, and the like – but ended with the image of the statesman self-taught, not by reading philosophy, but history. Two of the best-known tales from antiquity were the ascription of Scipio's victory over Carthage to his habit of reading Xenophon and Lucullus' feat of making himself into a successful general merely by reading history.[5] These models provided, so to speak, the practical political justification for studying history against the claims of those who considered history inferior to other

[5] The Scipio model was fixed by Cicero in *Tusc*. II, xxvi, 62 and the Lucullus model in *Acad*. II, i, 2. I am not suggesting that the idea of the philosophic adviser dropped out of ancient education or that the idea of the statesman-historian replaced that of the statesman-philosopher. For example, in Plutarch's essay, "That a Philosopher ought to converse especially with Men in Power", the philosophic-adviser model is perpetuated (*Moralia* 777A). Also in his (?) "The Education of Children" the perfect man, the traditional statesman-philosopher, is not advised to school himself specifically in history, though he is told to train above all his memory (*ibid.*, 7E, 7-8; 9E).

studies. The concept of learning from examples put this justification into a framework of moral philosophy.

(ii) *The idea of example*. The ancients' use of "example" was rich and varied, ranging from the sample of merchandise by which the seller tried to persuade the buyer of the quality of his wares to the precedent in law or history by which the orator tried to do the same thing with his arguments. Metaphorically, the Romans had long used *exemplum* to connote a sign or symptom of states of affairs, or of virtues and vices, or of character, and to denote some specific action or event or person that represented them. The Romans were particularly given to using historical figures to exemplify and define Roman virtues, often as a patriotic assertion of superiority over the Greeks – a habit which even Cicero, hard as he tried to vend Greek philosophy and rhetoric in Rome, did not escape.[6]

In theory, especially in rhetorical theory, the Greek concept of example (*paradeigma*) was more elaborate than the Roman. In practise, in the education of the young or in political speech-making, Greeks and Romans seem to have employed examples in much the same way.[7] The young Roman, as Horace and Terence present him, learnt, not from the ethics of the philosopher, but from his father, who would point to particular examples in the boy's experience and tell him which to avoid and which to imitate.[8] The significance of this pedagogic strategy in relation to the notion of political education is not difficult to see. The Younger Pliny, reminiscing about the good old days, tells us of an established rule among the Romans – the ruling circles, of course – whereby the elders were obliged to transmit to the younger generation the principles which it in turn would have to transmit to the next. This was not to be done merely by what they could hear, that is, by precept, but by what they could see, by example. They were taken to the Senate and there their fathers pointed out the actual procedures to them; they were prepared for politics "by the surest method of instruction, example".[9] The Roman "man of action" thus learnt from experience, and since experience was invariably referred to as consisting of "one's own and that of others",

---

[6] For the general significance of Cicero's use of examples, see Michel Rambaud, *Cicéron et l'histoire* (Paris, 1953), 36-7. For the point made here, see Karl Alewell, *Über das rhetorische* ΠΑΡΑΛΕΙΓΜΑ (Leipzig, 1913), 97-8, and Hans Schoenberger, *Beispiele aus der Geschichte, ein Kunstmittel Ciceros Reden* (Augsburg, 1910), 34-5.

[7] It is true that to Plato the *paradeigma* was an ideal pattern, and that he would have regarded the instilling of right conduct by reference to concrete examples mere (necessary) habit-forming and not education in the proper sense. But on Plato's own evidence (*Prot.* 325E-326A), in actual practice the young Athenian of the Periclean age was exposed to much the same method as the young Roman was later.

[8] Horace, *Sat.* I, 4, 105-128. Terence, *Adel.* III, 3, 415 and *Heaut.* I, ii, 210; II, 1, 221 — the father in Terence's first case being admittedly notable for his lack of success.

[9] Pliny, *Ep.* 8, 14, 4ff.

history, the experience of others in the past, served the same pedagogic purpose. When Terence has a father give his son the stereotyped advice "it is wise to draw from others' experience the lessons that may profit yourself", he has said almost *verbatim* what Polybius, Livy, Tacitus, and others were to say in justification of the study of history.[10]

From Greek rhetoric, the Romans took over certain technical details in the use of examples, which stayed largely within the rhetorical schools, and certain justifications for using them, which spread more widely. Aristotle had laid down that example was "rhetorical induction", just as the enthymeme was the "rhetorical syllogism" – rather second-rate procedures if compared to dialectic, for rhetoric after all deals with subjects, like human actions, for which we have no systematic rules. Nevertheless, there were rules pertaining to the use of examples, distinctions to be drawn between historical and invented examples, and the greater plausibility of rhetorical induction and the more compelling nature of the rhetorical syllogism, in comparison to their logical counterparts, had to be admitted and examined.[11] Of the three major Roman treatises on rhetoric, Cicero's, the anonymous *Ad Herennium*, and Quintilian's, the first still adhered to Aristotelian technicalities, such as distinguishing example from parallel and similitude as instruments for establishing probability by appeal to precedent; the second modified, and the third simplified, these matters.[12] What was happening was that in Rome, where rhetoric in any case soon became a declining art, the role of example in the formal structure of discourse was much less of an object of interest than the general justification for the use of examples which anyone – orator, historian, or poet – could readily employ. In part, this justification was negative, namely the denial of the efficacy of the alternative to example, precept or principle (*praeceptum*), as a teacher of prudence. Instruction by precept was associated with unpopular, Greek philosophizing; instruction by example offered a superior route to truth and virtue than did the sterile dogmas of the schools. (This was an argument which we shall find again in the seventeenth and eighteenth-century rejection of scholastic and religious philosophies.) "For if the Greeks are strong on precepts, the Romans are stronger on examples", Quintilian wrote, adding "which is a far greater thing".[13] If the orator's reasons do not make the facts obvious, he explained, example will lead us to the truth. With Livy the generals learn their tactics from examples; generals inspire the soldier to follow, not their instructions, but their personal example. The Stoic moralist Seneca, who probably used examples more frequently than any other writer of the Roman

---

[10]   Terence, *Heaut, loc. cit.*, Polybius, I, 35, 7-10, Livy, 22, 39, 10. Tacitus, *Ann.* IV, xxxiii. Cf. also *Rhet. ad Her.* IX, ix, 13.
[11]   Aristotle, *Rhet.* I, ii, 12 (1357a); II, xix, 2 (1393a); II, xx, 8 (1394a); I, ii, 7 (1356b).
[12]   Cicero, *De inv.* I, xxx, 49. *Rhet. ad Her.* IV, xlix, 62. *Quintilian*, V, xi, 1-2.
[13]   XII ii, 30.

imperial period, uttered a dictum well remembered by posterity: *longum iter est per praecepta, breve et efficax per exempla,* long is the way if we follow precepts, short and efficacious, if we follow example.

The justification for the use of examples had also a positive side. The rhetoricians held that its vividness made example persuasive, and soon it was claimed that example was not merely persuasive, but also irresistibly implanted motives of right conduct. This claim was made for examples of virtue, for in the opposition of virtuous precedent to ethical principle in terms of their efficacy, something stronger than mere forensic advantage might well have to be claimed for examples. I know of only one ancient who attempted something like a systematic, psychological account of the power of virtuous example. That was Plutarch in his justification for writing his *Lives*. He argued that examples of moral virtue (*to kalon*) create an urge in the observer to be virtuous also; this urge is self-inspired, for it derives not merely from an intuitive attempt, as with a child, at imitation (*mimesis*) of what is perceived; it is the investigation (*historia*) into the circumstances of the examples presented to us which engages our intellectual faculties and in so doing furnishes us with a moral purpose.[14]

Plutarch's argument was a gift to all later theorizers who defended the didactic purpose of history either in itself or in opposition to learning from the precepts of moral philosophy. One might almost say that it was to the persistence of Plutarch's *Lives* as the most popular classical reading from the sixteenth to the nineteenth century that the idea of exemplar history owed much of its persistence.

(iii) *The function of the historian.* If we follow the later theorizers, we must not derive ideas about the function of the historian from the general purposes of history-writing among the ancients – record, memorialization, invention of genealogies, patriotic justification, and the like. We have to derive these ideas in a simpler manner, namely, from authoritative pronouncements by specific ancient authors. We shall also have to confine ourselves to those authors whose later influence can be documented and not to adopt more recent judgments, however justifiable in the light of better knowledge, about who is worth citing and who is not.

Polybius' *Histories*, of all the major histories of antiquity, was the most method-conscious work. Besides representing older philosophical theories about cyclical recurrence and the role of fortune – theories revived in the Italian Renaissance but of little consequence subsequently – it offered so many explicit arguments with which to sustain the didactic purpose of history, that to have read Polybius is to have read most of the advocates of exemplar history, ancient and modern. As mentioned earlier, the "man of action" is

[14] *Pericles,* II, 3. Plutarch may have had Aristotle in mind here (*Eth. Nich.* VI, viii, 8-9), but that is merely conjecture.

Polybius' chief concern both as a writer and as a reader of history: "Plato tells us that human affairs will then go well when either philosophers become kings or kings study philosophy, and I would say it will be well with history either when men of action *(pragmatikoi ton andron)* undertake to write history . . . or regard training in actual affairs as necessary for writing history" (XII, 28, 1-5). Historians are praised according to whether they took part in politics and thus know what they are talking about or merely wrote for gain or from the seclusion of the study. Mere students of books are unlikely to produce works of utility to readers. And the utility of the historian's work lies in confining his attention to what would interest students of politics only. Polybius praises the great practical utility of such history, especially in his day "when the progress of the arts and sciences has been so rapid that those who study history are, we may almost say, provided with a method for dealing with any contingency that may arise" (IX, 2, 5). The method proceeds through vicarious experience; of the two experiences that instruct us in practical life, our own misfortunes and those of others, the latter is to be preferred as being safer and not exposing us to harm (I, 35, 7-10). Thus we are instructed not by precept but by reasoning from experience, especially experience reported in sufficient detail to include the situation and motives and reasons for the failures of past actions (XII, 25i, 6-9). This, then, is the practical, or as he calls it, pragmatic *(pragmatikos)* function of history. It raises two requirements. First, it requires truth as a necessary criterion of history, history without truth being a body without eyes (XII, 12, 1-3), incapable of teaching anything. The second requirement is apodeictic exposition, which does not mean, however, the philosopher's demonstration or proof by argument. When he calls his work apodeictic *(tes apodeiktikes historiai)*, he merely means by this historical narratives supported by citing of appropriate details and by adducing the causes of events (II, 37, 3; cf. IV, 40, 1-3). The apodeictic subserves the pragmatic function: "For the mere statement of a fact may interest us but is of no benefit to us: but when we add the cause of it, the study of history becomes fruitful. For it is the mental transference of similar circumstances to our own times that gives us the means of forming presentiments of what is about to happen, and enables us at certain times to take precautions and at others by reproducing former conditions to face with more confidence the difficulties that menace us" (XII, 25b, 1-3).

Cicero was no historian. But his pronouncements on history were quoted by everyone who wrote about history between the Renaissance and the later eighteenth century, and evidence for their quotation also before and after this period is by no means scant. Since these pronouncements look like *obiter dicta* of no particular profundity, one is tempted to ascribe their longevity primarily to the fact that it was Cicero who had made them. But that is not the whole story. Cicero attempted to weld into a common cultural ideal the systems of thought and instruction of his time – Greek with Roman, philosophy with rhetoric, the ideal of the contemplative with that of the active life. Philosophical rhetoric was to effect this synthesis. The Roman orator, tied to his law-court, was to be turned into a man of wider culture; he was to imitate the sophisticated Greek orators and to study, among other subjects, history. The relationship of history to rhetoric had therefore to be defined for his benefit. It was a peculiar relationship. On the one hand, the orator ought to annex history to oratory; it furnished him with true examples from antiquity which gave authority and credibility to his speech; it was the branch of literature closest to oratory, since it dealt in truths, whereas poetry, whose task it was to provide pleasure, necessarily dealt in falsehoods. On the other hand, rhetoric had no rules for history, nor history for rhetoric ("what Greek rhetorician was ever guided by Thucydides?"); the orator had to raid history at his convenience.[15] The upshot of this was that Cicero declared what was peculiar to history. The first of the two foregoing considerations issued in a recommendation of the particular value of history; the second, in saying what the rules of history were. The value of history was expressed in Cicero's famous definition: history was the witness of the past, the light shed on truth, the life-giving force to memory, the guide to life (*magistra vitae*), the herald of ancient days – and it was the orator's duty to commit her to immortality.[16] The rules of history were laid down in another famous passage. (Under the name of Cicero's laws of truth we shall encounter some of them, as well as the indestructible epithet *magistra vitae*, again later.) Every orator, Cicero says, can see that the first law of history is that the historian must not say anything that is false, the second that he must be bold enough to tell the whole truth; and further, there must not be anywhere in his writings a trace of partiality or malice.[17] The most influential elaboration of the notion that historical narrative must be true thus came from rhetoric, which need not surprise, since discourse on the theory and practice of writing history remained under the aegis of rhetoric for another millenium and a half, and discourse on virtually any academic subject, under the aegis of Cicero for even longer.

Dionysius of Halicarnassus' prolix history, the *Roman Antiquities*, would hardly have made him an influence to be reckoned with, despite his deliberately unacknowledged attempt to imitate Polybius' injunctions on the

[15] *Orator* xxxiv, 120. *De leg.* I, ii, 5. *De Orat.* II, xii, 51ff. Similarly Quintilian, II, iv, 2; X, i, 31-34.
[16] *De orat.* II, ix, 36.
[17] *Ibid.* II, xiv, 62. The strictly rhetorical purport of these remarks should not be forgotten, though subsequently it was. Unlike Thucydides or Polybius, Cicero was here defining the historian's craft and describing neither his importance nor his virtues. He evidently thought these laws applied to the historian's, but not to the rhetorician's, treatment of historical narrative (*Brutus* xi, 42), and himself did not hesitate to demand of his prospective biographer the maximum of eulogy "and in that respect disregard of the laws of history" (*Ad. Fam.* V, 12, 3).

apodeictic function of history (V, 56, 1). But as an outstanding literary critic and essayist on historical, biographical, and rhetorical subjects, he had a great deal to say about the writing of history and the criteria for evaluating good and bad historians. Harking back to classical Greek literature and examining Thucydides in terms of the best canons of style, he, like Cicero before him, did not find him a good model for orators to follow. In a *Letter to Pompey* he compared Herodotus to Thucydides, dividing history into a subject-matter and a stylistic part, and gave most of the honors to Herodotus. This rapprochement of history with literature is probably Dionysius' chief claim on our attention; he established, though not originated, the notion that the rules of history were literary rules, in their widest sense, and that such things as choice of subject matter, knowledge where to begin and end narration, decisions about what to include and what to omit, and whether to relate events in logical or chronological order, were governed by esthetic criteria. Moreover, in his *Art of Rhetoric* – a book today more properly attributed to Pseudo-Dionysius than Dionysius – he coined the oft-repeated phrase that "history is philosophy teaching by examples".[18]

Diodorus Siculus, another minor Greek figure of the first century B.C., is significant here for other reasons. Having spent thirty years compiling a history of the entire known world from the Creation to his own day, the *Historical Library*, he provided it with a preface, in which the moral function of history was elaborated at length. The justification he gives for writing a universal history is that of Stoic philosophy. Rome was realizing the Stoic idea of a world-state or world-city (*cosmopolis*), and Diodorus evidently thought that the historian ought to do the same with his pen. Historians, he says, restore the universal unity of mankind – a unity which time and space had broken up (I, 1, 3). Our lives are short but history ensures a kind of immortality; everything perishes, but history preserves the experience of all ages and is thus capable of making examples of good and bad available forever. In giving us these sentiments, which are virtually indistinguishable from Seneca's, Diodorus not only proves beyond a doubt the derivation of the notion of "vicarious experience" from Stoic thought. He also gives evidence for how well established the conventional and endlessly repeated catalogue of the virtues of history had become by his time: history gives the young the wisdom of the aged; for the old it multiplies the experience they already possess; it qualifies the private citizen for leadership; it entices to the imitation of good and the avoidance of bad; soldiers become more patriotic in the hope of posthumous encomia; the wicked are dissuaded from evil out

---

[18] XI, 2, 19-21. The author here ascribes to Thucydides the idea, but not the actual words, that history is philosophy teaching by examples. The reference is to Thucydides' famous remark that his history was meant to be profitable, since the probable recurrence of events makes the records of the past the guide to the future (Thuc. I, 22, 4). This was also the original pedagogic motif which Isocrates, Polybius, and others elaborated.

of fear of everlasting opprobrium (I, 1, 5). If the myth of Hades (in our period, the "fear of hell" was usually substituted for this) can scare people into adherence to piety and justice, much more so can history equip people for righteousness. In short, history was "the mother-city (*metropolis*) of philosophy" (I, 2, 3).

Among the Roman historians of the later Republican period, Sallust's prefatory reflections to his once enormously popular historical monographs show Stoic influences, but apart from conventional praises of intellect over physical prowess, and some phrases about the importance of the historian to society, he offered little that is relevant here. Livy in the preface to his history of Rome insisted strongly on the exemplar function of history. What makes history fruitful is its clear presentation of examples of every kind of conduct; it is from the moral lessons they present that we can select for ourselves, as well as for the state to which we belong, those that are honorable for imitation and those that are dishonorable for avoidance (I, pref., 10; 15-16).

Tacitus, the greatest historian of the imperial period, who unavoidably saw and heard much evil, struggled hard to write *sine ira et studio,* without anger and without preconception, and without affection or hatred – an echo perhaps of Cicero's injunctions, since as an orator himself, Tacitus freely worked with the stock epigrams accumulated by the rhetorical schools. In his *Annals,* he distinguished between learning right conduct by one's own lights and by the experience of others, and declared the latter more effective (IV, xxxiii). He conceived the first duty of the historian to be not merely the recording of meritorious deeds: firmly convinced that one of the few things that could restrain the villainous Caesars was the fear of what posterity might think of them, he wanted the historian to hold vice in check by threatening to commit it to record (III, lxv). (Later, historians, and in particular Tacitus himself, were sometimes referred to as a rod for tyrants – an extreme, but plausible, extension of the historian's role as an educator of princes.) In the *Histories* there is a passage on the apodeictic function of the historian, reminiscent of what we already encountered in Polybius: all the contributory conditions of events must be examined to give us a knowledge of motives and causes (I, 4). But Tacitus here says more than Polybius did, and certainly more than Cicero who defined contributory conditions of events as "originating in accident, discretion, or foolhardiness".[19] Tacitus' listed contributory conditions were social and psychological factors, and as such left the traditional confines of Roman political historiography. In part, Tacitus fitted the stock requirements of exemplar history; in part he went beyond it and influenced those who had other conceptions of history. A curious and perhaps not inappropriate comment specifically on this Tacitean passage was made by a German historio-

[19] *De orat.* II, xv, 63.

grapher early in the nineteenth century. The English historians of the second half of the eighteenth century, Hume, Gibbon, and others, he wrote, have become the models for the rest of Europe; their excellence is due to their attempt to live up to Tacitus' demand that the historian make history intelligible by penetrating into the condition of society and into the inner life of man.[20]

Lucian of Samosata, a Greek later in Roman service, shares the distinction with Dionysius and Diodorus of having stated his views on history at length – indeed, he wrote the only full-length treatise on history-writing which survives from antiquity, *How to Write History*. Telling the would-be historians of his day how they should go about their job, he defended the serious, truthful Thucydidean narrative against the Herodotean proclivity to narrate to please. Lucian represents a rather modern point of view, if harking back to Thucydides – who wrote just before the rhetorical invasion of history had begun – can be called modern. In any case, Lucian's insistence that narrative must be truthful owes little to the formulas of the rhetorical school on this particular point; these he undoubtedly knew well, having been a rhetorician once himself. Lucian is also less heavy-handedly didactic than Polybius in his insistence on the utility of history; Polybius' views were, as I have indicated, an elaboration of Thucydides' view, and Lucian went back to the source (41, 1).[21] Truth is not merely identified as a characteristic of history for the purpose of teaching rulers or for making clever distinctions between it and oratory and poetry. Lucian has much to say about these distinctions, but to him they arise from practical considerations. The historian, unlike the orator, does not look for what to say, but merely for how to say it; the facts are already there and speak for themselves, and he has to stick to them. If history is to be something serviceable or useful (*to chresimon*), and that is its sole purpose, the incidental function of being amusing or pleasing, and therefore any attempt at making it so, are inimical to history. He condemns all such attempts, be they motivated by a desire to please, to flatter, or to be patriotic, for "history cannot admit a lie, even a tiny one" (7, 4). This insistence drives him beyond Tacitus' measured assurance of writing history *sine ira et studio*. The historian is "in his books a stranger and a man without a country, independent, subject to no sovereign, not reckoning what this or that man will think, but stating the facts" (41, 1). We almost feel as if Lucian by reaching back to Thucydides, and by devaluing those intervening arguments which justified history in pedagogic, rhetorical, or other terms extrinsic to it, is reaching forward to a modern, perhaps even to a nineteenth-century conception of the subject. "The historian's task," Lucian wrote, "is to tell the tale as it happened" (39, 1). This, coming from

---

[20]   Ludwig Wachler, *Geschichte der historischen Forschung und Kunst* 2 vols. (Göttingen, 1818), II, 611.
[21]   See n. 18 above.

an oft-quoted author, must have sounded like a disappointingly low estimate of the historian's function to those who drew on Polybius rather than Thucydides, on Rome rather than Greece. It is to these exponents of exemplar history that we are now ready to turn.

## II. THE HEYDAY OF THE EXEMPLAR THEORY OF HISTORY

The conception of history in the centuries preceding the nineteenth was derived principally from reading the authors I have discussed. Rival conceptions of history, like Christian providential history, and rival authors, like Moses, universally acknowledged to have been the first historian, or Josephus, or the early Church Fathers, dealt with history as *res gestae* and not as *disciplina;* even Christian historiographers referred to the classical historians when speculation turned to history as a subject of study. Every major classical historian was available by the fifteenth and sixteenth centuries and translated into the vernaculars by the seventeenth. Translators used their prefaces, understandably, to praise the utility of the study of history, and to hold up as a model the particular author they had translated. Few doubted that in principle the only perfect historians (of secular history) were the classical historians, and that they and the ancient rhetoricians had said all there was to be said about the study of history. There was an awareness that there were also modern historians writing about the history of their own time, and it was generally allowed that some three or four of them – Guicciardini, Davila, de Thou, and Clarendon – could be exempted from the conviction that modern historians must necessarily be inferior to the ancients. This was a very strong conviction. In England, for example, it was reiterated with tiresome frequency, by Bacon, Temple, Bolingbroke, Warburton, and Walpole among others, "that the history of England has never yet been written" (as Hume put it), and that what passed for history was ridiculous compared to what there was from antiquity. Antiquity provided authoritative historians; a few moderns might be read because they had something interesting to say – exposing the wickedness of this or that religious or political party – but no modern historian could be taken as a guide to the science of history as such.[22]

But if Livy and Tacitus had no peers, Dionysius and Lucian did. A branch of scholarship had sprung up, practiced by the writers of historical manuals who undertook both to define history and to explain the method of studying and writing it. It is to them that we must look for the primary evidence of historical theorizing. There were a great many of these books,

---

[22] This last point was a very durable one. The opponents of the establishment of a school of Modern History at Oxford in the 1850's asked: "Is the subject suitable for Education? Is it an exercise of the mind? ... Where is the standard author like Thucydides, etc.?". Qu. in R. W. Southern, *The Shape and Substance of Academic History* (Oxford, 1961), 10.

and the complaint that there were more people designing systems for history than there were good modern historians was neither uncommon nor without foundation. These books originally were referred to as *Artes Historicae* and bore such titles as *How to Write History, The Conception of History, The Art of History,* or *The Study of History.* There was also another genre of manuals, books dealing with more technical problems, like source and textual criticism; although sometimes written by the same people who wrote the former type of book, they need not concern us here.[23]

The *Artes Historicae* as a recognizable species originated with the Italian humanists in the sixteenth century, but soon spread to other countries. At first much occupied with the literary or rhetorical approach to history, they developed into justifications of the pragmatic, Polybean approach and the problems connected with it, though as late as the eighteenth century many of them still showed considerable concern with such rhetorical problems as order of argument, arrangement of subject matter, and style. There are national differences between them, too; the early Italian ones, for example, were sometimes written by Platonists and cast in the form of Socratic dialogues; the German specimens contained more concern with scriptural history than the Italian, the French, or the English, since they were caught up in Reformation theology. The inspiration for these historical manuals is quite plain. An early collection of these works in two large volumes, the *Treasury of Historical Art* (1579), contains in one volume seven contemporary specimens and Dionysius' essay on Thucydides, and in the other, nine contemporary ones and Lucian's essay on how to write history.[24] Studded with citations from the ancients, imitative of them as well as of one another, often platitudinous and always didactic, the *Artes Historicae* were the principal disseminators of exemplar history. When they were written for more formally educational purposes – or when their arguments were retailed for these purposes – there was much emphasis on the Christian besides the classical conception of virtue, as befitted books written for the young; in point of time, that line goes back to the uses of exemplar history by medieval hagiographers and chroniclers. I wish to illustrate the contents of the *Artes* in our period by briefly citing the three major works of the genre as well as by reference to more specifically pedagogic works.

The most important history manual in the sixteenth century was that of the French legal theorist Jean Bodin, who is better known for his later work

---

[23]  Arnaldo Momigliano, *Contributo alla storia degli studi classici* (Rome, 1955), 81, describes the latter type.

[24]  *Artis Historicae Penus* 2 vols., ed. Johann Wolff (Basel, 1579). The collection is surveyed in P.C.F. Daunou, *Cours d'études historiques* 20 vols. (Paris, 1842), VII, 34-69; in John L. Brown, *The Methodus ad Facilem Historiarum Cognitionem of Jean Bodin* (Washington, 1939), 46-8; and most recently by Beatrice Reynolds, "Shifting Currents in Historical Criticism", *Journal of the History of Ideas* XIV (October 1953), 417-92.

on political theory. His manual, the *Method for the Easy Comprehension of History* (1566), influenced the English ones written in the seventeenth century, and was still cited in the eighteenth, by admirers who acclaimed Bodin as the discoverer of the geometric method before Descartes and by critics who thought him old-fashioned and unable to distinguish fact from fiction. The seventeenth century produced the most detailed manual, that by the Dutch classicist Vossius (Gerard Johann Vos), *The Art of History, or the Nature of History and Historics* (1623) – "historics" or "historic", a term in use until the nineteenth century, denoting the theory of historiography. The last considerable manual was Lord Bolingbroke's *Letters on the Study and Use of History* (1738), which is perhaps the only one still occasionally read today. The tradition of writing these manuals, in imitation of the earlier models, continued for some time, though usually as formal lecture-courses for students; Joseph Priestley's *Lectures on History and General Policy* (1798) was among the more prominent later patchworks of that sort. There are of course great differences between these three major *Artes Historicae*. Bodin represented the Renaissance humanist viewpoint in his subdivision of history into human, natural, and divine (which, since usually nothing much further was said about divine history, served as a device for excluding it from consideration), and rather atypically, attempted to establish naturalistic principles, such as climatic theories, for connecting the first two. Vossius, a classical philologist to the bone, developed the notion of the art of historics by a series of definitions, and offered a catalogue of all the possible characteristics of history, substantive and formal, using Cicero's injunctions as the basis. Bolingbroke, the only one of the three who did not write in Latin, reflected the aristocratic, belletristic mannerisms of the English Augustan age, and several contemporary themes – such as anticlericalism, pyrrhonism, and the theory of self-love – are mixed in, often inconsistently, with the conventional topics discussed. But granted these differences, all three uphold exemplar history after the manner of their Roman predecessors; in large part, they are little else but paraphrases and citations with suitable elaboration from the authors we surveyed in the preceding section: the "man of action", the function of examples to inspire or deter, history as *magistra vitae,* history as the prolongation of individual experience, the historian's concern with truth, the persuasiveness of example – these and all the rest occur with varying emphasis in each one of them.

A representative sample from more specifically pedagogic literature, in France and England, shows the same picture, but with greater stress on moral elevation conceived in Christian terms. Among the Jesuit authors, the poet Le Moyne (1670) has much on history as an "exemplary philosophy" and its role as a teacher of virtue especially for the young. Bishop Bossuet (1681), addressing his history to the Dauphin, stressed the use of examples of the past as a means of extending experience for princes in particular.

Locke's liberal friend Jean Le Clerc, who used the maxims of the ancient historians to fight the religious prejudices of the day, devoted much of his inaugural address (1712) as professor of ecclesiastical history at Amsterdam to the notion of example and its irresistible effect on virtue. The great French Catholic historiographer Lenglet du Fresnoy, in a massive survey of the entire known historical theory and practice of his day (1713), declared that the purpose of history is to instill prudential rules and the practice of virtue through representing persons possessed of it in an eminent degree. Rollin, the principal of the University of Paris, whose textbook on Belles Lettres (1726-28) went through innumerable editions in English and French and was still read in the nineteenth century, devoted much of one volume to his claim that history be studied before all other subjects on the grounds that it affords exemplar lessons of virtue. (Among men of letters more interested in wit than pedagogy, Saint-Réal (1671) introduced what was perhaps the only novel idea on the subject – namely, that since men are invariably motivated by prejudices and passions, it is more useful to study examples of vice than of virtue.)[25] With the English writers, the picture is the same. Degory Whear, the incumbent of the first endowed history professorship at Oxford (1622), proposed two ways in which historical examples can be used: for imitation of the deeds of good men and avoidance of those of the wicked, and for the extraction of morally elevating maxims from particular historical sequences. Hearne (1703), the Bodleian librarian famous as an antiquary, discoursed in his guide to history on the irresistible nature of historical examples even to those who are wicked themselves. And in a later textbook, Manwaring (1739), giving thirty-three rules for the study of history, limits the subject matter of history to matter novel and weighty, full of virtuous examples.[26]

It is true that most of the exponents of exemplar history raised issues which post-date antiquity, like divine providence, scriptural chronology, or periodization of history. But these formed mostly a small proportion of their discourse, the bulk of which dwelt on the problems with which the ancients had dealt. Polybius' "man of action" was a favorite not only with the Jesuit and other pedagogues, but even with the principal historians of the period,

[25] Pierre Le Moyne, *De l'histoire* (Paris, 1670), Diss. I, chs. vii, ix. Jacques Benigne Bossuet, *Discours sur l'histoire universelle* (9th Fr. ed., London, 1707), 5f. "An oration concerning the usefulness and excellence of Ecclesiastical History . . . By Mr. Le Clerc" in Jabez Hughes, *Miscellanies in Verse and Prose* (London, 1737), 235-8. N. Lenglet Du Fresnoy, *New Method of Studying History . . .*, trans. R. Rawlinson, 2 vols. (London, 1728), I, 24. [Charles] Rollin, *The Method of Teaching and Studying the Belles Lettres* (10th ed., London, 1804), II, esp. 232ff. "De l'usage de l'histoire", in *Oeuvres de M. L'Abbé* [*César Vichard*] *Saint-Réal* (The Hague, 1722), I, 68-73.
[26] Degory Whear, *The Method and Order of Reading both Civil and Ecclesiastical Histories,* trans. E. Bohun (3rd. ed., London, 1698), 343-4. [Thomas Hearne], *Ductor Historicus* 2 vols. (2nd. ed., London, 1705), I, 115. Edward Manwaring, *A Historical and Critical Account of the Most Eminent Classic Authors . . .* (London, 1737), 357f.

themselves often statesmen or office-holders. Polybius' apodeictic requirement is found in virtually every manual, as is the Stoic concept of vicarious
experience and the prolongation of life by history – and that not only in the
neo-Stoics of the seventeenth century but with influential churchmen like
Bossuet and Le Clerc. Tacitus' advice to explore motives held great appeal
for those forever advising historians to expose the inner springs and resorts
of historical characters – from Bacon to Saint-Réal and to Gibbon, the fascination with the springs of character attests to both the preoccupation with
psychological ethics and the fascination with an as yet not understood mechanical problem, the spring being an object that mysteriously stored energy.
Lucian's analysis of impartiality was to protect the reader of histories written
by partisans of religious and political factions. Dionysius of Halicarnassus
came in for his share, when one of his translators, deploring that Aristotle
had left rules for rhetoric, but not for history, proved at some length that
Dionysius' rules provided what Aristotle had left undone, and indeed ex-
ceeded what Lucian and even Cicero had laid down.[27] Nothing, of course,
could be written without reference to Cicero. Cicero's definition of history
as *magistra vitae* occurs in every manual for a period of over two centuries;
either it or his laws of truth even provided the standard motto or emblem
for the frontispieces of major historical works, like Raleigh's or Clarendon's,
or graced their dedicatory prefaces, like de Thou's.

In all these discourses, new ideas consisted of adding yet another virtue
which an example could instill, or yet another reason why examples were
irresistible; differences of opinion revolved around whether or not the study
of philosophy was a prerequisite to the study of history (denied by the
majority); differences of conception of the subject matter were reflected in
whether the rhetorical rules of arrangement, order, and style were included
(as in Vossius) or omitted altogether (as in Bolingbroke) and in advising
which classical historian offered the best model.

The practising historian had little hope of distilling any meaning from all
this. Wrote the Frenchman Rapin, the author of the best-known history of
England before Hume's: "When realizing that I had now undertaken to write
a formal history, I wanted to thoroughly instruct myself in the rules which
the masters had given for succeeding in this enterprise; but believe me, I did
not find there the aids I had expected. Some of these rules are so vague that
one can only regard them as useless; not that they are not excellent in themselves, but because they teach nothing in particular or nothing new, nothing
that does not come naturally to any person with common sense. Of this kind,
for example, are the following: That a historian must speak the truth. That
he be on no account biased . . . One advises to take Livy as a model. Another prescribes Caesar. A third would like all histories written in the manner

---

[27]   Edward Spelman, *The Roman Antiquities of Dionysius Halicarnassensis* 4 vols.
(London, 1758), I, xvff.

of Tacitus ... there is no less diversity in all the advice about the form of history, the arrangement of materials, the style, and similar matter. All this advice is absolutely unnecessary ... the most distinguished historians never tie themselves down to any rules except those dictated by reason and common sense." [28]

What, then, is the significance of this extensive literature? It does not suffice to say, though it is perfectly true, that the authors of the *Artes Historicae* and related literature simply copied the ancients (and one another). We have to ask what they thought they were doing when they did this. It is safe to interpret the irrelevance of this literature to the practising historian as *prima facie* evidence that we are dealing with philosophy of history, with propositions intelligible in the context of ethics or other philosophic concerns yet void of anything either sufficient or necessary to the study of history. And to this context the clue, here as with the ancients, is the juxtaposition of example to precept.

### III. THE SIGNIFICANCE AND DECLINE OF THE EXEMPLAR THEORY OF HISTORY

The many virtues imputed to learning from example – the quickness and irresistibility, the safety of vicarious, rather than personal, experience – were particularly evident in moral instruction. "In moral philosophy," a Christian humanist had declared long ago, "examples are of more avail than precepts; for everyone more promptly and more willingly imitates what he admires." We follow Christ "rather by the example of martyrs, than by the admonition of theologians". Le Clerc and other theologians engaged in opposing narrow dogmas said the same thing.[29] But not only theologians. Vossius, engaged in a polemic against a sixteenth-century German pyrrhonist who had asserted that history is no more than an imperfect record of singular events, not a discipline subject to a definite method, enlarged on the relation of singular to universal, and on the necessary confirmation of universal precepts by particular examples. Vossius did not maintain that we arrive at precepts by induction from historical particulars. History was merely "the knowledge of singular events whose memory it is useful to conserve in order to ensure a good and happy life"; all this knowledge does is to confirm the precepts (of morality) established by philosophy. It was a way of teaching philosophy. History "is philosophy teaching by examples. From this affinity and conjunction of philosophy with history it follows that the philosopher may

[28] Paul de Rapin Thoyras, *Histoire d'Angleterre* 10 vols. (2nd. ed., The Hague, 1727), I, ii-iii.
[29] Juan Luis Vives, *De tradendis disciplinis*, 1531, in *Vives: On Education, trans.* Foster Watson (Cambridge, 1913), 234. Le Clerc in Hughes, *Miscellanies* (note 25 above), 235.

illustrate his precepts with historical examples, and that the historian, in turn, may test (*expendere*) certain facts in the light of the philosopher's precepts." [30] Already Bodin had advised the construction of a commonplace book, in which the examples of history suitably graded as base or honorable, useful or useless, could be systematically arranged to yield something like a training manual in virtue. [31] Among his English followers, Whear had gone further and explained how, in addition to guiding us to the good, examples might be used in the actual construction of all kinds of precepts. Formally what he proposed was typical of the new scientific method, substantively it was rather unenlightening. We are told to take the story of those indestructible cast-out brothers Romulus and Remus from Livy. This story would yield two or three "axioms": the foreknowledge of the deity preserves those destined for great work later; or, the foundation of empires is sometimes laid in shameful beginnings but attended by miraculous events; or, the foundations of empires appear to us contemptible, but actually show the operation of divine providence. Then, to confirm the axiom, we have to look for other examples – like Cyrus's foundation of the Medo-Persian empire – to see whether other founders were similarly cast out and miraculously preserved. [32]

With Bacon and Hobbes, who wrote about the relation of historical example to precept at the same time as Vossius and Whear, these tendencies are carried further. Example begins to play a decisive role in the construction of a prudential ethic. Hobbes, it has been argued, used history in his rejection of traditional ethical norms just as he later used political philosophy to the same end. [33] Bacon, as might be expected, not merely used historical examples, but wrote at length on the validity of doing so. He held that moral philosophers had discoursed on virtue and vice but had found no convincing method for making their teaching effective. Their failure to relate their teachings to the emotional life and to the forces which composed it made them inferior to the historian as observers, and therefore teachers, of morals. "Aristotle's and Plato's moral doctrines are admired by many; but Tacitus utters observations on morals that are much truer to life." [34] The philosophers have had little to say about the emotions which, like factions in a state, are at war within man. "But the poets and writers of histories are the best doctors of

---

[30]  Gerardi Ioannis Vosii, *Ars historica, sive de historiae & historices natura . . . commentatio* (Leyden, 1623), 16; 30.

[31]  Jean Bodin, *Method for the Easy Comprehension of History,* trans. Beatrice Reynolds (New York, 1945), 35-6.

[32]  Whear, *op. cit.,* 344.

[33]  Leo Strauss, *The Political Philosophy of Hobbes* (Chicago, 1952), ch. vi, where Hobbes' preface to his translation of Thucydides (whose narrative instructs the reader "more effectually than can possibly be done by precept") is convincingly shown to be the key to the argument. Hobbes, incidentally, admitted to following Cicero and Lucian among others.

[34]  *Temporis Partus Masculus* in *The Works of Francis Bacon,* ed. J. Spedding, R. L. Ellis, and D. D. Heath 12 vols. (Boston, 1863), VII, 31.

this knowledge." History, poesy, experience, and not the precepts of traditional philosophy teach those things that are useful to life. Tacitus' astute case histories provided one part of the argument; the method of that great consumer of classical examples, Machiavelli, provided the other. The best method "is that which Machiavel chose wisely and aptly for government; namely, *discourse upon histories or examples*. For knowledge drawn freshly and in our view out of particulars, knoweth the way best to particulars again. And it hath much greater life for practice when the discourse attendeth upon the example, than when the example attendeth upon the discourse." [35]

Bolingbroke, a professed Baconian, and in his epistemology more radical than Locke but less radical than Hume, examined the notion of example in great detail. He did this both as a philosopher striving for something new to say and as a humanist anxious to show that he could quote whatever the ancients had said – a somewhat difficult undertaking. The two ways of experience, personal and historical, were not only quoted from Tacitus and Polybius, but examined and compared. The inefficacy of precepts, however true they might be, was considered in the light of Seneca's pronouncements, and also connected with the then current psychological theory, in which the passions – amenable to example, but impervious to precepts – received much attention. Indeed, Bolingbroke gave examples of examples to make his points, but seemed to have found only one argument that had not yet been "insisted on by those who have writ concerning the method to be followed". He noticed that ancient examples were singularly inapplicable to modern times. If a general were to imitate the Roman generals who committed suicide in order to fulfill an oracle's prediction of victory for their troops "he might pass for a hero, but I am sure he would pass for a madman". The correct use of examples was not to imitate the particular modes of action, which are the subject of custom and therefore the product of different periods and nations, but to study them philosophically, as exemplifications of general principles and rules of conduct. (This fertile notion was taken further by Bolingbroke's early follower Voltaire, and is sometimes identified as Voltaire's philosophy of history.) Such principles, we are told, must always be true because they are conformable to the invariable nature of things; they are discoverable by induction from historical example. "He who studies

---

[35] *Advancement of Learning, ibid.*, VI, 359. What I have quoted from Bacon does little more than hint at his elaborate arguments. For Bacon's defense of examples see VI, 97ff; on history, VII, 385; on Tacitus, VI, 235. It might be noted that admiration for Tacitus usually implied admiration, even if qualified, for Machiavelli. The orthodox opposed both as anti-Christian and subversive and sometimes averred that the teaching of Tacitus had produced Machiavelli's. Bolingbroke, a freethinker, chose Tacitus as his model for history and Machiavelli for political theory; others chose the other way about. Hume put a motto from Tacitus' *Histories* on the titlepage of the *Treatise* (which, according to its first learned reviewer, in 1739, "sufficiently betrayed the author's evil intentions"); he classed Machiavelli among the best historians. All this points to a connection of exemplar history with political theory, which is in need of study.

History as he would study Philosophy will soon distinguish and collect them, and by so doing will soon form to himself a general system of Ethicks and Politicks on the surest foundations, on the trial of these principles and Rules in all ages, and on the confirmation of them by universal experience." [36]

The drift of the arguments advanced by those who wrote about history should now be clear. History is, or ought to be, what came to be called in the eighteenth century "the empirical part of moral philosophy". Throughout the period surveyed, the term "moral" referred to both civic and private morality, to politics and ethics. (To the exponents of exemplar history, the Roman conception of virtue as public virtue was paramount; that specifically Christian virtues could be gained from the study of historical examples, was, for the most part, the stock-in-trade of Christian educators and authors of history schoolbooks, who retailed exemplar history for pedagogic purposes, as I have noted.) But the term "philosophy" by the end of this period, as is well known, had become detached from its scholastic moorings and was defined in terms of the characteristics which first Bacon and then Newton had assigned to natural philosophy.

This stage in the development of history as moral philosophy heralded the end of exemplar history as a serious intellectual endeavor. For history now had to be regarded as a science, or as part of a science, in the sense in which natural philosophy implied that term. The systematization which all along had been hinted at, feebly by Bodin and Whear, dogmatically by Bacon, and optimistically by Bolingbroke, was now demanded. It was one thing to oppose, just as the Romans had, precept to example and to define history as "philosophy purified from the pedantry of the schools and free from the encumbrances of division and arguments, and reduced to action and example". [37] It was another thing to show by what kind of systematic study of historical facts moral philosophy could be produced. Few thinkers, even among Englishmen who had never heard of Descartes', Malebranche's, or Bayle's scepticism of history, could find a basis for doing this. After Locke and Shaftesbury – Hobbes was still not respectable – any significant attempts at constructing scientific systems of ethics would have to be based on psychology and not on history; to put it epigramatically, on man, not men. Whoever wanted to convert the aspirations of exemplar history into rigorous scientific propositions would soon find either that the propositions he advanced were scientific only in name or that he had in fact abandoned history for social science. This did indeed happen. I shall mention, without further elaboration, an instance of each position.

The Scottish philosopher and pedagogue George Turnbull, who wrote about the same time as Bolingbroke, found himself inspired by a remark in

[36] Henry Saint-John, Lord Viscount Bolingbroke, *Letters on the Study and Use of History* (London, 1738), Let. III, 12-13.
[37] Le Moyne, *op. cit.,* Diss. I., Ch. viii.

Newton's *Optics* to the effect that the methods of the natural philosopher were applicable to those of the moral philosopher. He wrote first one book designed to prove that this was so and then another, in which he assigned to the study of history that role in moral science which observation and reasoning from observed facts played in the physical sciences. He thought he had established that history was the empirical part of moral philosophy. By the latter term he seems to have meant as often as not political science; for the (unstated) moral laws established inductively from historical examples are said to make prediction of political changes and the establishment of good government possible, and Aristotle as well as Polybius are mentioned as his predecessors.[38] What in fact he had done was to write an *Ars Historica* of the traditional kind on which the fashionable vocabulary of axiom, law, and hypothesis was superimposed. His principal original suggestion was that the study of history become the paradigm for the study of the physical sciences, since proceeding from "facts or examples" was better than experimental proof of preconceived hypotheses. Turnbull, evidently mindful of Newton's *Queries,* thought that such hypotheses, though used in the natural sciences, were ultimately "fatal" to the development of them as well as of moral science.[39] His work was uninfluential and little read.

A different approach was taken in a slightly later attempt to theorize about history in a scientific – in contemporary usage, "philosophic" – style. It emanated from a school of theorists composed chiefly of Scottish philosophers of the second half of the eighteenth century. Their approach was described by one of their contemporaries as *"Theoretical* or *Conjectural History,* an expression which coincides pretty nearly in its meaning with that of *Natural History,* as employed by Mr. Hume and with what some French writers have called *Histoire Raisonée".*[40] This school was principally devoted to historical sociology or anthropology. Its theory was to concentrate on the reconstruction of unknown stages in the development of society from known stages, by means of certain hypotheses about social, cultural, physiological, or economic phenomena. As one of its practitioners said, Montesquieu was the Bacon and Adam Smith the Newton of this new science of society. Contemporaries, for a while at least, saw in it an unexpected fulfillment of two centuries of speculation about history, an advance "which even the prophetic genius of Bacon could not foresee". But neither it nor the similar philosophy of history espoused by the *philosophes* of the French Enlightenment was

[38] *The Principles of Moral Philosophy* (London, 1740), 200-1.
[39] *Observations Upon Liberal Education in all Its Branches* (London, 1742), 391.
[40] Dugald Stewart, *Account of the Life and Writings of Adam Smith* [1793] in *The Collected Works of Dugald Stewart,* ed. Sir William Hamilton 10 vols. *(Edinburgh, 1858),* X, 34. The practitioners of this history have been surveyed by Gladys Bryson, *Man and Society: The Scottish Enquiry of the Eighteenth Century* (Princeton, 1945), who includes Hume among them *(ibid.,* 102-9); and by W. C. Lehmann, *Adam Ferguson and the Beginning of Modern Sociology* (New York, 1930).

destined to succeed the idea of exemplar history as the dominant speculation about history, though each exercised a profound influence on the practices, respectively, of social scientists and historians.

The exemplar conception of history survived; what had failed was the attempt to integrate it with current scientific assumption, except in a superficial way.[41] But since by the second half of the eighteenth century politics and ethics had been put, individually and jointly, on what seemed to be a secure scientific base, it had little to offer to the majority of the sophisticated. With history no longer the principal anti-scholastic source of moral enquiry, exemplar history no longer had a philosophic function. It was no longer plausible as a philosophy of history, though it could still purport to be a theory of its study — at least so long as history was a lay pursuit, whose chief interest, then as now, was in individuals and their behavior. As a moral philosophy, it could survive only in its Christian-pedagogic version, which was least likely to be affected by the decline of classical conceptions of moral and political enquiry. After about 1800, exemplar history was largely confined to schoolbooks — some of them reprints of early eighteenth-century manuals — since it was only for the education of children that the justification of the study of history in terms of its moral utility could now be plausibly upheld. (That was also Hegel's view, who, like Burke before him, denied that exemplar history was for statesmen.[42])

The authoritative position ascribed to the ancients, from which exemplar history derived, also survived, but again with significant changes. Among the classical historians, the philosophizing Polybius, the father of pragmatic history, was eclipsed by Herodotus and Thucydides, who were more con-

---

[41] A popularized notion like the principle of the uniformity of human nature was used to explain to the ordinary reader the exemplar value of the deeds of kings and generals, which, he is said to have often complained, had not the slightest bearing on his own problems. (With the *Artes* often defining history as "an exemplary philosophy invented for the instruction of the great", nothing much lower than kings and generals were admitted as examples for imitation.) The typical reply to this complaint was that, morally, high and low were constituted alike, "that the frame of men's minds is much the same, let their condition be what it will. The passions, virtues and vices, operate in all alike, though upon different objects." John Oldmixon, *The Critical History of England* ... (London, 1726), 2.

[42] "It may be allowed that examples of virtue elevate the soul and are applicable in the moral instruction of children for impressing excellence upon their minds. But the destinies of peoples and states ... present quite another field. Rulers, statesmen, nations, are wont to be emphatically commended to the teaching which experience offers in history. But what experience and history teach is this — that peoples and governments never learned anything from history, or acted on principles deduced from it." G. W. F. Hegel, *The Philosophy of History,* trans. J. Sibree (New York, 1956), 6. Burke, reacting against the attempts at systematization which I have described, declared that if history were studied "as a repertory of cases and precedents ... a thousand times better that a statesman had never learned to read". *The Works of the Right Honourable Edmund Burke,* ed., John C. Nimmo 12 vols. (London, 1887), IV, 468. Nietzsche, going back to Polybius, was to take a different view, and in his *Use and Abuse of History* resurrected the "man of action" (*Thätige*) as the chief beneficiary of exemplar history.

sonant, not merely with the intensified interest in Greek antiquity, but with the new view that history be studied for its own sake.

This new view – new in its acceptance only, but long underlying the work of scholars and antiquarians – succeeded in deposing exemplar history even as a theory of study, because history as a subject of study had ceased to be what it had been in the heyday of the *Artes Historicae*. It was rapidly becoming a professional enterprise written by professors for students. That metamorphosis hailed from Germany, especially from Göttingen, where scholars in the late eighteenth and early nineteenth centuries were able to appropriate quietly the fruits of English, Dutch, and French historical scholarship, without concern for a lay public (to which, unlike their French and English counterparts, political history had in any case not been a *Bildungswissenschaft*), and where essentially different intellectual and social conditions obtained. From there and later from universities elsewhere, the tendency to make historical studies strictly professional was spread. The perennial struggle between the antiquarian and the philosophic historian, the pedantic scholar and the educated gentleman, fought in antiquity and again since the Renaissance, was coming to an end. The *érudit* was triumphing over the *philosophe,* and only a few transition figures – Gibbon, it has been suggested, was one of them – succeeded in being both.[43]

The view that history be studied for its own sake was not a philosophic view, though it received that gloss from the romantics; it sprang from practice, not from theory. It was a fact of professional life which, so to speak, falsified the exemplar theory, though it was soon called upon to support other and perhaps less harmless delusions. By the early nineteenth century, the moralist who had equated the study of history with the high-minded art of instructing the public in drawing lessons from the past, would be confronted with the identification of the study of history as the lowly pursuit of past facts. The reality and the significance of this confrontation have become forgotten. But the sentence which was passed on the old view and which heralded the triumph of the new is still remembered: "To history has been attributed the office to judge the past and to instruct the present to make its future useful;" Ranke wrote in his first work in 1824, "at such high functions this present attempt does not aim – it merely wants to show how things really were".[44]

*The Warburg Institute, University of London*

---

[43]  For Gibbon see Momigliano, *op. cit.,* 199. A review of the late eighteenth-century German translation of Bolingbroke's *Letters* declared that it was preferable to study history "as mere dates and dry narration" than as philosophy teaching by examples, since emphasis on individuals and their behavior had proved a handicap to technical, historical subjects like administrative history; Bolingbroke was for beginners, not for professionals. *Göttingische Anzeigen von gelehrten Sachen* 199 (1794), 1991-3.
[44]  Leopold von Ranke, *Geschichten der romanischen und germanischen Völker,* ed. W. Andreas (Wiesbaden, 1957), 4.

# 5.

## CAUSATION AND THE AMERICAN CIVIL WAR

## TWO APPRAISALS

### I. *By* LEE BENSON

"And then... and then..."

In his *Aspects of the Novel*, E. M. Forster observes that "what the story does is to narrate the life in time". Beginning with primitive man, storytellers have held their audiences by making them want to know what happens next. Something happens. "And then?" Something else happens. "And then?" So it goes until they end the story.[1]

Although historians also use the narrative device, "and then", to tell what happened to men over time, they aim to do more than tell a story or present a chronicle of events. For a history and a chronicle differ in essentially the same manner that a plot and a story differ in the novel. To quote Forster:

Let us define a plot. We have defined a story as a narrative of events arranged in their time-sequence. A plot is also a narrative of events, the emphasis falling on causality. "The king died and then the queen died" is a story. "The king died, and then the queen died of grief" is a plot. The time-sequence is preserved, but the sense of causality overshadows it... Consider the death of the queen. If it is in a story we say "and then?" If it is in a plot we ask "why?" That is the fundamental difference between these two aspects of the novel.[2]

Using Forster's criterion, we can define a historian as a plot-teller. Unlike the chronicler, the historian tries to solve the mystery of *why* human events occurred in a particular time-sequence. His ultimate goal is to uncover and illuminate the motives of human beings acting in particular situations, and, thus, help men to understand themselves. A historical account, therefore, necessarily takes this form: "Something happened and then something else happened *because*..." Put another way, the historian's job is to explain human behavior over time.

### 1. General Laws of Causal Dependence

To do his job successfully, the historian has to assume the existence of general laws of causal dependence. That is, he has to adhere to certain logical principles

---

[1] E. M. Forster, *Aspects of the Novel* (New York, 1954), 25-42.
[2] *Ibid.*, 86.

(or laws) which, I suggest, govern any explanation of human behavior, whether the attempt finds expression in a poem, a novel, or a historical monograph. Suppose we were to concede that Aristotle is right and that poetry is more philosophic and of graver import than history. Nevertheless, the proposition asserted here holds that poets, novelists, and historians must adhere to essentially the same principles to achieve plausibility – although they may not know that they are doing it. Perhaps this point is best made by analyzing Forster's plot: "The king died, and then the queen died of grief".

If we read a novel built around that plot, what logical principles would we invoke before we accepted its causal inference?

The first logical principle that governs causal explanations is associated with the time-sequence of events. The alleged causal event must actually occur and it must precede the effect; in Forster's plot, the king must die before the queen. An elementary principle, of course. So elementary, in fact, that to cite it is to invite the charge of stating the obvious. And yet, despite its elementary character, perhaps because of it, that principle is sometimes ignored in historical explanations.

The second explanatory principle is an extension of the first. For us to accept Forster's plot, the king must not only die before the queen, the queen must know of the king's death. If the queen could not have known, or did not actually know, we would reject the "grief-stricken" explanation, even though it satisfied the time-sequence requirement. Stated more generally, the second principle asserts that human beings must be aware – consciously or unconsciously – of antecedent events that allegedly produce certain effects upon them. True, if the queen were killed instantaneously by a falling gargoyle while she was walking around the castle walls, we might accept an explanation that "she did not know what hit her". But, obviously, that is not the kind of cause-effect sequence Forster was describing.

It is equally obvious that this principle does not require us to assume that men are aware of all the "historical forces" that affect them, directly and indirectly. Suppose the king had died in the Crusades. We might regard Forster's plot as plausible if he showed that the queen knew the king had died; he would not have to show, for example, that the event could be traced to the Moslems' loss of control of the Western Mediterranean. Suppose, however, that the plot centered on the idea that changes in control of the Mediterranean were ultimately responsible for the queen's death. To achieve even minimal plausibility, Forster would still have to show that the queen knew, or believed, that the king had died while on Crusade. If he failed to do so, his plot would be incredible, even if his historical scholarship were impeccable. I am suggesting here that we cannot treat so-called historical forces as though they were things in themselves, in some metaphysical way, independent of men's awareness. Men may not control their destinies, but "historical forces" can only operate through men who act on the *belief* that certain events have occurred, or will occur, or are more or less likely to occur. (For our present purposes, it is immaterial whether men's beliefs correspond to reality.)

Granted that Forster's explanation of death from grief passes the first two tests, we would then test it further by invoking general laws of human behavior. Despite its scientific ring, the term "general laws of human behavior" should not raise the tempers of humanistically-oriented scholars, nor raise the ghost of Henry Adams, who was convinced that the second law of thermodynamics could function as the first law of history. Aristotle, it will be recalled, ranked poetry above history on the ground that poetry is concerned with universal and pervasive phenomena; in other words, the art of poetry expresses, and bases itself upon, general laws of human behavior. Similarly, when Forster devised a plot based on the queen's dying of grief, it was predicated on the assumption that men believe human beings can die of grief. In short, when authors create plots that ring true, they are satisfying what we regard as general laws of human behavior.

The fourth and final explanatory principle is an extension of the third. To be convincing, a novel built around Forster's plot must not only pass the tests associated with time sequence, actors' awareness of antecedent events, and *general* laws of human behavior, it must satisfy us in respect to the *uniqueness* of the characters, relationships, and circumstances it has depicted. From all that the author has told us, we must feel that the plot, characters, relationships, and circumstances, are not only generally credible, but that they ring true in this particular novel.[3]

Since my discussion of the complex problems involved in the analysis of historical inquiry is designed to be suggestive rather than exhaustive, this essay makes no attempt to identify all relevant explanatory principles, nor to discuss any one in detail. But a concrete illustration may help to support the contention that historical, like literary, work must conform to the principles cited above.

Fortunately for our purposes, the most celebrated hypothesis in American historiography affords direct parallels with the plot Forster sketched. Forster said: "The king died, and then the queen died of grief." Frederick Jackson Turner said: "The frontier ended in 1890, and then American society experienced a series of fundamental shocks and changes". To quote, not paraphrase, what Turner wrote in 1893: "And now, four centuries from the discovery of America, at the end of a hundred years of life under the Constitution, the frontier has gone, and with its going has closed the first period of American history".[4] And,

[3] In effect, Forster invoked the fourth principle while hailing George Meredith as "the finest contriver" ever produced by English fiction. "A Meredithian plot is not a temple to the tragic or even to the comic Muse, but rather resembles a series of kiosks most artfully placed among wooded slopes, which his people reach by their own impetus, and from which they emerge with altered aspect. Incident springs out of character, and having occurred, it alters that character. People and events are closely connected, and he does it by means of these contrivances. They are often delightful, sometimes touching, always unexpected. This shock, followed by the feeling, 'Oh, that's all right', is a sign that all is well with the plot..." *Ibid.*, 90-91.

[4] Frederick Jackson Turner, *The Frontier in American History* (New York, 1950), 38.

in 1896 – by then prepared to state his hypothesis more explicitly – he wrote that the rise of the Populist movement was due to the death of the frontier and the end of "free land":

> In the remoter West, the restless, rushing wave of settlement has broken with a shock against the arid plains. The free lands are gone, the continent is crossed, and all this push and energy is turning into channels of agitation... now the frontier opportunities are gone. Discontent is demanding an extension of governmental activity in its behalf.[5]

I need not belabor the point that the Turner hypothesis has powerfully shaped American historiography. The hypothesis breaks down, however, when we invoke the first, elementary explanatory principle. Just as the king had to die if the queen was subsequently to die of grief, the "free lands" had to disappear if the Turner hypothesis was to be credible. Failure to invoke that elementary principle, I suggest, has burdened American historiography with a hypothesis based on a demonstrable error. It is not necessary here to assemble the data which show that "free land" had not disappeared by 1890, 1896, or 1900. An authoritative recent study, whose dedication paid homage to "the traditions of Frederick Jackson Turner", acknowledged that the "economic impact of the passing of the frontier was comparatively slight, largely because the westward movement continued after 1890 as before. Good land still waited newcomers in the West, for despite the pronouncement of the Census Bureau ['that there can hardly be said to be a frontier line' in 1890], only a thin film of population covered that vast territory".[6]

The example of the frontier hypothesis has been cited to illustrate the general proposition that the same logical principles govern causal explanations of human behavior, whether they are advanced by historians or by novelists. Having sketched some of these principles, I shall now be concerned with discussing one major difficulty that arises when historians attempt to put them into practice.

Though historians and novelists must adhere to the same logical principles, a crucial difference exists between the kinds of explanations they are likely to offer. Since novelists frequently build their plots around an individual, or around a relatively small number of individuals, they may conceivably present single-factor explanations of behavior. But historians deal with the complex interactions of relatively large numbers of individuals and groups, and, therefore, always face the difficult task of assessing the relative importance of more than

---

[5] *Ibid.*, 219-220.
[6] Ray A. Billington, *Westward Expansion* (New York, 1950), 749. Conceivably, one might rescue the frontier hypothesis by invoking the principle that truth in history is not only what actually happened, but what people believe to have happened. In this case, however, the rescue operation cannot succeed. In a study that has not yet been published, I have shown that, during the 1890's no significant segment of the American people were even aware that the frontier was supposed to have passed into history. Actually, the Populist Revolt came and went before Turner's erroneous assertions trickled down to the public by way of historians who did not subject them to adequate logical and empirical tests.

one factor. In short, historians can neither resort to monistic explanations of specific events, nor substitute eclecticism for monism.

Because it contradicts our experience, an eclectic, unweighted list of "causes" fails to satisfy our need to know why an event followed some prior event. Ignoring the philosophical question of free will, we cannot deny that man has greater capacity than other forms of matter to choose between alternative goals and between alternative ways of attaining specific goals. Life plainly demonstrates to us, however, that men are subject to many influences and that, on occasion, some determine their choices or actions more than others. Everyday speech reflects our intuitive attempts to rank causes in some order of significance. We freely talk of "the most important cause", "the major factor", "a significant reason", "an unimportant consideration". Thus, even if impelled by no other consideration than personal experience, historians who try to reconstruct and explain the real-life complexity of human affairs must try to give relative weight to causal factors. An excellent example is provided by one of the classics of historiography, Thucydides' *History of the Peloponnesian War*.

## 2. The Example of Thucydides

Like his predecessor, Herodotus, Thucydides wrote about a great war. But, according to Francis Godolphin, they differed radically in their conception of historiography: "For Thucydides, above all, causes exist inside the human sphere, and it is the historian's business to find them and relate them to events. He rejects absolutely the external causation of Herodotus. He clearly objects to Herodotus' use of the single principle and the general hypothesis to explain particular events. The naiveté of the myths in Herodotus is likewise unworthy of history. For Thucydides a plurality of causes related to problems of economic wants and political power must replace the Herodotean Nemesis... The irrational does exist for Thucydides... and he shows the profound effect it may have on established patterns, but it is chance only in the sense of the contingent or accidental, never the abstract power, Fortune or Providence, later deified by the Romans".[7]

As Thucydides' introduction demonstrates, however, he did not regard a plurality of causes as synonymous with an unweighted list of causes.

War began when the Athenians and the Peloponnesians broke the Thirty Years Truce which had been made after the capture of Euboea. As to the reasons why they broke the truce, I propose first to give an account of the causes of complaint which they had against each other and of the specific instances where their interests clashed; this is in order that there should be no doubt in anyone's mind about what led to this great war falling upon the Hellenes. But *the real reason for the war* [italics added] is, in my opinion, most likely to be disguised by such an argument. What made war inevitable

[7]    Francis R. B. Godolphin, *The Greek Historians* (New York, 1942), xxiii-xxiv.

was the growth of Athenian power and the fear which this caused in Sparta. As for the reasons for breaking the truce and declaring war which were openly expressed by each side, they are as follows.[8]

And then he traced in detail the sequence of events that culminated in the declaration of war by Sparta and her allies against Athens and her allies.

Thucydides took the end of the Persian War as the starting point of his narrative. Structurally, Book One is built around three closely related themes: the state of public opinion over time and in different places; the processes whereby public opinion was formed; and the impact of public opinion upon events.[9] With skill and economy, he traced the increasing tensions between the Athenian and Spartan coalitions; and, in building his narrative to its war climax, he distinguished between the "real" causes of conflict and superficial "pretexts". He differentiated between immediate and underlying causes, and made unequivocal judgments about the "chief reasons", or "chief reason", for specific decisions and actions.

Thucydides' practice of assigning relative weight to causal factors shows up most clearly in a passage describing the climactic meeting of the Spartan Assembly. At this meeting, leading Spartans, as well as delegates from Sparta's allies and from Athens, presented arguments for and against a declaration of war. Finally, the question was put to the Assembly by a Spartan leader: "'Spartans, those of you who think that the treaty has been broken and that the Athenians are aggressors, get up and stand on one side. Those who do not think so, stand on the other side', and he pointed out to them where they were to stand. They then rose to their feet and separated into two divisions. The great majority were of the opinion that the treaty had been broken". [I, 61].

But a number of different arguments had been presented to the Assembly in favor of a declaration of war. Appeals had been made to the Spartans to honor their treaty obligations, to redress their allies' wrongs, to rebuke the arrogant Athenians, and to protect their own interests. Which arguments controlled the action of the "great majority", and to what degree? What accounted for the persuasive force of those arguments? Here is Thucydides' summary statement of the considerations determining public opinion in Sparta on the issue of war or peace.

The Spartans voted that the treaty had been broken and that war should be declared, not so much because they were influenced by the speeches of their allies as because they were afraid of the further growth of Athenian power, seeing, as they did, that already the greater part of Hellas was under the control of Athens. [I, 62]

As the quotation suggests, Thucydides' treatment of causation rejects both the

[8]  I, 25. The translation used here is that by Rex Warner (Penguin Book ed., Great Britain, 1956).
[9]  My discussion refers only to the account in Book I, 13-96. Not being a specialist in the field, I do not presume to offer an account of Thucydides' concept of causation as such. His work is drawn on solely for illustrative purposes.

oversimplifications of monism and the indecisions of eclecticism. In essential respects, his book is written much as men talk in daily discourse and think in real life. And, like men in real life, he concluded that decisions were made and actions were taken "partly" because of one reason but "chiefly" for another. (The validity of his particular interpretation, of course, is irrelevant to my argument.)

Thucydides has been cited here as a classic representative of historians whose work rests upon three propositions: 1) causation is present in human affairs; 2) it therefore cannot be avoided in accounts which purport to tell what human beings did; 3) like other students of men in society, historians who attempt to explain the occurrence of events must make judgments concerning the relevance and significance of different causal factors.

Though these propositions have been acted upon since Thucydides' time, they involve difficulties which, in my opinion, historians have scarcely begun to attack systematically, much less resolve.[10] It is true that in everyday speech we do not hesitate to make the claims conveyed by expressions such as, "the chief reasons", "partly because", "mostly because". When we use them, we undoubtedly have some more or less definite idea in mind, and, succeed in communicating that idea to others. But it is extremely difficult to employ such terms in connection with specific historical events. When historians attempt to appraise the relative significance of causal factors, at least four questions arise:

What do historians intend to convey when they assert that one factor was the "main" or "principal" cause of an event such as the Peloponnesian War or the American Civil War, and another factor was of "minor" or "limited" significance? What data do they offer to support their assignment of relative weight? What procedures do they use to obtain the data? On what grounds can estimates be made of the degree in which data support a conclusion *when judgments conflict* about the relative importance of different factors?

These questions bring us to the core of historical inquiry, and the difficulties they involve may explain the sparseness of the theoretical literature which attempts to answer them concretely.[11] Confronted by this problem, and unable to wait for a theory, historians have had to proceed as though they already knew the answers to the questions. Such a practical approach seems both defensible and desirable. Yet it also seems desirable that historians attempt to

[10] "When as students of history we approach the subject of 'causation', we find ourselves in difficulties, for the problem is not one that has received sustained consideration. In accounting for historical events, every historian has been a law to himself." Frederick J. Teggart, "Causation in Historical Events", *Journal of the History of Ideas*, III (1942), 3-11.

[11] See the penetrating essay by Ernest Nagel, "The Logic of Historical Analysis", *The Scientific Monthly*, LXXIV (1952), 162-69, reprinted in several anthologies. As recently as 1957, Professor Nagel expressed the view that, although "philosophic students of historical method have written much on problems of historical causation, in my opinion, the extant literature is on such a high level of generality that the conclusions reached do not effectively illuminate the logic of historical inquiry". Letter from Ernest Nagel to Charles Y. Glock, March 26, 1957, cited with the writer's permission.

advance beyond the practical by attacking some general problems of historical causation while dealing with specific events.

### 3. Causes of the American Civil War

A substantive example may again serve to focus the discussion. In this case, it is provided by the historical literature relevant to the coming of a war, rather than one historian's explanation of a war.

The number of studies touching upon the causes of the American Civil War has already reached awesome proportions. The number of different explanations advanced is not as large but is almost as awesome.[12] Yet a reasonably comprehensive survey of the literature[13] indicated that the structure of these explanations is strikingly similar to that found in Thucydides. Like him, historians of the Civil War build their narratives around three themes: the state of public opinion over time and in different places; the processes whereby public opinion was formed; and the impact of public opinion upon events. Again, like him, they trace the rising tension between rival coalitions and the interaction between public opinion and events. In most accounts, the rivals are grouped into two major coalitions, North and South; but in a few, the West (or Northwest) is designated as a third.

Each historian whose work was examined employed some variant of the "and then" formula. Each selected some more or less specific date when tensions were low as the chronological starting point. Either the account was given in straight chronological order, i.e., beginning with the starting point and marching to the war climax; or a version of the "flashback" was used, i.e., beginning with the war, back to the starting point, and once again arriving at the war climax. The starting points differed widely but the narrative framework was essentially the same.[14]

According to some historians, different and clashing economic systems constituted the major source of conflict between the rival coalitions. Other historians found conflicts between different "cultures" to be the chief cause of tension. Still others stressed antagonisms stemming from divergent political theories and moral codes. In short, historians disagree about which groups were responsible for the rising tension, or about the issues over which groups

[12] See the excellent analyses by Howard K. Beale, "What Historians Have Said About the Causes of the Civil War", in Social Science Research Council, *Theory and Practice in Historical Study: A Report of the Committee on Historiography* (New York, 1946), 55-102; and Thomas J. Pressly, *Americans Interpret Their Civil War* (Princeton, 1954).
[13] This survey was partially reported in Lee Benson and Thomas J. Pressly, *Can Differences in Interpretations of the Causes of the American Civil War be Resolved Objectively?* (Bureau of Applied Social Research, Columbia University, 1956, mimeographed.)
[14] Of course, works focused entirely on the secession crisis did not follow this pattern. Nevertheless, even those works made implicit assumptions about the factors bringing tension to a high point from some prior date when relative calm prevailed.

fought, or about both. But in each account the outcome is the same. Opinions crystallize and significant segments of the population living in the rival areas become increasingly antagonistic until the war climax is reached. With rough accuracy, this is the structure of the works examined which touched upon causation in the Civil War.

A crucial difference exists, however, between Thucydides' explanation of the Peloponnesian War and those offered by historians of the Civil War. Possibly because he was concerned with small homogeneous city-states, some of them governed by direct democracy, Thucydides drew little distinction between elite groups and masses in tracing the events leading to war. Though he indicated that leaders influenced the masses, he ascribed their influence to the force or clarity of their arguments in public debate and to their record of accomplishment, not to their authority of office, disproportionate command of material resources, or conspiratorial skill. Discussing the Athenian answer to the Spartan ultimatum, for example, he noted that Pericles had suggested the answer in his speech to the Assembly. "The Athenians considered that his advice was best and voted as he had asked them to vote." [I, 96]. Thucydides did not argue that, prior to the outbreak of the war, members of the public on either side were lashed into frenzy by trusted leaders or skilled agitators who induced them to act irrationally. The Spartan decision for war was presented as the rational, inevitable reaction of thinking citizens to the developments affecting their collective interests. Neither the formation of public opinion, nor its impact upon decisions or events, was described as controlled by small elite groups seeking private or concealed objectives. In his account, the masses were not only theoretically sovereign, they appear to have effectively exercised their sovereignty.

Unlike Thucydides, historians of the Civil War deal with large political units whose form of government was *representative*, rather than *direct*, democracy. It is understandable, therefore, that with few exceptions, the historians whose works were examined tended to emphasize the disproportionate ability of certain men (or groups) to influence and control governmental decisions and actions. Some accounts made only rough distinctions between leaders and followers; other accounts established more precise categories. Whatever the system of classification, significant distinctions were made between men, both in respect to their decision-making power and in respect to their ability to shape public opinion. Thus in all works examined, public opinion was held to be a significant cause of events. But it was not viewed as the only determinant of government legislation or policy, not even by historians most inclined to invest the masses with sovereign power; it was recognized that certain men possessed disproportionate power to shape public opinion along lines most favorable to their convictions, interests, or prejudices.

Compared to Thucydides, Civil War historians clearly face a more complicated task when they try to determine the relative importance of causal factors. They must assess the relative power of "elite groups" and masses in the decision-making process. (Here the term "elite groups" refers to political, economic, and cultural leaders on all social levels.) And they must assess the role played by members of elite groups in the formation of public opinion prior to the acts of secession in the Southern states; they cannot assume that the evolution of public opinion was the rational, inevitable, reaction of informed citizens to developments affecting their collective interests.

But the task of Civil War historians is identical with Thucydides' in respect to one aspect of the causation problem. Just as he had to determine the proportion of Spartans who favored declaring war on Athens, Civil War historians must determine, for example, the proportion of Northerners who favored legislation to halt further geographic expansion of slavery. And just as Thucydides had to determine the extent to which the Spartans' decision for war was influenced either by fear of growing Athenian power or by pressure from their allies, Civil War historians must estimate the extent to which Northerners' opinions on the expansion of slavery were influenced by economic, political, moral, or other objectives. In more general terms, Civil War historians, like Thucydides, must make judgments concerning the state of public opinion on specific issues at a given time and place, and they must assign relative importance to the different "reasons" (motives, considerations) that led men to arrive at certain opinions. In my view, an attack upon this aspect of the public-opinion problem is not only the most effective way to *begin* an attack upon the overall problem of Civil War causation, but it may help us eventually to attack some general problems of historical causation. A summary and expansion of the discussion may justify these conclusions.

## 4. Public Opinion as a Cause of the Civil War

The survey of Civil War studies offering causal explanations found that all treated certain factors as more important than others, explicitly or implicitly. Though every historian treated public opinion as a significant determinant of events ultimately resulting in the war, there was considerable difference in the emphasis placed upon it. Moreover, historians presented widely different estimates of public interest in certain issues, and they presented widely different – sometimes directly contradictory – descriptions of the state of public opinion on the *same* issue.

For example, historians made different or contradictory assertions about the extent, intensity, and motivation of popular support for, or opposition to, adoption of such policies as the abolition of slavery, limitation of the territory legally open to it, re-opening of the African slave trade. Depending upon the specific assertions made, public opinion on certain issues was held to be a more or less significant determinant of decisions or actions taken by individuals, organized groups, and government agencies. In turn, those events (decisions and actions) were said to have brought about changes in the state of public opinion, which then led to still other events that ultimately resulted in the Civil War. Thus, although all historians viewed the interaction between public opinion and events as occurring in a specific, causally related sequence whose terminal point was the outbreak of war, the specific sequences they described differed widely.

If the analysis is correct, the following conclusion seems justified: Verifying claims concerning popular support for, or opposition to, certain government actions is a crucial, preliminary step in the verification of historical explanations that emphasize the impact of public opinion upon events. No causal relationship *necessarily* exists between the state of public opinion and the occurrence of a particular event, or set of events. If a historian asserts that such a relationship exists, it seems reasonable, therefore, to ask him to justify his description of public opinion before appraising his argument about its impact upon events. In other words, it would be logical to appraise the data and procedures used to *ascertain* public opinion on given issues before appraising the data and procedures used to *assess* its effect. To paraphrase Mrs. Glasse's celebrated advice on how to cook a hare, the recipe suggested here for assessing the role of public opinion as a cause of the Civil War begins, "First, catch your public opinion".

Thus, we come back to the first explanatory principle discussed in connection with Forster's plot and Turner's hypothesis. Brought to bear upon the Civil War, that principle requires historians to demonstrate the state of public opinion on specified issues before they assert that public opinion produced specified effects ultimately resulting in war and assign it relative weight as a causal factor. Unfortunately, at present, historians are poorly equipped to demonstrate the state of public opinion on any issue; adequate rules do not exist to help them to ascertain it.

As I see it, a critical weakness in American historiography becomes apparent when we recognize that the traditional rules of historical method were not devised by scholars dealing with mass behavior, and that these have not been amended in any systematic form by later scholars concerned with such phenomena. As a result, historians have few guide lines when they set out to assess the role of public opinion in a mass society. Lacking such guide lines, but forced to cope with the problem, historians have employed procedures of dubious validity to arrive at equally dubious conclusions.

For example, spurred on in recent decades by the popularity intellectual history has enjoyed, American scholars have relied heavily upon the assumption that writers serve as the antennae of the race. More specifically, they have assumed that the values, attitudes, and opinions they find expressed in certain books, or other works of art, accurately reflect the climate of opinion dominating a given time and place. This assumption rests on a still more basic one;

namely, that the writer, or intellectual, accurately reflects public opinion because he powerfully shapes it. Are those assumptions warranted? At present, how do we know that specified writers serve as sensitive antennae at a particular time and place? Granted that poetic insights reveal truths obscure to less prescient men; when poets disagree, which poet (or poets) are we to select as our guide? How do we know that specified books had specified effects? How do we know which books changed which people's minds in what ways, where, how, and why? In my opinion, at present we do not really know the answers to any one of those questions, but we have acted on the assumption that we know the answers to all of them. The result is that explanations of the Civil War rest upon extremely shaky foundations. One example, perhaps, makes the point.

No matter what else they disagree upon, Civil War historians agree that one book, Harriet Beecher Stowe's *Uncle Tom's Cabin*, reflected and shaped American public opinion and significantly influenced the course of events. True, Abraham Lincoln was disposed to speak of the Civil War as "Mrs. Stowe's War". I suggest, however, that despite such authority, no credible evidence now exists to substantiate the alleged influence of *Uncle Tom's Cabin*. Actually, scattered, impressionistic evidence indicates that historians have tended to exaggerate greatly the book's role as a reflection of, or influence upon, public opinion. More to the point, and more significantly, I do not know of any *systematic* attempt to study the book's influence. Ringing assertion has substituted for credible demonstration.

Stated in more general terms, my argument holds that no set of systematic propositions have yet been developed to define the relationships between literature and life, and that historians, therefore, cannot now use literature as a valid and reliable indicator of public opinion.

This view does not imply a nihilistic position on the relationships between literature and life. To say that historians have not yet systematically attempted to define those relationships, is not to say that they do not exist or that no possibility exists of establishing them. Further, the example of *Uncle Tom's Cabin* has not been used as a blunt instrument to attack intellectual history. Quite the contrary. I think we need more, but better, intellectual history – and I think that we may get it, if we try to adapt to historical materials and problems certain theories, concepts, and methods developed in other disciplines (e.g., the theory of "reference group", the concept of "social role", the method of "content analysis").

My main point, however, is that causal explanations require observance of certain logical principles. Even the most elementary principle, I have suggested, has been overlooked in explanations of the Civil War. That is, certain phenomena are alleged to have produced certain effects, but insufficient effort has been made to demonstrate that the phenomena actually occurred in the proper time sequence. We would not place credence in an explanation of the Civil War whose description of the state of public opinion was demonstrably erroneous;

but, we would believe that, at least, a possibility existed of verifying an explanation whose description was accurate.

Whether historians will ever be able to verify estimates of the relative importance of public opinion (or any other factor) as a cause of an event can only be regarded as an open question at present. Conceivably, however, progress in historiography may eventually narrow the range of disagreement. That happy day would come about if certain explanations offered for an event could be eliminated on the ground that they made erroneous claims concerning the state of public opinion, and, therefore, violated the principle of causal dependence that holds that a causal factor alleged to exist must have preceded the alleged effect. In similar fashion, the other three general principles (actor's awareness, laws of human behavior, intrinsic plausibility) sketched at the outset could be invoked to narrow the range of potentially verifiable explanations of the American Civil War (or of any other "major event"). And narrowing the range of potentially verifiable explanations for the Civil War, I assume, would put us in a better position to assign relative weight to causal factors than the one we are in now.[15] It seems reasonable, therefore, to conclude with this observation: Historians of the Civil War might progress most directly and rapidly if they applied the general logic of historical inquiry to the systematic, explicit, and precise study of concrete events, and, in the process, deliberately attempted to develop more powerful conceptual and methodological tools with which to reconstruct the behavior of men in society over time.

*Columbia University*

## II. *By* CUSHING STROUT

A specter haunts American historians – the concept of causality. After nearly a hundred years of passionate and dispassionate inquiry into "the causes of the Civil War" the debate is still inconclusive. Even more discouraging, according to the editor of a recent anthology of historical writings on the problem, "twentieth-century historians often merely go back to interpretations advanced by partisans while the war was still in progress".[16] Despite the impasse, historians are not often discouraged. Some take refuge in professional patience or the firm confidence that their opponents have simply hardened their hearts to truth. Others are reconciled to skepticism by the historical relativism, defended by Carl Becker and Charles Beard, which characterizes all historical inter-

---

[15] It is worth emphasizing that the ultimate verification of any particular explanation of the Civil War will imply the elimination of all other explanations. *Cf.:* "...verification involves not only confirmation but the exclusion or disproof of alternative hypotheses". Morris R. Cohen, "Causation and Its Application to History", *Journal of the History of Ideas*, III (1942), 12-29.

[16] Kenneth M. Stampp, *The Causes of the Civil War* (Englewood Cliffs, N.J., 1959), vi.

pretations as determined products of a temporary, dominant "climate of opinion". A few, like Beard himself, have drastically tried to cut the knot by surgical removal of the causal category itself from history, though his own practice of economic determinism flatly contradicted this Draconian proposal. When the investigation of the answer to a question has led to such frustrating difficulties, it is necessary to re-examine the question, even if it leads the historian into philosophical territory where he naturally fears to tread.

Historians are often vulnerable to Henry Adams's charge that their causal assumptions, "hidden in the depths of dusty libraries, have been astounding, but commonly unconscious and childlike",[17] yet they can find no real help from the eccentric results of his own search for a historical physics which would unify the course of events under one abstract formula, "a spool upon which to wind the thread of the past without breaking it".[18] For all his brilliance his speculative theory has quite rightly struck most historians as an exotic hybrid of history and science, spoiling the integrity of each. The "scientific school of history" ended either in fanciful speculation about historical laws or a naive cult of fact-finding as the essence of scientific method. If even the scientist, at the level of sub-atomic particles, must substitute statistical probability for causal universals, the historian has always been embarrassed by the effort to discover conditions which invariably produce certain results not otherwise accounted for. He cannot discriminate with exactness constants and variables by experimentation on a past forever gone, nor can he always confidently turn to social scientists for causal rules when their findings, even when valid and relevant, are limited historically to particular times and places. Grateful as the historian may be for generalizations about, say, the voting behavior of Americans, he is ruefully aware that recurring evidence for the behavior of Americans in civil wars is fortunately not available.

The historian conventionally speaks of "multiple causes" because he knows he has no monistic formula to explain the course of history and no single generalization to cover all the necessary and sufficient conditions for a civil war. This fashion of speech is, however, misleading because he cannot escape his difficulties by multiplying them. If he does not believe that each of the many "causes" could have produced the Civil War by itself, then he must assume that the whole collection of them acted together as one in bringing about that effect. He is then left with the familiar problem of accounting for this causal relationship by reference to confirmed generalizations. What he cannot do for one "cause", he cannot do for a set of them acting as one.

Historians sometimes seek to avoid the problem of generalized causal rules by talking of a necessary chain of events.[19] Yet the events which are put into

[17] *The Education of Henry Adams* (New York, 1931), 382.
[18] *Ibid.*, 472.
[19] Adams described his own history of the United States as an effort to state "such facts as seemed sure, in such order as seemed rigorously consequent", so as to "fix for a familiar moment a necessary sequence of human movement". *Ibid.*, 382.

the so-called chains clearly have more determinants than are recognized by so placing them, and the same event can be put into a number of possible chains. The election of Lincoln, produced by a large number of small events, might well appear in two alleged chains of events which suggest quite different interpretations of the coming of the war. The chains are not, furthermore, really "necessary" unless their linkage is explained by theories or generalizations which the makers of chains seldom make clear, even to themselves.[20]

A deeper difficulty of the causal query is that it may be defined so as to conflict with the historical attitude itself. If the historian were to deduce consequences from antecedents, there would be nothing in the former not found in the latter. How then could he speak of anything new happening at all? The special sensitivity of the historian is to the novel elements, the discontinuities, emerging in a situation. He discovers the relevant antecedents retrospectively with the help of the illumination of the consequences, which call out for a past. Looking backwards, he discerns a process that does not logically or inevitably follow from certain antecedents, but takes its life and form only from its development. There is no point at which the historian can declare that the Civil War became inevitable, even though he might find it increasingly probable. Those who have said it was inevitable have either deduced it from a dogmatic general proposition about the "necessary" conflict of classes in society, according to the determinism of historical materialism, or they have pointed instead to the stubborness of the slavery problem and the moral and ideological imperatives which made certain policies humanly "necessary" (granted their premises), rather than historically inevitable in terms of an impersonal process.[21] In studying the Civil War the historian must know about such antecedents as the origins and expansion of slavery, for example, but he cannot deduce the war from the existence of that institution. "American historians have been too clever by half", Carl Becker once said, "in finding other causes of the Civil War",[22] but the cleverness has been stimulated by knowledge of the fact that slavery existed and was eliminated elsewhere without civil war.

The serious difficulties of exact causal determination have led some thinkers to suggest that the historian make reasonable estimates of causes, based upon his judgment of what *would* have taken place in the absence of a particular

[20]   Mario Bunge, *Causality: the Place of the Causal Principle in Modern Science* (Cambridge, Mass., 1959), 126.
[21]   Arthur M. Schlesinger, Jr. sees the Civil War as a "log-jam" which had to be "burst by violence", a common feature of the "tragedy" of history; but surely only commitment to policy positions deemed necessary and worth the price of force explains the "log-jam" he describes. See his "The Causes of the Civil War: a Note on Historical Sentimentalism", *Partisan Review*, 16 (1949), 969-81. Pieter Geyl, who also attacks the "revisionist" thesis of a "needless war", carefully avoids making the claim that it was inevitable, leaving the issue moot. See his "The American Civil War and the Problem of Inevitability", *New England Quarterly*, 24 (1951), 147-68.
[22]   Letter to Louis Gottschalk, Sept. 3, 1944, in C. Becker, *Detachment and the Writing of History*, ed. Phil L. Snyder (Ithaca, 1958), 88.

factor being tested for causal relevance.[23] If the course of events would have been much the same, the factor is assumed to have had no causal significance. Some critics have replied that history is, as Beard maintained, "a seamless web"; but surely it is not so seamless that historians must follow Beard in believing that there is no more reason to explain American intervention in the First World War by reference to the German policy of unlimited submarine warfare than by reference to the Kaiser's moustaches.[24] This extreme position denies to the historian that realistic sense of relevance which the study of history and direct experience of human affairs have traditionally provided. Many explanations in history certainly do reflect and depend upon this trained sense of relevance.[25] Modern historians have stressed slavery rather than states rights in explaining the crisis of 1860 because they know that the legal position of states rights has often sheltered Northerners and Southerners alike, depending on the more substantial interests it has been designed to protect. Beard himself rejected Turner's stress on the importance of free land to American development on the ground that though slavery, capitalism, and free land were "woven in one national mesh", yet "slavery would have been slavery and capitalism capitalism in essence even had there been no free land with its accompaniments".[26] He could only arrive at this conclusion by imaginatively breaking the web he considered "seamless". (Even so, this procedure does not convincingly support Beard's thesis of the Civil War as a necessary conflict between capitalism and agrarianism, not only because the economic issue of the tariff had been gradually composed since 1832, but because it was during the competition for and debate over the western territories that relations between the sections became embittered to a state of crisis out of which the war came.)

Sidney Hook has persuasively argued for the importance of hypotheticals contrary to fact in establishing the interrelation of events. Yet he admits that though we have the right to make such predictions when they rest upon valid generalizations about individual and social behavior, still "we have no logical guarantee that they will continue to hold or that something new and completely unforeseen will not crop up..."[27] The difficulty is that in dealing from a hypothetical point of view with a particular series of events we are assuming that it will not be intersected by other seemingly unrelated series of events. For

---

[23] See Max Weber, "Critical Studies in the Logic of the Cultural Sciences", reprinted in English in *The Methodology of the Social Sciences*, ed. Edward A. Shils and Henry A. Finch (Glencoe, Ill., 1949), esp. 164-88.

[24] See his *The Discussion of Human Affairs* (New York, 1936), 79, where he characterizes causal judgments as subjective, arbitrary ruptures of the "seamless web" of history.

[25] The relevance of training to the use of "guarded generalizations", neither purely analytic nor purely synthetic, is argued convincingly by Michael Scriven, "Truisms as the Grounds for Historical Explanations", in *Theories of History*, ed. Patrick Gardiner (Glencoe, Ill., 1958), 463-68.

[26] Letter to Frederick Jackson Turner, May 14, 1921, Box 31, Turner Papers, The Huntington Library.

[27] *The Hero in History: a Study in Limitation and Possibility* (New York, 1943), 132.

this reason our calculations, even at their best, may be "well grounded and reliable but not certain". Is the process sound enough to justify our saying that slavery was the cause of the Civil War if by assuming its absence we could reasonably demonstrate there would have been no armed conflict? We would then have to show that none of the other issues between the sections was intractable or explosive enough to generate war. The problem is that slavery was so entangled with the other grievances of a political, economic, and social character that it is artificial to separate it out, nor do we have at hand a confirmed set of generalizations about the causes of war to apply. Whatever our calculations might be, we could not satisfy the unknowns in the formula "if *a* and *only a*, then *b* and *only b*". We might well grant that though the North fought for the Union, and the South for the right of secession, still it was slavery which menaced the Union and needed Southern independence to protect its growth; even so, we could only conclude that the war was essentially fought *about* slavery, not that it was *produced* by it.

The hypothetical method of discovering causal relevance has awkward difficulties whenever the issues become complex. The historian is trained to think with respect to documentary evidence, which exists only for what did happen, not for what would have happened. He can reflect upon what might have happened in order better to evaluate what actually did happen, but to speculate on what would have happened often puts him in the position of building his hypothesis on a nest of bottomless boxes of untestable hypotheses. It is clear that the historian may sensibly ask if slavery might have expanded into the newly acquired territories in the 1850's and after. Whether or not Americans were quarrelling about "an imaginary Negro in an impossible place" has turned on a discussion of the relevance of a staple-crop system inappropriate to the arid lands of the West, the potential use of slavery in mining, the expansionist ambitions of Southerners, or the fears of some future technological invention as potent as the cotton gin in bolstering slavery.[28] The question serves to highlight the possibilities contained within the situation of crisis, and it has a bearing on the historian's appreciation of the Republicans' position of containment of slavery.

Doubt over the significance of an event tends to generate the conditional query as a way of resolving it. If the historian wonders why the South seceded after Lincoln's election, he might ask himself what would have happened if Senator Douglas had been elected. Since Southern Democrats had already rejected Douglas at the Charleston Convention, they *might* have found him intolerable as president. The historian cannot be sure, but the question points up the South's demands and highlights the importance to Southern eyes of Lincoln's being the leader of a sectional party committed to containment of slavery. Since men who act in history must calculate the possible consequences

---

[28] See Harry V. Jaffa, "Expediency and Morality in the Lincoln-Douglas Debates", *The Anchor Review*, 2 (1957), 199-204.

of various alternatives, the historian in trying to understand them is led to do the same. Questions of what would have happened can be answered, of course, only by judgments of probability based on knowledge of the actual situation. They emphasize the significance of certain happenings without pretending to an impossible certainty, specificity, or scope.

A merely utopian conditional question allows equally plausible but contradictory answers. It has, for example, been argued that if the North had let the South secede in peace, the two nations would have enjoyed future friendly relations, thus saving the terrible costs of war.[29] It is not surprising that a Southerner might find this assumption convincing, but it clearly includes too many imponderables to justify any firm judgment. To raise questions that cannot be reasonably answered is an exercise in futility unless they are treated only as the indirect means of drawing attention to elements of an actual situation. Asking what would have happened if the North had "let the erring sister go", only serves to force a weighing of Lincoln's policy reasons for holding a symbol of federal authority in the South, as well as of the nationalistic sentiments of the Northerners who supported him. Provided the historian maintains his primary interest in what actually did happen, he may with propriety, under certain conditions, ask what might have happened or what would have happened. Such questions are especially useful for evaluating policy.

The most frequent type of historical explanation usually appears in causal disguise, which helps account for the historian's reluctance to banish the idea of cause. *Cause* often functions as *reason* or *purpose*. Explanation in terms of purpose is the natural way participants in a situation account for what happens. Thus the interpretations of the Civil War that prevailed at the time were couched by the North in terms of the aims of a "conspiracy" of aggressive slave-holders and by the South in terms of the ambitions of a radical group of abolitionist "Black Republicans". These simple theses were too obviously partisan charges of blame to find acceptance by later historians, whose professional confidence is rightly based on the principle that those who come after an event can, with the help of emotional distance, awareness of consequences, and wider perspective, know more about it than any participants. But even later historians have extensively used the language of purpose. The "revisionist" thesis of a needless war produced by "blundering statesmanship" essentially interprets the war in that way, as the consequence of human judgments and passions, though it condemns them as "irrational".

The historian cannot dispense with "cause" in this sense because, as Becker put it, "men's actions have value and purpose; and if we write history in such a way as to give it meaning and significance we have to take account of these

[29] Richard H. Shyrock, "The Nationalistic Tradition of the Civil War: A Southern Analysis", *South Atlantic Quarterly*, 32 (1933), 294-305. There is a useful extract in Stampp, *op. cit.*,45-9.

values and purposes, to explain *why* men behave as they do, what they aim to accomplish, and whether they succeed or not".[30] The critic might well say that a man's purpose may not be the cause of his action – yet apart from this "humanistic" concern history threatens to become a merely impersonal process which "might have occurred at any time and in any place, given a sufficient number of persons to operate the events".[31] It is this intense commitment to the purposive dimension of history which leads many historians to feel a strong sympathy with literature and a sullen suspicion of social science. The occasional philistinism and arrogance of some propagandists for the social sciences have made many historians understandably defensive.

Yet in cooler moments the humanistic historian must acknowledge that this purposive dimenstion does not exhaust history. Historians have also been keenly interested in the explanatory relevance to American history of such relatively impersonal factors as De Tocqueville's "equality of condition", Turner's "frontier hypothesis", Beard's "capitalism and agrarianism", Potter's "abundance", and Hartz's "atomistic social freedom". These explanations need not be antagonistic when they are formulated without monistic claims. Turner, despite the dogmatism of his famous essay, was committed in principle to a "multiple hypothesis" approach; Beard was increasingly led to modify the monistic and deterministic implications of his economic interpretation; and both Potter and Hartz have explicitly repudiated the sufficiency of a single-determinant explanation.[32] The force of these various theories lies in their capacity to illuminate structure and continuity in American history, as demonstrated by specific historical illustrations, numerous enough to give significance to the generalizations. As such, they are not so much "causes" of specific events as they are ways of segregating out long-term conditions and tendencies of American culture and development. They give contour and meaning to the stream of events insofar as the historical evidence supports the generalizations.

The causal problem becomes acute when the historian faces the task of explaining a complex series of events which have the ideal unity of a single event, like the Civil War. The general causal question is then propounded: what was "the fundamental cause" of the event? The notorious disparity of opinion on the answer to this question should suggest that there is some fallacy in seeking to find a prime mover that can be abstracted from the process to account for it, like slavery, rival economic systems, or the "blundering statesmanship" of agitators and leaders. None of these alleged fundamental causes can be understood apart from their specific historical context, nor could

---

[30]   Letter (n. 22 above), 87.
[31]   Becker, "Harnessing History", *New Republic*, 22 (1920), 322.
[32]   For Turner and Beard see my *The Pragmatic Revolt in American History: Carl Becker and Charles Beard* (New Haven, 1958), 21-3, 105-6. For the others see David M. Potter, *People of Plenty: Economic Abundance and the American Character* (Chicago, 1954), 165; Louis Hartz, *The Liberal Tradition in America* (New York, 1955), 20-3.

any person be said to understand the Civil War who only knew that its funda-mental cause was any or all of these things. Otherwise history would merely be a cook-book for those sworn to fásting. These judgments of fundamental causality are only retrospective assessments of a reconstructed story and never a substitute for it. Actually they should be taken only as clues to the story being told. The pragmatic meaning of the assertion that slavery was "the fundamental cause" is only that the institution was so deeply entangled in the issues that divided the sections that it provides a valuable focus for examining the skein of events which culminated in war.

The historian does his work in good conscience, despite the difficulties of causality, because so much of his labor does not depend upon causal judgment. Whatever some philosophers may say, he knows that explanation is broader than causal explication. He may tell his readers much about the issues between Lincoln and Douglas, the legal status of slavery, the structure of classes in society, the economic interests of the sections, the character of the abolitionist movement, the balance of power in the Senate, the social and ideological differences between North and South, and the chronology of events without venturing beyond descriptive analysis into causal judgment. Characteristically, the historian explains by showing how a certain process took shape, answering the "why" with more of the "what" and "how". "The careful, thorough and accurate answer to the question *How*", writes the English historian C. V. Wedgwood, "should take the historian a long way towards answering the question *Why*..."[33] The historian is inescapably committed to narrative.

The relativists may quickly point out that the stories historians have told clearly reflect the "climate of opinion" in which they were constructed. Beard's economic interpretation grew out of a Progressive milieu in which the critics of industrial America had been drawn increasingly to economic analysis of contemporary problems; the "revisionism" of J. G. Randall betrayed some of the liberals' disillusionment with World War I and the fear of involvement with World War II; Arthur M. Schlesinger, Jr.'s criticism of the "revisionist" thesis of "a needless war" openly compares the Nazi and Southern threats to an "open society" and reflects the post-war "hard" policy towards Soviet imperialism; and Avery Craven's latest analysis, a modified "revisionist" view, strikes a Cassandra pose by comparing the Civil War crisis to the frightening "cold war" situation of today, where huge power-blocs compete for "satellites" and are deeply estranged from mutual understanding.[34] Inevitably, the historian's experience of present history will suggest questions and hypotheses, and in the attempt to relate his story to his public he will naturally try to find

[33]  *Truth and Opinion: Historical Essays* (London, 1960), 14.
[34]  Schlesinger specifically refers to the problem of dealing with a "closed society" in both periods in "The Causes of the Civil War: a Note on Historical Sentimentalism", *Partisan Review*, 16 (1949), 969-81; and the "cold war" analogy is extensively developed in Avery O. Craven, *Civil War in the Making, 1815-60* (Baton Rouge, La., 1959), esp. xiii-xiv.

terms appropriate to his own age. Yet he must always be on guard against the insidious tendency of analogy to blur the important nuances of difference between a past age and his own. His fundamental premise as a historian must be that human experience significantly changes in its form and meaning, that his present is only a phase of a process which calls out for historical analysis precisely because it is not uniform and continuous. The historian may believe that while one generation passes away and another generation comes, the earth abides forever, but it is his special obligation to note that the sun also rises on a new day.

The relativism of Becker and Beard was a valuable attack on the pretensions of nineteenth-century historical positivism, but its force was blunted by remnants of the same determinism they challenged. Becker considered historical judgments transient and arbitrary because he saw the mind of the historian as a mere product of the social forces active in his setting, projecting onto the blank screen of the past his own image, shaped by the hopes and fears generated by his "climate of opinion". Beard was nostalgic for the dream of an omniscient grasp of the totality of all happenings. He knew the dream was utopian; therefore, he settled instead for an "act of faith" in historical progress towards a specific future as the basis for interpretation of the past, a prediction which future history would validate or refute. But one must reply: if involvement in present history gives the historian his need to know the past, it does not necessarily prevent him from having enough detachment to apply articulate and impersonal standards to the evidence he examines; if the historian cannot know everything, it does not follow that he cannot know anything of historical importance; if the future is opaque, the past cannot be illuminated from a source which, being still indeterminate, will not furnish any light; if the historian is truly honored, it is because of his power of hindsight, not his power of prophecy.

If historians seem to have rented out a large hotel of "rooms with a view" in order to tell their story of the Civil War, it should be remembered that the sign out front should often read, "philosophy, not history, spoken here". Much of the recent debate over the Civil War centers on philosophical issues about economic determinism or rationalist politics. The historical materialists reduce the political, ideological, and moral questions to the "inevitable" conflicts of classes in society; the "revisionists" assume that violence is abnormal and that an event as bloody and tragic as civil war must have been avoidable by "rational" men; their critics point to the intractability of moral issues and the normality of non-rational factors in history.[35] Historians cannot escape such philosophical questions, but they need not entail a skepticism about historical truth.

The philosophy of history in America, as Morton G. White has pointed out, has been a very poor relation indeed. (Not even the Pragmatists, who did

[35] Illustrative examples of these three positions can be found in Stampp, *op. cit.*, 56-65, 83-7, 113-22.

much to stimulate interest in history, paid it the honor of systematic attention. It is therefore encouraging that Mr. White should seek to lead philosophers to consider the "special kind of discourse" which is narration.[36]) The causal problem would be greatly clarified if both historians and philosophers realized that in telling a story the historian is committed to the "logic" of drama. In explaining the Civil War he necessarily seeks to recreate the strife of opposing forces out of which the war came. The connective tissue of his account then has a dialectical form: a person or group takes a position and performs an action because of and in relation to the position or action of another person or group. The historian's story becomes a narrative of this reciprocal response. Thus, by a crude sketch, the explanation of the event would have this character: Lincoln saw in the South's pro-slavery position a threat to the democratic traditions of the American community; the South saw in his election the menace of future interference with their "peculiar institution" and growing domination by an industrial North; Lincoln and the North saw in Southern secession a challenge to federal authority and the prestige of national union; the South saw in the provisioning of Fort Sumter an intolerable danger to independence of the Confederacy... In such terms, but with much greater richness and concreteness, the historian tries to reconstruct the dramatic "logic" of a sequence of events which demands to be humanly understood rather than scientifically explained.

This dialectical method does not entail any Hegelian scheme or "bloodless dance of the categories"; on the contrary, it keeps the historian in touch with the familiar existential world of human action, too concrete and passionate for final abstract accounting. Like the action of a novel or play, it can be imaginatively experienced as a meaningful plot in which character, events, and circumstances are woven together in a process made intelligible in human terms of tradition, interest, passion, purpose, and policy. This kind of historical action is understood in the same way as a novel's plot is understood, though the former must be faithful to given evidence and the latter to aesthetic standards. To ask the question "why?" is then meaningful only as a demand for enlightenment on some particular passage of the story which does not "make sense". The general causal question remains at worst an irrelevant basis for interminable disagreement, at best a generator of hypotheses to stimulate research which may promote understanding by leading to a richer, more coherent story.

In reconstructing the dramatic "logic" of a situation which eventuated in civil war, historians cannot expect to achieve a flawless coherence in their stories. They have no warrant for making history neat and tidy when experience itself has ambiguities. Often there is uncertainty about motives, even for the actor himself, because the flaw lies not in the historian's impotence but in the documents or life itself. Even if historians cannot agree, to cite a classic

[36] "A Plea for an Analytic Philosophy of History", in Morton G. White, *Religion, Politics, and the Higher Learning* (Cambridge, Mass., 1959), 74.

controversy created by conflicting evidence, whether Lincoln sent a relief ship to Sumter in the cunning expectation that the South would commit aggression by firing on the fort, or, on the contrary, discovered by the attack how inaccurately he had measured the secessionist temper, nevertheless, they can still reach a common understanding of his policy reasons for risking war in the first place, whatever he expected or hoped would happen, after he had done what he felt had to be done. Historians will never escape the need for critical debate on their findings to help them move towards a consensus of understanding, but this fate is no ground for despair. It is rather the dogmatic insistence on scientific explanations, especially when they are beyond historical competence, that dooms historians to endless and fruitless contention.

Mr. White prophesies "a new era in the philosophy of history" when "the tools of linguistic philosophy" shall be brought to bear on "clarifying the logic of narration".[37] Sharp as these instruments are, however, they involve the risk that the operation may kill the patient. In explaining narration it may be forgotten that narration is a form of explanation, which aims not at logical rigor of implication but at dramatic comprehensibility, appropriate to the untidy, passionate, and value-charged activities of men. Historians may be said to be engaged in constantly teaching that lesson, yet, as much of the long inconclusive debate about "the causes of the Civil War" makes clear, without really knowing it. It is time they directly confronted the specter that haunts them.

*California Institute of Technology*

---

[37] *Loc. cit.*

# 6.

## NAMIER AND NAMIERISM

JOHN BROOKE

"The great historian", wrote Sir Lewis Namier in his essay on *History*, "is like the great artist or doctor: after he has done his work, others should not be able to practise within its sphere in the terms of the preceding era." No one who works within Namier's chosen sphere – British parliamentary history in the eighteenth century – can do so in terms of the pre-Namier era; and such has been his authority that for some time to come historians of that period will be differentiated from each other on a pro and anti-Namier basis, with respect both to methods and conclusions. In the field of modern European history Namier's contribution was less substantial, nor has this aspect of his work aroused the same degree of controversy over methods and outlook. Still, human history is a unit, however we may divide it up for convenience of study or research; and a historian's purpose is likely to be the same whatever period he studies. To Namier "the crowning attainment of historical study" was "an historical sense – an intuitive understanding of how things did not happen". (How they did happen was a matter of specific knowledge.) For Namier the main purpose of history was to help man "to master the past immanent both in his person and in his social setting and induce in him a fuller understanding of the present".

It is not the object of this essay to examine Namier's findings in detail nor to test the validity of his conclusions within his chosen sphere: that is a matter for research, not for an essay in historiography. Namier himself modified many of his earlier findings in the light of his later work, and further research will no doubt bring more changes. There can be no such thing as definitive history, and the historian's contribution to the understanding of humanity is not to be measured by the degree to which his work is outdated by subsequent research. An undergraduate today has access to a body of scientific knowledge which was beyond the reach of Newton, but that does not make him a greater scientist than Newton. It is the purpose of this essay to consider the Namier method and outlook, his conception of history and the way it should be written; something which even in his lifetime was known as "Namierism", and which has influenced historians of all periods. This involves an examination of the implications behind Namier's work, of ideas taken for granted but rarely given expression, and is based primarily on an understanding of his method and purpose gained during nine years' collaboration with him on the *History of Parliament*.

The student of Namier is at once confronted by the fact that his writings are all beginnings to vast enterprises which were never concluded. *England in the Age of the American Revolution* ends with the establishment of Bute's ministry in December 1762: it did not even reach the Stamp Act, which historians usually regard as the outset of the revolution. *Diplomatic Prelude*, Namier's study of the origins of the Second World War, written before most of the relevant diplomatic documents were published, was intended as preliminary to a larger and fuller work which never appeared. "For forty years", Namier says in his introduction to *Vanished Supremacies*, "I have wanted to write a history of Europe 1812-1918" – but he never wrote it. The last nine years of his life he devoted to the task of editing the *History of Parliament* for the years 1754-1790, the period he had made peculiarly his own, and this he intended to be his *magnum opus* – he died with the work unfinished. His books are full of promises to write about this subject or that, promises which were rarely fulfilled. Behind each work by Namier there was a vision which never became reality.

Yet the quantity of his work was considerable. In a period of roughly thirty years he published two long books on eighteenth-century politics; *Diplomatic Prelude*, together with two supplementary volumes of essays; a study of the revolutions of 1848; and a number of essays on British and European history, some of considerable significance. There was his work on the *History of Parliament* (his contributions to these volumes must amount to near half-a-million words), and a biography of Charles Townshend, also left unfinished. Throughout his life he was a frequent contributor to the press and learned journals. His work for the Zionist movement and for the resettlement of Jewish refugees during the Hitler period took him away from historical research, and for twenty years he held the chair of modern history in the University of Manchester. The writing of history was only one of many occupations (and to him not always the most important) in a long and full life.

Namier's writings may be divided into two types: long books, based on detailed research and covering only a short period of time; or brief essays on vast subjects. *England in the Age of the American Revolution* is a book of over four hundred pages which narrates the events of only the first two years of George III's reign, while *Monarchy and the Party System*, a lecture delivered in an hour, spans the period from George II to Victoria. *Diplomatic Prelude* covers the eleven months from Munich to the outbreak of war in four hundred pages, while *Basic Factors in Nineteenth-Century European History* – from Napoleon to Hitler – is an essay of twelve pages. "What matters in history", Namier wrote, "is the great outline and the significant detail: what must be avoided is the deadly mass of irrelevant narrative." [1] A searchlight concentrated at the focal point, he used to say, will give more illumination than rows of candles.

It has become a common criticism of Namier's work to say that while he had mastered what has come to be known as the "analytic" method of writing history, he could not narrate a sequence of events in the manner of the classic historians. Behind this is the assumption that history is, or ought to be, primarily narration, and that the literary qualities associated with a good story-teller count for much in the make-up of the historian. Yet no historian is able to narrate events in the way a novelist does; he must also analyze institutions and ideas, and provide co-ordinates for the outline of events. "While ideas outlive reality, names and words outlast both", was a favorite aphorism of Namier; and in the essay from which this is quoted (*History*) he gave two examples: "There were bishops in the fourth century, and party names were in use in eighteenth-century England; yet conclusions must not be drawn from either fact without a thorough understanding of what those terms then covered." The criticism that Namier had no gift for narration is scarcely true (*Diplomatic Prelude* is a masterly example of how to narrate a complicated series of events), but masks a more formidable criticism: that Namier was not interested in those matters that are usually thought the proper concern of historians. One distinguished British historian has compared Namier to the Duke of Newcastle, the central figure in his eighteenth-century books, who "wasted his life on trifles", and has remarked on the oddity of Namier's preferring to write about the intrigues of Newcastle and Bute rather than Pitt's foreign policy.

When Namier was working on the *History of Parliament*, it seemed to me significant that he preferred to write about small men, who made little impression on the history of their times, or obscure transactions without great effects. When I asked him why he was interested in the lives of small men, he told me that as a child he had been neglected by his parents, had found companionship only with servants, and had thus developed an interest in the lives of people who never held to center of the stage. When asked what the phrase "Namierizing history" really meant, Namier would laugh and reply: "It means finding out who the guys were." The Members of Parliament whose lives were obscure roused his interest, and it is difficult for anyone who did not work with him to appreciate the amount of time he would devote to them or how engrossed he could become in what to others seemed trivial events. Behind a good deal of the criticism directed at Namier and his methods there is exasperation at an historian of his intellectual gifts apparently misapplying them on trifles. The question why Namier did so is crucial to an understanding of the man himself and of his conception of history.

---

[1] *Avenues of History* (London, 1952), 8.

Namier began historical research before the First World War, in the political atmosphere of the New Imperialism. Ideas of imperial union were in the air, and Namier's first historical work (which he never published), submitted in 1912 for the Beit Prize Essay at Oxford, was a review of plans for imperial federation. When he went to America in 1913 to take up a business appointment, he began to work on the imperial problem during the American revolution; and, as he recounts in the preface to the *Structure of Politics*, decided to study the House of Commons, "which, in so ill-fated a manner, undertook the work of preserving the First British Empire". For the rest of his life, whatever diversions were presented by other historical problems, British parliamentary history remained, as he wrote in 1952 in the preface to *In the Nazi Era*, "my own chosen field". Many misconceptions about Namier's work disappear when it is realized that he was primarily a historian of Parliament. It was not the eighteenth century as such that particularly attracted him (many aspects of the history of that period did not interest him at all), but Parliament; and it is significant that both his eighteenth-century books begin with a sentence about the importance of Parliament in British life. Within Namier's frame of reference the story of how Bute wrested from Newcastle control of the House of Commons is relevant; an account of Pitt's foreign policy or the conduct of diplomatic negotiations, is not.

When Namier began his work, modern British parliamentary history (from the Revolution onwards) was not a field of study which attracted historians. There was one scholarly work on the eighteenth-century Parliament, *The Unreformed House of Commons*, by Edward and Annie G. Porritt, which, as Namier says, necessarily dealt with "the constant rather than with the changing elements"; there were biographies of the leading parliamentary figures; badly-edited and incomplete editions of their papers (generally with election correspondence omitted); and a few scholarly works on parliamentary reform. No attempt had been made at a comprehensive edition of parliamentary debates since the early nineteenth century; for information about back-bench Members there was little except the pioneering works of local antiquarians; and for the constituencies, one had to turn to the propaganda of parliamentary reformers. Historians generally followed Macaulay and pronounced moral strictures against both eighteenth-century Members and electors, without asking how the unreformed Parliament had worked and why it managed to escape reformation until 1832. The history of the most vital and enduring of all political institutions was largely unrecorded, and to this day there is no chair of parliamentary history in any British university.

Namier originally intended to call his book "The British Parliament in 1761", and it was to be followed by a further study of the British Parliament during the American Revolution. The original title foreshadowed the subject matter of the work better than *The Structure of Politics at the Accession of George III*, the one he later adopted. He took for his motto a quotation from Aeschylus:

I took pains to determine the flight of crook-taloned birds, marking which were of the right by nature, and which of the left, and what were their ways of living, each after his kind, and the enmities and affections that were between them, and how they consorted together.

The point of this quotation was in the final phrase: Namier's aim was to study an institution, the House of Commons, as it existed between 1761 and 1784, through the lives of its members – he wanted to find out "how they consorted together". These were not so many individuals who happened to have flourished at about the same time: their lives were interlocked, and the highest common factor was their membership of the House of Commons. An institution has a life and personality of its own, transcending those of the individuals who compose it; but to re-create it as a living organism Namier had to go beyond the bare records of its corporate life and study the lives of its Members. His task was, in his own words, "to find out all I could about every single Member who sat in the House between 1761 and 1784"; and he soon realized that he was acquiring information not merely about Members of Parliament but about the social and economic life of the period. For the 558 Members of the House of Commons formed a representative sample of the governing class – or, to use Namier's expression, the political nation – of their day, and a sample chosen neither by chance nor with any subjective inclinations. Through a study of their biographies it was possible to re-create the mental and moral atmosphere in which they lived, to eliminate the preconceptions of a later age, and to see political problems in their proper context. Namier hoped that an incidental result of his work would be to rescue eighteenth-century history from contemporary memoir and letter writers, whose object was to amuse rather than to search for truth, and from nineteenth-century Whig historians, concerned to trace the ancestry of their political creed – in short, to penetrate to the reality behind anecdotes and ideas.

What Namier did was to employ a new technique of historical research, with results that may be seen from a comparison with similar phenomena in the history of science. Whether Namier discovered this technique himself, or whether others had preceded him, is not of great consequence. Galileo did not invent the telescope nor Freud the free-association method in psychology. And it is with the invention of the telescope that the Namier method of historical research may best be compared, nor is the parallelism between history and astronomy made merely for literary effect: both are attempts to investigate conditions in the past in the belief that these will lead to an understanding of the present. The Namier method is simply a more efficient technique for investigating the past, just as the telescope is a more efficient instrument than the naked eye for investigating the heavens. But neither will tell the student all he wants to know; the Namier method is inappropriate for the investigation of certain problems and periods, and it remains a mere instrument, its findings subject to interpretation. It will give the investigator new facts, but it will not supply explanations or construct theories.

The Namier method was founded on the extensive study of contemporary materials, printed or manuscript – "I hardly remember having come across any contemporary materials", he wrote in the preface to the *Structure of Politics*, "or any book reproducing such materials, which did not contribute something to my information." Historical research, as he conducted it, could hardly be combined with University teaching; it was an occupation in itself, demanding the historian's full time and concentration; and during the years which Namier devoted to historical research he lived on borrowed money and a grant from the Rhodes Foundation. If, as Gibbon maintains, diligence and accuracy are the only merits to which a historian may lay claim, then Namier was justified in both: his transcripts of manuscripts (taken down in shorthand) fill over thirty large note books, and his copies of contemporary memoirs and correspondence are all carefully checked against the originals. In his *Additions and Corrections* to volume I of Fortescue's edition of the correspondence of George III, published in 1937, he outlined the standards he expected from editors of historical documents: textual accuracy; the careful checking of dates; the correlation of the documents with other sources; and an attempt to explain obscure transactions and identify lesser-known persons. He spent a great deal of time, especially after he had begun work on the *History of Parliament*, in searching for documents – "cross-country paper chases", as he used to describe these journeys to country houses and record offices. And during the last twenty years of his life he was handicapped by paralysis of the right hand which made writing almost impossible.

Before the *Structure of Politics* had been published, Namier had realized, to continue the metaphor, that he must acquire a larger telescope; and in a remarkable essay, written in July 1928 (and republished in his posthumous book *Crossroads of Power*), he outlined the way such an instrument should be fashioned. "The biography of the ordinary man cannot be profitably attempted", he wrote, "unless one writes the history of a crowd . . . The student has to get acquainted with the lives of thousands of individuals, with an entire ant-heap, see its files stretch out in various directions, understand how they are connected and correlated, watch the individual ants, and yet never forget the ant-heap." His plan was for a Dictionary of Parliamentary Biography, arranged not alphabetically but according to periods, "organized on a national scale, given national standing, and financed from national resources", the work not of one man but of a team.

In 1929 Namier became a member of a committee appointed by the First Lord of the Treasury to report on the materials available for a record of the Members of the House of Commons and on the cost and desirability of publication. The Wedgwood committee (so called from the name of its chairman Colonel Josiah C. Wedgwood, M.P.) recommended the compilation of a biographical history of the House of Commons, arranged according to "significant historical periods". But no provision was available from national resources, and only two volumes of the history (dealing with the fifteenth century) had been published when war broke out. When the work was resumed in 1951, it was under the direction of an editorial board of parliamentary historians and was financed by a Treasury grant. Namier became a member of the editorial board and editor of the section 1754-1790; and after his retirement from Manchester University in 1953 settled at the Institute of Historical Research in London to direct the work of his section.

Namier saw the *History of Parliament* as the continuation of the work he had begun with the *Structure of Politics*, but with a bigger and more sensitive instrument. Whereas formerly he had worked alone, he now had a staff of three research assistants, and could count also on the co-operation of students and scholars outside his staff. The larger the telescope, the farther it can penetrate into space; and though Namier led an able and devoted research team, he dreamt of an even bigger and finer instrument and chafed at the unavoidable restraints of time and money upon his research. Only a few days before his death, he wrote in an unfinished introduction to the *History:*

Experience shows that there is hardly a Member whose life could not be written if more collections, local records, newspaper files, etc. were examined. But there was neither time nor the means to carry researches so much further. . . . We have to say with the narrator in *Moby Dick*:

Small erections may be finished by their first architects; grand ones, true ones, ever leave the copestone to posterity. . . . This whole book is but a draft – nay, but the draft of a draft. Oh, Time, Strength, Cash, and Patience!

It seems unlikely that future historians will sit down, as did Macaulay, Lecky, Froude, or Gardiner in the nineteenth century, to write the history of a hundred years in a dozen volumes. A wide reading public for that kind of history no longer exists, nor is it probable that any one historian could satisfy scholars over so long a period treated in such detail. Modern technological inventions – the typewriter, the microfilm reader, and the electronic computer – are revolutionizing the writing of history, and a change has also come over the position of the historian: he is now primarily a teacher rather than a researcher, and the most profitable kind of history book is one designed for schools and universities and not based on original research. Detailed research on a large scale, in history as in science, can now only be done by a team, and has to be financed by a university, a Government department, or an educational foundation; it is designed primarily for scholars, and conforms to a standard of scholarship unrealizable fifty years ago. Such works are the *Victoria County History*, the *Complete Peerage*, and the *History of Parliament* in Britain; the civil and military histories of the Second World War, both British and American; and the great American editions of Horace Walpole, Jefferson, Franklin, and others. This is the historical research of the second half of the twentieth century: Namierism carried to its logical conclusion. It bears the same relationship to the methods of the *Structure of Politics* as the Mount Palomar telescope does to the home-made reflector: the instrument is bigger and the technique more refined, but the principle and purpose are the same. In most spheres of human activity – and historical research must now be counted among them – the individual can achieve little outside the group. The problem which occupied Namier all his life was how individuals could be induced to work together for a common good, transcending and yet satisfying their separate desires – how they could be made "to consort together". It was this interest in group activity which led him to study first imperial federation, and next the House of Commons, and which generated the idea of collective research.

Yet bigger and more sensitive instruments of historical research do not by themselves convey a deeper understanding of the past; the results of research must be filtered through the human mind. The observations of the astronomer lead to the formation of a hypothesis, and the end product of historical research is narrative and explanation. No amount of telescopic observation will account for the movements of the planets round the sun or the continuous outpouring of energy by the stars. To explain these phenomena the astronomer has to call in the aid of the ancillary sciences of physics and mathematics, and indeed there is hardly any branch of science which does not at some time bear upon his work. For his grandest purpose – a theory of the universe which shall explain how it arose and how it has developed – observational data must be supplemented by mathematical analysis.

Namier believed that psychology bears the same relation to the humanities as mathematics does to the sciences: a separate discipline, and also an instrument to serve the student of other disciplines. "Analytic insight into the tangle of human affairs", he wrote in *History,* "coupled with a consciousness of his own limitations is the mark of the real historian." He must acquire an understanding of how human beings behave, both individually and collectively, and trace the springs of action back into the human mind.

War advances the sciences which devise its weapons; the quest for a better control of man thus armed must turn to the new "humanities": foremost to history illumined by psychology and the social sciences, and directed to a pragmatic purpose.[2]

Just as it would be unthinkable for a scientist to attempt to evaluate the findings of twentieth-century technology with nineteenth-century mathematics, so to Namier it was unthinkable for the historian to interpret human conduct by the concepts of pre-Freudian psychology. The revolution in psychological thought at the beginning of this century must revolutionize the writing of history, and for students of the humanities the concept of the unconscious

[2]   *Facing East* (London, 1947), 27.

mind (to mention only the fundamental of Freud's theory) was as great a discovery as the displacement of the earth from the center of the universe had been for the scientist in the seventeenth century. History must absorb the findings of psychoanalysis and adapt them for its own purposes.

The most obvious application of the new psychological knowledge was in the assessment of historical characters, and the difference it made may be seen from a comparison of Macaulay's portrait of the Duke of Newcastle with Namier's. Both historians agree that Newcastle was avid for power, jealous of his colleagues, incessantly occupied with trifles, and unfit to bear political responsibility. But Macaulay depicts Newcastle as a fool, a fit object for ridicule; Namier as a neurotic, a fit object for pity. The concluding passage of Namier's portrait of Newcastle is an example of analytical research adapted for historical purposes:

Newcastle frequently referred to himself as a "galley-slave" – why then did he remain in office? Men are said to seek pleasure and shun pain; but as "there is no accounting for tastes", the statement is tautological – they seek what they seek. It was proudly believed in the past that the earth was the centre of the universe; that man was created on a different day from other animals; that he was a reasonable being, "the captain of his soul". Men still cling to this last fundamental belief and they continue to give "reasonable" explanations for their actions, i.e., to "rationalize" them ... There are men who crave for mortification; "la mia allegrez' è la maninconia". But unless this desire assumes a standardised religious form – hair-shirt or hermit's hut – and can be represented as a profitable bargain for another world, men dare not admit it, not even to themselves ... There was unconscious self-mortification in Newcastle's tenure of office.[3]

Here Freud's concept of the sense of guilt appears in the portrait of an historical character; and in Namier's account of events at the accession of George III, Newcastle's neurosis and the King's emotional immaturity are more potent factors than political ideas. These events were to Namier a historical comedy: a conflict of characters, with consequences for history, rather than a conflict of political principles. Namier has been accused of "taking the mind out of history"; it would be more correct to say that he was among the first to take into history the post-Freudian conception of the mind. That is what his critics so much disliked.

"Biographies", Namier wrote in his essay on history, "have become the ritualist form of English historiography"; and he went on to criticize the typical political biography as being neither good history nor good biography.

But to deal with the human mind would require knowledge of ancillary disciplines, foremost of psychology, both normal and pathological, and insight into the human mind and character; while most biographers if asked for their qualifications could only answer more or less like the girl who applied for the post of nurse to children: that she herself was once a child.

---

[3]   *England in the Age of the American Revolution* (2nd ed., London, 1961), 82-3.

In the later years of his life Namier was working towards a new form of biography which would correlate political ideas and action with emotional life. Such were the longer biographies he wrote for the *History of Parliament* and his essay on King George III. Most ambitious of all was his study of Charles Townshend, in which he traced the psychological origins of Townshend's American policy to impressions of his early life. Townshend, as a young man in rebellion against an oppressive father, himself became the heavy father in his dealings with the American colonies, and their subjection to the government of the parent country was the one political idea which he constantly followed. Yet Namier understood that there are limitations to the psychological analysis of historical characters: only rarely is there sufficient material, and even then, as he wrote at the end of his biography of Townshend, it is easier "to analyse the shortcomings and mistakes of a man than to convey an idea of his genius, charm, or eloquence". And in his essay *Human Nature in Politics* he uttered a warning:

The unqualified practitioner must not be let loose, not even on the dead, and a mere smattering of psychology is likely to result in superficial, hasty judgements framed in a nauseating jargon ... When dealing with the mysteries of the human mind, we had best say with the preacher: "And now, brethren, let us boldly face the difficulty, and then pass it over."

The commonest charge against Namier was that he was indifferent to the influence of ideas in history: and if ideas are regarded as intellectual concepts, the charge has substance. "History, when viewed in terms of pure ideas", Namier wrote in his essay *Communities*, published in 1927, "becomes a record of human folly. But men are seldom so absurd as words make them appear; seldom, if ever, do they fight and die, or even kill, for a mere shibboleth." And later, in the same essay:

To some the subject-matter of medicine is disease, and of history ideas, as if these were extraneous things which visit or befall human beings. But disease is merely a condition of the human body defined and circumscribed by medical thought, and some diseases vanish, whilst others appear, only because of changes in medical conceptions and terminology. Nor have nationality and religions an independent existence and permanent, immutable contents; they reflect certain things in the lives of communities, and often the same things under changed names.

Ideas are not like the forces of nature – the wind, the sun, the stars – which determine the conditions of man's existence and are beyond the control of his will. They exist only in the minds of men (and are not the same for each individual man); their living content is instinctive and emotional, though their outward form may be rational; and for this reason they may outlive the circumstances which produced them, retaining only their emotional relevance.

To treat them as the offspring of pure reason would be to assign to them a parentage about as mythological as that of Pallas Athene. What matters most is the underlying emotions, the music, to which ideas are a mere libretto, often of very inferior quality; and once the emotions have ebbed, the ideas, established high and dry, become doctrine, or at best innocuous *clichés*.[4]

What are usually termed political ideas are but the resultants on a rational plane of a number of conflicting, sometimes unconscious, emotional forces, and are rarely themselves the determinants of human action. "It is hard to believe", wrote Namier in his essay *Human Nature in Politics*, "that on the Paris barricades men died in 1830 in order to preserve the Charter, or in February 1848 in order to obtain an extension of the franchise"; and he declared it would be naive "to judge of the essence of mass movements by the pronouncements or professions of those who manage to filch them". To believe that men tortured and murdered each other in fourth-century Constantinople because of the difference between the *homoousion* and the *homoiousion*, or that the wars of religion in sixteenth-century Europe can be accounted for by disputes over dogma and church government, is to rate man's concern for abstract thought too high and his understanding of common things too low. As for the mass passions of the twentieth century – nationalism, racialism, and anti-Semitism – they can be understood, if at all, only in terms of mental pathology, not of political thought.

The study of ideas stripped of their emotional contents was to Namier a mere intellectual exercise: theology without faith. The Christian doctrines of the nature of God – the Trinity and the Incarnation – to an atheist are absurd; to a believer they are God's revelations to man of the truth about Himself. The fascination of ideas for the intellectual owes something to the fact that they are documented, and the historian has an overweening respect for what can be found in books; their pedigrees can be reconstructed and collateral lines developed; they can be classified, as a philatelist classifies stamps by their perforations and watermarks, or used to build systems as a child plays with bricks. They appeal to mankind's love of constructing order out of chaos, and bolster up human vanity. Namier in his essay on *Democracy* (1941) wrote about a "democracy of conceit, based on the self-adoration of man: on an enthusiastic belief in the light of human reason, the omnipotence of human thought, and the infinite perfectibility of human nature"; and warned against those who "envisage an idea, play with it, profess it, even flaunt it, without truly embracing it".[5] The strength of ideas is not in their logic or consistency but in the emotional pressure behind them, which is usually both illogical and inconsistent (but not necessarily unreasonable or ill-founded).

In 1945 in an essay on anti-Semitism Namier wrote:

What is it that has aroused those passions and phobias in so many lands, through so many centuries? Understand and explain the problem as much as you may, there remains a hard, insoluble core, incomprehensible and inexplicable.

4  *Personalities and Powers* (London, 1955), 4.
5  *Conflicts* (London, 1942), 195.

And the same year, in a review of Mr. A. J. P. Taylor's book *The Course of German History:*

He has carried his brilliant analysis to the border of psychological and sociological inquiry, without directly tackling the problem of what it is that makes the Germans behave in such, for us bewildering and incomprehensible, ways.

The thought behind both these quotations is the same: that there are limits to historical analysis as a tool for the understanding of human conduct; that the historian ultimately comes to a region where his training and technique are in vain, and where he has to hand over to the psychologist and the sociologist; and farther along the road there is the mile-stone where psychology and sociology can go no further, and where man can walk by faith alone.

The limitations of historical analysis may be seen – to choose a classic example – from an examination of the evidence for and against the resurrection of Jesus, an event fixed in time and place and apparently verifiable. Of the historical truth of the resurrection only two views are possible (the attempts of nineteenth-century German theologians to find a naturalistic explanation may be summarily rejected): either the Gospel story is substantially true and an event of such consequence for mankind that every other fact recorded by history is dwarfed into insignificance; or else it is false – the biggest deception ever practised upon credulous humanity. The Gospel evidence for the resurrection may be countered by the lack of evidence from any source not concerned to propagate it as truth; while the argument that this was an event contrary to the laws of nature, is met by the Christian claim that it was not contrary to the laws of God. Each argument runs up against an objection impossible to overcome yet insufficient to render it nugatory. No fact known to history is of such consequence, whether true or false, yet historical analysis is powerless to determine one way or the other. Faith will induce belief, and scepticism doubt; and the reasons for both have nothing to do with historical truth.

The resurrection is one single historical fact, here isolated out of its context. But every historical event is the accumulation of a number of facts, which are accepted or rejected, emphasized or relegated to a place of minor importance, according to the judgment (or some would say, the taste and fancy) of the historian. On a cloudless night about six thousand stars, of varying degrees of brightness, are visible to the naked eye; and man's imagination has constructed pictures and patterns out of these isolated points of light: Orion, the great hunter; Andromeda, the maiden; Perseus, her deliverer; Pegasus, the winged horse; and others. The observer at the same spot on the earth's surface will see the constellations unchanged throughout the course of his life, and thus the impression exists that the patterns in the sky are 'eternal' – natural phenomena like the stars themselves. But if the observer could be shifted to the other end of the galaxy, or to a point in time a million years from our own, even if he saw the same stars they would not be in the same patterns; for the constellations have no reality, they are the products of time and space. And the patterns historians weave out of facts vary also with time and space and lack objective truth.

It is obvious that a Catholic historian's account of the Reformation will differ from that of a Protestant, or that the Russian Revolution will be seen from different angles by historians in Moscow and Washington. The effects of time on the historian's vision are also obvious: those historians who wrote in the aftermath of the Reform Act of 1832 could hardly appreciate the merits of the unreformed Parliament; and historians of the twentieth century have emphasized social trends in the Puritan Revolution which once seemed not of prime importance. Less obvious is the extent to which the historian's objectivity may be corroded by unconscious mental attitudes. He brings to the facts he has discovered the sum total of his experiences of life, of all he has felt and absorbed, in the present and from the past, both conscious and unconscious: his interpretation of life, the terms on which he accepts it, which differ in every human being and are not always to be accounted for by differences in education or mental environment. History is almost necessarily subjective, a projection of the personality and faith of the historian against the background of his chosen period – and even the choice of period or subject is characteristic. Such a work as Toynbee's *A Study of History* is really the autobiography of a mind, and the first section of Namier's *England in the Age of the American Revolution* ("The Social Foundations") tells the discerning reader at least as much about Namier as it does about eighteenth-century England. In 1944 Namier wrote in answer to the question: "Will it be possible for historians ever to arrive at an impartial, reasonably accurate, view of the events of World War II?":

I see no basic difference between World War II and any other set of historic happenings: the bias is in men and not in events, and there is nothing which cannot be dissected with cold detached objectivity, or which is intrinsically beyond the range of aggressive controversy. It all depends on what emotions are at work in the student: for objectivity itself is not necessarily unemotional (or dull). It may spring from breathless curiosity, which can attain the pitch of intellectual sadism. On the other hand, the spectro-analysis of the human mind can break up a ray of light into fantastic colour patterns. In fact, really intense research and analysis require some correlation between the student's emotional life and experience and his subject. But it depends largely on his mind and character whether the correlation is fruitful or harmful. A Nazi can hardly write an objective history of Sparta, once the supposed analogy with Hitler's Germany has struck him – and presumably will not write it at all unless it has. The Nazi mind (which is not confined to Germany) will never take an impartial view of World War II, or for that matter of any other subject. As for accuracy, it is a conception which I would associate with statements rather than with views. And there will be room and material for an infinite amount of "accurate" investigation into World War II – but what will result from it? Shall we get any nearer to explaining the senseless irrelevancy of so-called human thought and action? Behind your question seems to lurk a very justifiable doubt, brought out by World War II (but which should not be limited to it) whether we shall ever know anything which is worth knowing.

History to Namier had a pragmatic character. Early historians wrote to the glory of God; latter-day ones to the glory of a social class, a political and social philosophy, or of a nation-state. History is the perpetuation of a series of myths, which after they have served their purpose are gradually unravelled and the truth in them brought to light. British historiography on the American revolution, to give one example, was long concerned to explain the loss of the American colonies as due to no fault of the British Parliament or governing class. There was need to find a scapegoat, and so George III was charged with attempting to subvert American liberty as part of a design to overthrow the British constitution. The loss of the American colonies was the price the nation had to pay for the preservation of its system of representative government, which conclusion served as some sort of solace to latter-day Whigs (as did also the persistent denigration of American life and culture common in Britain during the nineteenth century). While there remained in the British political nation a group who regarded themselves as spiritually descended from the Whigs who had opposed George III, this myth satisfied an emotional need and worked against an impartial assessment of the American problem. Namier's own work on the diplomatic origins of the Second World War was prompted by moral revulsion, not only against the Nazis but against the "janissaries and appeasers" in western Europe who had had "neither the faith, nor the will, nor even sufficient repugnance, to offer timely, effective resistance". It was "a failure of European morality", and Namier duly called his second book on pre-war diplomatic history *Europe in Decay*. By then he had accomplished his purpose and the impetus to continue this work was lacking. "I myself am getting sick [of diplomatic history]", he wrote to me on 15 May 1950. "I shall drop it soon. Then I, too, shall return to the Rockinghams." And so, after having discharged a duty, he went back to his chosen field.

Little is achieved if the historian who destroys a long-standing myth sets up another in its place, as he may well do, for the incentive to destroy an old religion comes from faith in a new one. It was to guard against this that Namier developed the instrument of collective research – the patterns in the sky which appear so natural to the naked eye are obliterated by the detail to be seen in a telescope, and with the help of mathematics a more realistic survey of the heavens can be made. For the same reason Namier stressed "consciousness of his own limitations" as one of the marks of the great historian. For no period of history is the material available complete for all the historian's purposes, and it is often at the most critical junctures that the supply dries up. Contemporary documents concerning a particular transaction can only diminish in quantity with the progress of time, and later accounts of participants or eye-witnesses have almost invariably been submitted to conscious or unconscious mental revision – "emotion recollected in tranquillity". It is difficult to discover precisely what was happening in the minds of the chief actors: decisions are rarely taken in so clear-cut a manner as later appears; there are changes and shifts of emphasis, unrecorded and almost impossible to record – the things that really matter are hardly ever committed to paper. We shall never know what factor counted for most in determining Chamberlain's foreign policy in the autumn of 1938, precisely when and why Stalin opted for an alliance with Germany in the summer of 1939, or the explanation of Hitler's oscillations in the last week of peace. The historian may deduce what appears to him probable, but his deductions can never be submitted to any objective test such as is available to the scientist.

The result of Namier's work (he was aware of it himself) was to depreciate the value of history. If asked, what do men learn from history?, he would reply: Precisely what they wish to learn. In 1941 he wrote:

One would except people to remember the past and to imagine the future. But in fact, when discoursing or writing about history, they imagine it in terms of their own experience, and when trying to gauge the future they cite supposed analogies from the past: till, by a double process of repetition they imagine the past and remember the future.[6]

"Man is a repetitive, aping animal", Namier wrote in *History*, "and to basic irregularities and individual variations he adds the element of imitation and of expected repetition"; and he gave this example:

When the Russian revolution broke out in March 1917, there were people who expected that the Russian armies would now fight with a new *élan*, forgetting that in 1792 war broke out in the third year of revolution, while in 1917 revolution broke out in the third year of war; the French peasant-soldier – to mention but one factor – went to the front to retain the land he had seized, while the Russian peasant-soldier went home to seize it.

And this was his conclusion: "One of the aims of sound historical education must be to wean men from expecting automatic repetition and from juggling with uncorrelated precedents and analogies." But he did not think it could be easily, or perhaps ever, attained. Namier was fond of comparing history to psychoanalysis: both set out to reveal the repressed past in order to heal the disease of the present, and both are better able to diagnose than to cure – "the beneficial therapeutic effects of history have so far been small; and it is in the nature of things that it should be so".[7] Whatever therapeutic value there may be in psychoanalysis can hardly be obtained simply by reading about it, and similarly the value of history as an intellectual discipline lies almost wholly in the attempt to write it.

Namier defined faith as "the response of human nature, not of human

6  *Conflicts*, 69.
7  *Avenues of History*, 5.

understanding" [8] – not necessarily a specific religious or political creed. Throughout Namier's work, from his earliest writings to his last, there is one firm article of faith: a belief in what he called predestination, both of men and things.

"Every man has only one method", Namier wrote about Hitler in 1940, "as he has only one face; he is born with both." [9] There is a predestination of character, regardless of formal creeds. He wrote in his essay *Human Nature in Politics*:

A man's relation, for instance, to his father or to his nurse may determine the pattern of his later political conduct or of his intellectual preoccupations without his being in the least conscious of the connexion; and self-deception concerning the origin and character of his seemingly intellectual tenets enables him to deceive others.

There was also predestination with respect to the affairs of nations: "National policy is seldom determined, in the long run, by calculation and thought . . . States, like planets, move in predestined courses." [10] About the imperial problem in the eighteenth century, Namier wrote: "No great historic problem has ever been settled by means of a brilliant idea – an invention in the sphere of politics – when its solution was not latent in circumstances, but many a problem has found settlement by not being pressed at such a moment." [11] In *1848: the Revolution of the Intellectuals* he analyzed the early manifestations of German aggressive nationalism, and found in the attitude of the Frankfort Parliament towards the Czechs and Poles a foretaste of that of Hitler: liberals and Nazis behaved towards the Slavs in the same way.

In 1929 Namier wrote of Theodor Herzl, the founder of Zionism, that "having had no intimate experience of politics", he "did not know how very little the mighty can do, how little they dare, how they play with ideas but seldom act on them, except when forced by circumstances or the will of the masses".[12] To Namier mass action was the most potent force in politics: "the masses are invincible whenever they have a clearly defined, feasible aim in view"; and mass psychology was "the most basic factor in history".[13] In *England in the Age of the American Revolution* he wrote:

But whatever theories of "free will" theologians and philosophers may develop with regard to the individual, there can be no free will in the thinking and actions of the masses, any more than in the revolutions of planets, in the migrations of birds, and in the plunging of hordes of lemmings into the sea.

"The mob had come out in revolt", Namier wrote of 1848, "moved by

---

[8]   *Diplomatic Prelude* (London, 1948), 3.
[9]   *Conflicts*, 53.
[10]  *Conflicts*, 13.
[11]  *England in the Age of the American Revolution*, 35.
[12]  *Skyscrapers* (London, 1931), 141.
[13]  *Skyscrapers*, 147; *Personalities and Powers*, 4.

passions and distress rather than by ideas: they had no articulate aims, and no one will ever be able to supply a rational explanation of what it was they fought for, or what made them fight". The determinants of mass action were basic, instinctual forces, and its expression revolution or war.

Namier set little value on human achievements; he had infinite pity for human suffering.

*Institute of Historical Research,*
*University of London*

# III

## HISTORY AND
## SOCIAL THEORY

# 7.

## ON THE ETIOLOGY OF INTERNAL WARS

HARRY ECKSTEIN

### THE CONCEPT "INTERNAL WAR"

The term "internal war" denotes any resort to violence within a political order to change its constitution, rulers, or policies.[1] It is not a new concept; distinctions between external and internal war (*guerre extérieure* and *guerre intérieure*) were made already in the nineteenth century by writers on political violence.[2] Nor does it mean quite the same thing as certain more commonly used terms, such as revolution, civil war, revolt, rebellion, uprising, guerrilla warfare, mutiny, *jacquerie*, *coup d'état*, terrorism, or insurrection. It stands for the genus of which the others are species.

Using the generic concept alongside, or even in place of, the more specific terms is justifiable on several grounds. Most obviously, all cases of internal war do have common features, however much they differ in detail. All involve the use of violence to achieve purposes which can also be achieved without violence. All indicate a breakdown of some dimension in legitimate political order as well as the existence of collective frustration and aggression in a population. All presuppose certain capabilities for violence by those who make the internal war and a certain incapacity for preventing violence among

[1] Elsewhere I have used more cumbersome specifications for the term, holding that internal war is "a kind of social force that is exerted in the process of political competition, deviating from previously shared social norms, 'warlike' in character (that is, conducted practically without mutually observed normative rules), and involving the serious disruption of settled institutional patterns." *Internal War: Problems and Approaches* (New York, 1964), 12. The differences between the two formulations are due to the fact that here I am defining a term, while in the other essay I was delimiting a theoretical subject. (For what I mean by delimiting a theoretical subject, see *ibid.*, 8-11). – I am grateful to the Center of International Studies at Princeton University for supporting the work that went into this study as part of a wide-ranging set of inquiries into internal war. The Center's internal war studies, in turn, have been supported by grants from the Carnegie Foundation. Another, very different, version of the paper was published in a report prepared by the Research Group in Psychology and the Social Sciences, Smithsonian Institution, Washington, D.C., *Social Science Research and National Security* (government circulation only).

[2] For example, in Pierre Kropotkin, *Paroles d'un révolté*, ed. by Elisée Reclus (Paris, not dated, but circa 1885). The term was used by Count Fersen as early as 1790 and occurs also in the writings of Sismondi and the Federalist Papers.

those on whom it is made. All tend to scar societies deeply and to prevent the formation of consensus indefinitely. There is, consequently, at least a possibility that general theories about internal war may be discovered – general theories which may also help to solve problems posed by specific instances.

Another justification for grouping internal wars in a single universe is that actual instances of internal war often combine different types of violence, in space and time. Guerrilla warfare in one area may be combined with terrorism in another; it may be preceded by insurrections and develop into full-scale civil war, or culminate in a mere *coup d'état*. Indeed the large-scale and prolonged instances of internal war that we generally call revolutions are notable chiefly for the fact that they combine, in strikingly similar sequences, many different types of violence.[3] To focus analysis from the outset on particular species of internal war therefore makes it necessary to abstract from actual internal wars occurrences which may not in fact be strictly separable. This may be fine for working out abstract theories, but will not do for developing theories closely relevant to historical (i.e., concrete) cases in all their complexity.

A third justification for studying internal wars generically is furnished by the very limited results so far obtained in comparative historical studies of revolutions, particularly the pre-war studies of L. P. Edwards, Crane Brinton, and George S. Pettee, and the more recent study of Hannah Arendt.[4] These studies deal only with the so-called Great Revolutions of history – conspicuous and much-studied disturbances that occurred in relatively advanced, mildly autocratic, western societies, between 1640 and 1917. Consequently, they seem to say little that is reliable about, or even relevant to, much of the political violence of our more far-flung and variegated world, or of pre-modern times, or, for that matter, of the period they cover. They draw mammoth inferences from very few cases; and they ignore not only the vast spectrum of *coups*, *Putsches*, uprisings, riots, and so forth, but also Mr. Hobsbawm's hero, the "primitive rebel", once so important, and again come to the center of affairs.[5] Thus, they are neither very "scientific" nor very historical. A more extensive view of the subject should yield not only knowledge more relevant to many particular cases but generalizations more trustworthy, by sheer weight of

[3] "The [French] Revolution is a series of shocks, each shock displacing power from Right to Left, from larger groups, to smaller and more determined groups, each shock taking on more and more the aspect of a *coup d'état*, less and less that of a widespread, spontaneous outbreak of the people, until finally, in a commonplace *coup d'état* hardly worthy of a good operetta, power comes to rest in the hands of the dictator Bonaparte." Crane Brinton, *A Decade of Revolution, 1789-1799* (New York, 1934), 1. This inspired characterization of the French Revolution might well serve as a rudimentary developmental model for any internal war that begins in large-scale, mainly spontaneous, popular violence.
[4] L. P. Edwards, *The Natural History of Revolutions* (Chicago, 1927); Crane Brinton, *The Anatomy of Revolution* (New York, 1958 – first published 1938); George S. Pettee, *The Process of Revolution* (New York, 1938); Hannah Arendt, *On Revolution* (New York, 1963).
[5] E. J. Hobsbawm, *Primitive Rebels* (London, 1960).

numbers, for the cases covered in the classic comparative histories. Pettee does say that by studying the more egregious cases he intends to illuminate all the rest – but he never does, and one doubts that he can.

Finally, the terminologies presently used to distinguish types of internal war vary greatly, are generally ambiguous, often define overlapping phenomena or phenomena difficult to distinguish in practice, and are rarely based on clearly discernible analytical needs. For few phenomena do social science, history, and conventional language offer so various and vague a vocabulary. Consider a few examples – a mere small sample of what there is to consider. Lasswell and Kaplan divide internal wars into palace revolutions, political revolutions, and social revolutions. Palace revolutions, as they define the term, are changes in rulers contrary to the "political formulas" of governments (that is, their formal constitutions), are usually effected by members of the ruling group themselves, and rarely lead to important changes in policy; political revolutions are changes in "authority structures" (formal power structures), and social revolutions changes in the overall "control structures" (effective power structures) of society, usually effected by men not already in ruling positions. A conventional distinction often made is that between revolutions and rebellions, the former being something broader in purpose and more tightly organized, as well as longer in duration and more violent, than the latter. Gabriel Bonnet, perhaps the most illustrious exponent of the French military doctrine of "revolutionary warfare", distinguishes between civil wars of liberation, and revolutionary wars, with civil wars further divided into riots, insurrections, pronunciamentos, and revolutions – terms which perhaps speak sufficiently for themselves.[6] Huntington talks about revolutionary wars and *coups d'état*, the key distinctions between them being their duration (*coups* are decided quickly, revolutions not) and the extent to which the insurgents already participate in the existing system of power (they do in *coups*, but not in revolutionary wars); *coups* are then further distinguished into governmental *coups*, which lead to no significant changes in social or political institutions; revolutionary *coups*, which do attempt to achieve such changes; and reform *coups*, which fall somewhere between the other two.[7] George Blanksten speaks of "real" revolutions, "near" revolutions, and mere non-constitutional changes of government in Latin America,[8] and Stokes uses a still more complicated typology to characterize Latin American political violence: *machetismo, cuartelazo, golpe de estado*, and *revolución*.[9]

One can derive from these and similar classificatory schemes a sort of composite typology, distinguishing between relatively unorganized and spon-

[6]   Gabriel Bonnet, *Les guerres insurrectionelles et révolutionnaires* (Paris, 1958), 34 ff.
[7]   S. P. Huntington, ed., *Changing Patterns of Military Politics* (New York, 1962), 22 ff.
[8]   George I. Blanksten, "Revolutions", in Harold Eugene Davis, *Government and Politics in Latin America* (New York, 1958), Chapter 5.
[9]   W. S. Stokes, "Violence as a Power Factor in Latin American Politics", *Western Political Quarterly*, Summer 1952, 445-68.

taneous *riots* by crowds with low capabilities for violence and modest aims, *coups d'état* by members of an elite against other members of the elite, full-scale *political revolutions* to achieve important constitutional changes, *social revolutions* to achieve large-scale socio-economic as well as constitutional changes, and *wars of independence* to achieve sovereignty in a previously dependent territory. But this typology is not necessarily better than the others. It does relate the various typologies by including most of the terms of the complicated schemes and adding more terms to the simple ones; but this alone does not make it more precise, easier to apply or more suited to the substantive tasks of study.

For all of these reasons it can do no harm and might do much good to consider internal wars as all of a piece at the beginning of inquiry and to introduce distinctions only as they become necessary or advisable. In this way, the possibilities of developing general theories are increased, as is the likelihood that the distinctions made will be important and precise. In any event, that is how I shall proceed here, showing at the end how a general theory about the genus "internal war" can be adapted to give an account of special cases.

### THE PROBLEM OF ETIOLOGY

The theoretical issues raised by internal wars can be classified according to the phases through which such wars pass. They include problems about their preconditions, the way they can be effectively waged, the courses they tend to take, the outcomes they tend to have, and their long-run effects on society.

Curiously enough, the later the phase, the less there is to read about the issues involved. Despite the protracted normative argument between pro-revolutionaries and anti-revolutionaries, initiated by Paine and Burke, almost nothing careful and systematic has been written about the long-run social effects of internal wars, least of all perhaps about some of the most poignant and practical problems they raise: how political legitimacy and social harmony may be restored after violent disruption, what makes internal wars acute or chronic, and what the comparative costs (and probabilities) are of revolutionary and evolutionary transformations. Little more is available on the determinants of success or failure in internal wars. A fair amount has been written about the dynamic processes of revolutions, above all in the comparative historical studies already mentioned and in a very few more recent books, like Crozier's *The Rebels*.[10] But in regard to etiology, to "causes", we are absolutely inundated with print.

This abundance of etiological studies is not, however, an unmixed blessing. If studying other aspects of internal wars poses the basic problem of thinking

---

[10] Brian Crozier, *The Rebels: A Study of Post-War Insurrections* (London, 1960), Parts III-V and Postlude.

of theoretical possibilities, studying their etiology poses a difficulty equally great: how to choose among a rare abundance of hypotheses which cannot all be equally valid nor all be readily combined. This problem exists because most propositions about the causes of internal wars have been developed in historical studies of particular cases (or very limited numbers of cases) rather than in broadly comparative, let alone genuinely social-scientific, studies. In historical case-studies one is likely to attach significance to any aspect of pre-revolutionary society that one intuits to be significant, and so long as one does not conjure up data out of nothing one's hypotheses cannot be invalidated on the basis of the case in question.

That most studied of all internal wars, the French Revolution, provides a case in point – as well as examples in abundance of the many social, personal, and environmental forces to which the occurrence of internal wars might be attributed. Scarcely anything in the French *ancien régime* has not been blamed, by one writer or another, for the revolution, and all of their interpretations, however contradictory, are based on solid facts.

Some interpreters have blamed the outbreak of the French Revolution on intellectual causes, that is to say, on the ideas, techniques, and great public influence of the *philosophes* (who were indeed very influential). This is the standard theory of post-revolutionary conservative theorists, from Chateaubriand to Taine, men who felt, in essence, that in pre-revolutionary France a sound society was corrupted by a seductive and corrosive philosophy.

Other writers have blamed the revolution mainly on economic conditions, although it is difficult to find very many who single out as crucial the same conditions. The revolution has been attributed to sheer grinding poverty among the lower classes (who were certainly poor); to financial profligacy and mismanagement on the part of the government (of which it was in fact guilty); to the extortionate taxation inflicted on the peasants (and peasant taxation verged upon brutality); to short-term setbacks (which actually occurred and caused great hardship) like the bad harvest of 1788, the hard winter of 1788-89, and the still winds of 1789 which prevented flour from being milled and made worse an already acute shortage of bread; to the over-abundant wine harvests of the 1780's (one of the first historic instances of the harmful effects of overproduction); to the increased wealth and power of the bourgeoisie in a society still dominated to a significant extent by aristocrats, the growth of the Parisian proletariat and its supposedly increasing political consciousness, and the threatened abrogation of the financial privileges of the aristocracy, particularly their exemption from taxation – all unquestionable facts producing manifest problems.

Still another set of writers locates the crucial cause of the revolution in aspects of social structure. Much has been made, and with sufficient reason, of the fact that in the last years of the *ancien régime* there occurred a hardening in the lines of upward mobility in French society – for example, a decline in grants of patents of nobility to commoners and the imposition of stringent social requirements for certain judicial and administrative positions and the purchase of officerships in the army. This, many have argued (following Mosca's and Pareto's famous theory of the circulation of elites), engendered that fatal yearning for an aristocracy of wealth and talent to which the *philosophes* gave expression. Much has also been made, with equal reason, of popular dissatisfaction with the parasitic life of the higher nobility, with its large pensions and puny duties, its life of hunting, love-making, watch-making, and interminable conversation. And much has been attributed to the vulnerability of the privileged classes to the very propagandists who wanted to alter the system that supported them ("How," asked Taine, "could people who talked so much resist people who talked so well?"), reflected in the Anglomania which swept through the higher aristocracy toward the end of the *ancien régime* and in the rush of many aristocrats to the cause of the Americans in their war of independence.

There are also certain well-founded "political" explanations of the French Revolution: that the revolution was really caused by the violation of the tacit "contract" on which the powers of the monarchy rested (a contract by which the aristocracy surrendered its powers to the monarchy in return for receiving certain inviolable privileges), or that the revolution was simply a successful political conspiracy by the Jacobins, based on efficient political organization. Personalities, needless to say, get their due as well: the revolution has been blamed, for example, on the character, or lack of character, of Louis XVI (who was in fact weak, vacillating and inconsistent), the supposed immorality of the Queen (who indeed was the subject, justly or not, of many scandals), the effect on the public of the dismissal of Necker, and, of course, on the "genius", good or evil, of unquestionable geniuses like Mirabeau, Danton, Marat, and Robespierre.

We could take other internal wars and arrive at the same result – similarly large lists of explanations, most of them factual, yet inconclusive. The more remote in time and the more intensively analyzed the internal war, the longer the list of hypotheses. Yet even so recent a case as the Chinese Communist Revolution has given rise to a fearful number of plausible hypotheses, many directly contradictory.

The Chinese Revolution has been blamed on plain conspiracy: a plot by a small number of Kremlin agents or power-hungry Chinese intellectuals. It has been blamed on social forces, like the rise of an urban working class or a "new" urban middle class, large-scale mobility from countryside to cities and the attendant weakening of traditional social patterns (the growth of a "mass" society),[11] or the effects of a "population explosion". Its genesis has been located in political culture, structure and decisions: in hyper-nationalism

---

[11] For an explanation of this term and its use in the explanation of large, illegitimate political movements, see W. Kornhauser, *The Politics of Mass Society* (New York, 1959).

and the hatred it engendered of those cooperating with "imperialist" powers; in the corruption of the incumbent regime; in that regime's supposedly selfish and reactionary policies, ignoring the interests of land-hungry peasants, urban workers, and the new urban middle class; in administrative incompetence; in exorbitantly harsh policies toward all actual and potential opposition. Economic explanations are available too; the revolution, it has been argued, was caused by general poverty, by the exploitation particularly of the peasants, by the breakdown of the peasant crafts due to Western imports, by intellectual unemployment, and by various natural disasters. Finally, there are the usual theories about great and puny men and, not least, the interpretation perhaps most familiar to us of all: that the revolution was caused by insufficient and untimely external support for the incumbents compared to the external support available to the insurgents.[12]

How can this embarrassment of interpretative riches (one hesitates to say theoretical riches) be reduced? If the examination of any single case allows one to determine only whether an interpretation of it is based on facts, then broad comparative studies in space and/or time are needed to establish the significance of the facts on which the interpretations are based. Was a blockage in the channels of social mobility a significant precondition of the French Revolution? We can be reasonably confident that it was only if it can be shown that elite circulation and political stability are generally related. Was the Chinese population explosion really an important cause of the Chinese revolution? Surely this is unlikely if demographic pressures do not generally affect the viability of regimes.

This is the simplest conceivable methodology, and easy to indicate abstractly. But actually to find the broad general relationships on the basis of which particular interpretations can be assessed is not so easy. For this purpose we need a tremendous amount of historical work that comparative historiographers of internal wars have hardly even begun to do. There are so many possibilities to be tested against so many cases. A general etiology of internal wars, at this stage, can only be a remote end of inquiry, and neither limited comparative studies nor interpretations of particular instances of internal war should pretend otherwise.

But even prior to undertaking that work, theoretical reflection can introduce some order into the chaos that internal war studies present. Most important, it can produce useful judgments as to the more economic lines to pursue in empirical inquiry. We can in a small way approach an etiology of internal wars by classifying the theoretical possibilities available, indicating the ana-

---

[12] I am indebted to my colleague Davis B. Bobrow for this list; his, I should mention, was in fact much larger. For a similar, still more extensive, treatment of the literature on the American Civil War, which is also very instructive on the general problems of causation of historical events, see Lee Benson and Cushing Strout, "Causation and the American Civil War. Two Appraisals", *History and Theory*, I, 2 (1961), 163-185. See also Thomas J. Pressly, *Americans Interpret their Civil War* (Princeton, 1954).

lytical choices they require and do not require to be made, and attempting to determine what lines of analysis are most likely to prove rewarding. Where the theoretical possibilities are as varied and chaotic as in the case of internal war, such reflection, to organize and restrict inquiry, is a necessary preliminary to the more definitive work of rigorously testing well-formulated propositions.

## "PRECONDITIONS" OR "PRECIPITANTS"?

Perhaps the first thing that becomes apparent when one tries to classify causal explanations of the sort sketched above is that many of the explanations do not really require a choice to be made by the analyst. The propositions do not always contradict one another; often, in fact, they are complementary, differing only because they refer to different points in the time-sequence leading to revolution, or because they refer to different kinds of causality, or because they single out one factor among many of equal significance.

The most important distinction to make in this connection is between preconditions and precipitants of internal wars. A "precipitant" of internal war is an event which actually starts the war ("occasions" it), much as turning the flintwheel of a cigarette lighter ignites a flame. "Preconditions" of internal war, on the other hand, are those circumstances which make it possible for the precipitants to bring about political violence, as the general structure of a lighter makes it possible to produce a flame by turning the flintwheel. Some of the causal explanations of the French Revolution already mentioned clearly fall into the first category, while others fall equally clearly into the second; and between explanations singling out precipitants and explanations emphasizing preconditions of internal war there obviously is no genuine contradiction. The distinction between precipitants and preconditions can therefore prevent much pointless argument between those who stress short-run setbacks and those who emphasize long-term trends in the etiology of civil strife. Clearly no internal war can occur without precipitant events to set it off; and clearly no precipitants can set off internal war unless the condition of society makes it possible for them to do so.

The greatest service that the distinction between precipitants and preconditions of internal war can render, however, is to shift attention from aspects of internal war which defy analysis to those which are amenable to systematic inquiry. Phenomena which precipitate internal war are almost always unique and ephemeral in character. A bad harvest, a stupid or careless ruler, moral indiscretion in high places, an ill-advised policy: how could such data be incorporated into general theories? They are results of the vagaries of personality, of forces external to the determinate interrelations of society, of all those unique and fortuitous aspects of concrete life which are the despair of social scientists and the meat and drink of narrative historians.

Closely related, the distinction between precipitants and preconditions of internal wars will also help one to avoid what is perhaps the most misleading theory about their causes: an unqualified conspiracy theory of internal war. To be sure, conspiracy seems to play an essential role in certain types of internal war, particularly those previously referred to as *coups* and palace revolutions. As well, one undoubtedly finds conspiratorial organizations in every internal war of any consequence – in one case Jacobins, in others fascists, in still others communists. This is precisely what tempts so many to attribute internal wars solely or mainly to conspirators, and thus to regard them, in the manner of Malaparte, essentially as matters of technique – plotting on one hand and intelligence and suppression on the other. In many cases, however, the conspirators seem to do little more than turn the flintwheel in volatile situations, or indeed not even as much as that; sometimes they merely turn the revolutionary conflagration to their own purposes. Internal wars do not always have a clear aim, a tight organization, a distinct shape and tendency from the outset. Many seem to be characterized in their early stages by nothing so much as amorphousness. They are formless matter waiting to be shaped, and if there is an art of revolution, it involves, largely at least, not making or subduing it, but capitalizing on the unallocated political resources it provides.

This reference to techniques of revolution leads to another point. If one leaves precipitants aside and focuses solely on data the social scientist can handle, one does not even leave out of consideration anything that matters from a practical standpoint. Preconditions are the crucial concern of men of affairs, revolutionaries or anti-revolutionaries, no less than of social scientists. After all, they have an interest in the etiology of internal wars in order to anticipate such wars in good time, prevent them when they are preventable, further their actual occurrence, or otherwise prepare for them. But unique and ephemeral phenomena cannot, by their very nature, be anticipated; they simply happen. The vital knowledge to have concerns those conditions under which almost any setback or vagary, any misguided policy or indiscretion, can set society aflame.

Certain kinds of precipitants of internal war have a special importance of their own, however, in what one might call "practical etiology" – the anticipation of internal wars for policy purposes. A precipitant may be found so frequently on the eve of internal wars that its existence can be treated as a particularly urgent danger signal, particularly if its effects are delayed sufficiently to allow some adaptation to the danger. As far as we know, both of these conditions are satisfied by economic precipitants of internal war. The point deserves some elaboration, particularly in view of the persistent emphasis on economic conditions in writings on internal war.

It now seems generally agreed that persistent poverty in a society rarely leads to political violence. Quite the contrary. As Edwards points out, following an argument already developed by de Tocqueville, economic oppression, indeed all kinds of oppression, seems to wane rather than increase in pre-revolutionary periods.[13] Brinton makes the same point. While not under-estimating the amount of poverty in the societies he analyzes in *The Anatomy of Revolution*, he does point out that all of these societies were economically progressive rather than retrograde. He points out also that revolutionary literature, at any rate in the pre-Marxist period, hardly ever dwelt on economic misery and exploitation – one hears about economic grievances, to be sure, but not the sort of grievances which arise out of "immiseration".[14] Even some Marxists seem to share this view. Trotsky, for example, once remarked that if poverty and oppression were a precipitant of revolution the lower classes would always be in revolt, and obviously he had a point.

It is equally difficult to establish a close link between economic improvement and internal war. Pre-revolutionary periods may often be economically pro-gressive, but economic progress is not always (or even often) connected with internal war. From this, however, one need not conclude that economic tendencies are simply irrelevant to the occurrence of political violence. Only the long-term tendencies seem, in fact, to be irrelevant. The moment one focuses on short-term tendencies, a fairly frequently repeated pattern emerges – and one which tells us why it is that some writers adhere stubbornly to the immiseration theory of internal war and others, with just as much conviction, to the economic progress theory. It so happens that before many internal wars, one finds both economic improvement and immiseration; more precisely, many internal wars are preceded by long-term improvements followed by serious short-term setbacks.[15] The bad harvests and unfavorable weather conditions in pre-revolutionary France, the American recession of 1774-1775, the bad Russian winter of 1916-1917 (not to mention the economic impact of the war on Russia) and the marked rise of unemployment in Egypt before Naguib's *coup* are cases in point. All dealt serious short-term blows to economic life and all followed long periods of economic progress, especially for those previously "repressed".

It is this dual pattern which really seems to be lethal, and it is not difficult to see why. In times of prolonged and marked economic progress, people become accustomed to new economic standards and form new economic expectations, which previously they could scarcely imagine. Confidently expecting continuous progress, they also tend to take risks (like accumulating debts) which they might not take otherwise. All this greatly exaggerates the impact of serious temporary setbacks; both psychologically and economically the costs of such setbacks are bound to be greater than if they occurred after long periods of stagnation or very gradual progress.

[13]  Edwards, *The Natural History of Revolutions*, 33.
[14]  Brinton, *The Anatomy of Revolution*, 29-37.
[15]  See James C. Davis, "Toward a Theory of Revolution", *American Sociological Review*, 27 (1962), 5-19. This paper traces the pattern in Dorr's Rebellion, the Russian Revolution, and the Egyptian Revolution.

Occasionally, perhaps, the study of precipitants of internal war may play a minor role in "theoretical" as well as "practical etiology". It could conceivably shed some light on the preconditions themselves in that there might be a connection between revolutionary conditions and how internal wars are actually brought about. For example, someone may blame internal war on dissatisfactions in the rural population of a society; but if we find peasants playing no role in the fomenting of violence, then we have good reason to doubt the interpretation. Precipitants may not directly tell us what the preconditions of internal war are, but they can sometimes indicate what they are not – be useful for falsifying hypotheses, or at least shedding doubt on them. But this does not alter the basic point: that the task of an etiology of internal wars is to discover their preconditions.

## COMMON HYPOTHESES ABOUT THE PRECONDITIONS OF INTERNAL WAR

We can profitably relegate to a secondary role most of those greatly varying, unique, and largely fortuitous events which occasion the outbreak of internal wars. But even if we do, a great variety of hypotheses remains – great enough if we confine ourselves to general treatments of internal war, and greater still if we deal with hypotheses formulated to deal with particular cases. In this connection, it might be useful to supplement the explanations of particular revolutions listed above with a sample of propositions frequently found in the more general literature on internal war. These include:[16]

a) *Hypotheses emphasizing "intellectual" factors*:
   1. Internal wars result from the failure of a regime to perform adequately the function of political socialization.
   2. Internal wars are due to the coexistence in a society of conflicting social "myths".
   3. Internal wars result from the existence in a society of unrealizable values or corrosive social philosophies.
   4. Internal wars are caused by the alienation (desertion, transfer of allegiance) of the intellectuals.

b) *Hypotheses emphasizing economic factors*:
   1. Internal wars are generated by growing poverty.
   2. Internal wars result from rapid economic progress.

[16] The hypotheses come from a large variety of sources, including: Lasswell and Kaplan, *Power and Society* (New Haven, 1950); the works by Edwards, Pettee, and Brinton cited above; Rudé, *The Crowd in the French Revolution* (Oxford, 1959); Trotsky, *The History of the Russian Revolution* (Ann Arbor, Michigan, 1957); De Grazia, *The Political Community* (Chicago, 1948); Gaetano Mosca, *The Ruling Class* (New York, 1939); and Vilfredo Pareto, *The Mind and Society* (New York, 1935).

3. Internal wars are due to severe imbalances between the production and distribution of goods.

4. Internal wars are caused by a combination of long-term economic improvement and short-term setbacks.

c) *Hypotheses emphasizing aspects of social structure*:
1. Internal wars are due to the inadequate circulation of elites (that is, inadequate recruitment into the elite of the able and powerful members of the non-elite).
2. Internal wars result from too much recruitment of members of the non-elite into the elite, breaking down the internal cohesion of the elite.
3. Internal war is a reflection of *anomie* resulting from great social mobility.
4. Internal war is a reflection of frustration arising from little general social mobility – from general social stagnation.
5. Internal wars result from the appearance in societies of new social classes.

d) *Hypotheses emphasizing political factors*:
1. Internal wars are due to the estrangement of rulers from the societies they rule.
2. Internal war is simply a response to bad government (government which performs inadequately the function of goal-attainment).
3. Internal wars are due, not to the attacks of the governed on those who govern, but to divisions among the governing classes.
4. Internal wars are responses to oppressive government.
5. Internal wars are due to excessive toleration of alienated groups.

e) *Hypotheses emphasizing no particular aspects of societies, but general characteristics of social process*:
1. Political violence is generated by rapid social change.
2. Political violence results from erratic and/or uneven rates of social change, whether rapid or not.
3. Internal war occurs when a state is somehow "out of adjustment" to society.

From this sample of propositions, all of them at least plausible, we can get some idea of the overwhelming ambiguities that general studies of the preconditions of internal war have created to supplement those originating in case studies. These ambiguities arise most obviously from the fact that many of the propositions are manifestly contradictory; less obviously, from the sheer variety and disparity of factors included, not all of which, surely, can be equally significant, or necessary, in the etiology of internal wars. For this reason, even when precipitants are subtracted, a considerable range of choices between theories remains to be made.

## INSURGENTS OR INCUMBENTS?

One crucial choice that needs to be made is whether to put emphasis upon characteristics of the insurgents or incumbents, upon the side that rebels or the side that is rebelled against. Not surprisingly, the existing literature concentrates very largely on the rebels, treating internal war as due mainly to changes in the non-elite strata of society to which no adequate adjustment is made by the elite. This would seem to be only natural; after all, it is the rebels who rebel. At least some writings suggest, however, that characteristics of the incumbents and the classes that are usually their props must be considered jointly with characteristics of the insurgents, indeed perhaps even emphasized more strongly. Pareto, for example, while attributing revolution partly to blockages in a society's social mobility patterns, considered it equally necessary that certain internal changes should occur in an elite if revolution was to be possible; in essence, he felt that no elite which had preserved its capacity for timely and effective violence, or for effective manipulation, could be successfully assailed, or perhaps assailed at all. One must, according to this view, seek the origins of internal war not only in a gain of strength by the non-elite, but also in the loss of it on the part of the elite. Brinton makes the same point: revolutions, in his view, follow the loss of common values, of internal cohesion, of a sure sense of destiny and superiority and, not least, of political efficiency in elites, and thus must be considered results as much as causes of their disintegration. And in Edwards's and Pettee's studies as well, revolutions emerge as affairs of the elites (if not always directly of the actual rulers): the crucial roles in them are played by intellectuals, by men rich and powerful but "cramped" by their lack of status or other perquisites, and by the gross inefficiency of the ruling apparatus.

Significantly enough, this view is stated perhaps more often in the writings of actual revolutionaries than in those of students of revolution. Trotsky, for example, believed that revolution requires three elements: the political consciousness of a revolutionary class, the discontent of the "intermediate layers" of society, and, just as important, a ruling class which has "lost faith in itself", which is torn by the conflicts of groups and cliques, which has lost its capacity for practical action and rests its hopes in "miracles or miracle workers".[17]

The joint consideration of insurgent and incumbent patterns thus would seem to be the logical way to proceed in the early stages of inquiry into the causes of revolution. But one should not overlook the possibility that suffi-

---

[17]   Trotsky, *The Russian Revolution*, 311.

cient explanations of the occurrence of many internal wars might be found in elite characteristics alone. A ruling elite may decay, may become torn by severe conflict, may be reluctant to use power, may come to lack vital political skills – and thus make it perfectly possible for a relatively weak, even disorganized, opposition of a sort that may exist in any political system to rise against it and destroy it. Indeed, there are theories which maintain that internal wars are always caused solely or primarily by changes in elite characteristics, and that one can practically ignore the insurgents in attempting to account for the occurrence of internal wars.

One such theory is propounded in Mosca's *The Ruling Class*. If the elementary needs of human life are satisfied, argued Mosca, one thing above all will cause men to rebel against their rulers, and that is their feeling that the rulers live in a totally different environment, that they are "separated" from their subjects in some profound sense. In other words, the estrangement of the elite from the non-elite is inseparable from the alienation of the latter; only the elite itself, consequently, can undermine its political position. In this regard Mosca made much of the feudal societies of Poland, Ireland, England, and Russia. The Polish nobles of the Middle Ages, for example, practiced extreme economic extortion, taking in levies almost all the peasant produced; they were ruthless and violent; they scrupulously extracted the *droit du seigneur*; and despite all that, and more, the peasants never rebelled – as long as the nobles "lived among them, spoke their language, swore the same oaths, ate the same kind of food, wore the same style of clothes, exhibited the same manners or lack of them, had the same rustic superstitions".[18] But a drastic change occurred when the nobility acquired French manners and tastes, "gave luxurious balls after the manner of Versailles and tried to dance the minuet". Despite more humane treatment, vicious and frequent revolts attended the estrangement of the nobles from their people.

This interpretation certainly makes sense in light of French experience: the French Revolution was far more an attack upon the refined and parasitic court nobility than upon the coarse, and little less parasitic, provincial nobility. It makes sense also in the case of Britain, for the British nobility (in the main) always preserved close ties to the soil and to the manner and morals of its tenantry; Squire Western is the embodiment of that fact. That is why it was for so long the butt of jokes among the more sophisticated, and shorter-lived, continental aristocracies.

Perhaps the most prolonged period of civil unrest in American history, the late nineteenth century, can be, and has been, interpreted in much the same manner – not only by political sociologists like De Grazia, but also by acute literary observers like Mark Twain and historians like Miriam Beard.[19] One

---

[18]　De Grazia, *The Political Community*, 74-75.
[19]　De Grazia, *The Political Community*, esp. 117 ff. and Miriam Beard, *A History of the Business Man* (New York, 1938).

of the more conspicuous features of that period was the compulsive attempt of the American plutocracy to imitate European "society". At no other time in American history was the elite so profoundly estranged from American life. Mark Twain gave this period a name which fits it exactly and has stuck to it ever since. It was the Gilded Age, the age of English clothes and accents, Roman orgies, continental travel, title-mongering, art-collecting, butlers and footmen, conspicuous consumption of every sort – the age which invented those now much more Americanized institutions, the debutante and the society page. Not until the American plutocracy had returned to its old habits of thrift and earthiness, of being plain Americans, was there a return to relative civil calm in the United States.[20]

More examples of the instability that ensues from the estrangement of elites are furnished in profusion by the westernized elites of many currently under-developed areas. The elites referred to in this case are not those who learn Western skills but remain identified with their native context; rather it is the westernized in lifeways, the visitors to the Riviera and the riders in Cadillacs, who try to lead a life totally different from that of their people. For such estranged elites, living abroad may indeed be a course preferable to the imi-tation of alien ways at home; at any rate, they are in that case rather less con-spicuous.

It is worth noting that in the postwar period internal wars have been rela-tively rare in two kinds of societies: either thoroughly modernized countries or very underdeveloped countries whose elites have remained tied closely to the traditional ways and structures of life.[21] Of course, a generalization of this kind is becoming increasingly harder to test, since the number of societies without a gulf between highly modernized elites and much less modernized masses seems to be rapidly shrinking. Nevertheless the notion is given cred-ibility by the fact that, while transitional societies seem to suffer more from internal wars than either traditional or modern societies – as one would expect upon many hypotheses – a very few seem to have strikingly low rates of violence compared to the rest. Egypt is one example, and Pakistan another. These societies seem to differ from the rest in one main respect. They have had "secondary" revolutions, so to speak, in which men of rather humble origins and popular ways (colonels' regimes) have unseated previously victorious transitional elites.

All this is not meant to validate the idea that elite estrangement is the main cause of internal war but only to show why it should be taken very seriously. The possible consequences of elite estrangement are not, however, the only reason for emphasizing studies of the incumbents at least as much as studies

---

[20] For evidence of acute unrest in the United States in this period, see De Grazia, *The Political Community*.
[21] Cases in point are the stable, highly developed democracies on the one hand, and countries like Ethiopia and Somalia on the other.

of insurgents in the etiology of internal wars. Another is the fact that internal wars are almost invariably preceded by important functional failures on the part of elites. Above all is this true of difficulties in financial administration – perhaps because finance impinges on the ability of governments to perform all their functions.[22] And finally, insurgent groups seem rarely to come even to the point of fighting without some support from alienated members of incumbent elites. On this point, agreement in the literature on internal war is practically unanimous.

## STRUCTURAL OR BEHAVIORAL HYPOTHESES?

A second strategic choice to be made in constructing an etiology of internal wars is between structural and behavioral hypotheses. A structural hypotheses singles out, so to speak, "objective" social conditions as crucial for the occurrence of internal war: aspects of a society's "setting", such as economic conditions, social stratification and mobility, or geographic and demographic factors. A behavioral hypothesis, on the other hand, emphasizes attitudes and their formation – not setting, but "orientations" (such as degrees of strain and *anomie* in societies, the processes by which tension and aggression are generated, and the processes by which human beings are "socialized" into their communities). The great majority of propositions regarding the causes of internal war are, on the basis of these definitions, structural in character. But, in concentrating upon structural explanations have writers on internal war taken the more promising tack?

At first glance, there would seem to be little to choose between structural and behavioral approaches. Since most human action is motivated, not reflexive, one always wants to know, if one can, about attitudes underlying men's actions. At the same time, there can be little doubt that attitudes are always formed somehow in response to external conditions. The difference between structural and behavioral theories would therefore seem to be, at best, one of emphasis or point of view. Yet emphasis can make a difference. Certain research results do seem to be associated with one point of view or the other. Behavioral approaches, for instance, may lead to theories stressing "intellectual" and voluntaristic factors in the etiology of political violence, or to theories attributing internal war mainly to efficient revolutionary indoctrination or inadequate value-formation by the incumbents. Structural

---

[22]  One of the most common conditions found before large-scale political violence is the financial bankruptcy of government, due to profligacy, over-ambitious policies, or the failure of a traditional tax structure in an inflationary situation, followed by an attack upon the financial privileges of strata which were previously the main props of the regime. R. B. Merriman, in *Six Contemporaneous Revolutions, 1640-1660* (Oxford, 1938) points out that the seventeenth-century revolutions in England, France, the Netherlands, Spain, Portugal, and Naples all had this point in common.

explanations may lead to theories of mechanical imbalance in society, or to theories attributing internal war mainly to specific situational conditions, attitudes being treated as mechanical responses to such conditions.

Which approach is preferable? Despite the fact that there is a danger that the behavioral approach might lead to naive conspiracy theory (the belief that internal wars are always the results of insidious indoctrination by subversive elements, and could therefore always occur or always be avoided) the arguments against a primary emphasis on structural theories are very strong.

One such argument derives from the general experience of modern social science. Purely structural theories have generally been found difficult to sustain wherever they have been applied, and one fundamental reason for this is that patterns of attitudes, while responsive to the settings in which men are placed, seem also to be, to an extent, autonomous of objective conditions, able to survive changes in these conditions or to change without clearly corresponding objective changes. This is one of the basic insights underlying the sociological theory of action, which, to be sure, assigns an important role to the situations in which human action occurs, but treats "culture" largely as a separate variable and attaches particularly great significance to agencies of socialization and acculturation. It underlies as well the relatively successful use of mediational models, rather than simple S-R models, in behavioral psychology.

No doubt this point should be much elaborated.[23] But one can make a cogent case for stressing behavioral theories of the causes of internal wars without going lengthily into the general nature and past experiences of social science.

The most obvious case for behavioral theories of internal war derives from the very fact that so many different objective social conditions seem capable of generating it. We may have available many interpretative accounts of internal wars simply because an enormous variety of objective conditions can create internal-war potential. Certain internal wars do seem to have followed economic improvement, others seem to have followed closely the Marxist model of internal wars, however many more have followed some combination of the two. Some internal wars have in fact been preceded by great, others by little social mobility; some regimes have been more oppressive and others more liberal in the immediate pre-revolutionary period, some both and some neither. Is it not reasonable to conclude that one should not seek explanations of the occurrence of internal wars in specific social conditions, but rather in the ways in which social conditions may be perceived? Instead of looking for direct connections between social conditions and internal war, should one not look rather for the ways in which an existing cognitive and value system may change, so that conditions perceived as tolerable at one point are perceived

[23]  Useful summaries of action and behavior theories can be found in Roland Young, ed., *Approaches to the Study of Politics* (Evanston, Illinois, 1958), 217-243 and 285-301.

as intolerable at another; or, concomitantly, look for the ways in which old systems of orientation are in some cases maintained rather than adapted in the face of social change, so that changes which one society absorbs without trouble create profound difficulties in another?

The point is not that objective conditions are unrelated to internal war. Rather it is that orientations mediate between social setting and political behavior, and – because they are not simply mirrors of environment – so that different objective conditions may lead to similar political activities, or similar conditions to different activities in different contexts; that in a single context a considerable change in political activity may occur without significant changes in objective conditions or changes in objective conditions without changes in activity. What should be avoided is linking aspects of social setting *directly* to internal war or *mechanically* to orientations. Internal wars are best conceived as responses to political disorientation (such as "cognitive dissonance", *anomie*, and strains in the definition of political roles), particularly in regard to a society's norms of legitimacy; and political disorientation may follow from a considerable variety of conditions, due to the variable nature of the orientations themselves and of the agencies that implant them in different societies.

One conspicuous point of agreement in comparative studies of revolution gives further credence to this argument. This is that revolutions are invariably preceded by the "transfer of allegiance" of a society's intellectuals and the development by them of a new political "myth" If intellectuals have any obvious social "functions", in the sense social scientists understand the term function, they are surely these: to socialize the members of a society outside of the domestic context, in schools and adult learning situations; to reinforce and rationalize attitudes acquired in all social contexts; and to provide meaning to life and guidelines to behavior by means of conscious doctrines where events have robbed men of their less conscious bearings. Intellectuals are particularly important in the education of adolescents and young people, and it has been shown quite definitely that political socialization occurs (or fails) mainly in the years between early childhood and full maturity.[24] It could also be shown that among revolutionaries the young tend to predominate, sometimes quite remarkably. Together these points go far to explain why the alienation of intellectuals is, in Edwards's language, a "master-symptom" of revolution: a condition that makes revolutionary momentum irreversible.

Another point that speaks for behavioral propositions is that internal wars can, and often do, become chronic. In some societies, the most manifest cause of internal war seems to be internal war itself, one instance following another, often without a recurrence of the conditions that led to the original event. This means that political disorientation may be followed by the formation

---

[24] For evidence, see Herbert H. Hyman, *Political Socialization* (Glencoe, Illinois, 1959).

of a new set of orientations, establishing a predisposition toward violence that is inculcated by the experience of violence itself. In such cases, internal wars result not from specifiable objective conditions, and not even from the loss of legitimacy by a particular regime, but from a general lack of receptivity to legitimacy of any kind. Violence becomes a political style that is self-perpetuating, unless itself "disoriented".

The very fact that elite estrangement so often precedes acute political unrest itself fits the case for behavioral propositions. It fits in part because the Establishment of any society includes its intellectuals, but also for a more important, rather technical, reason. Orientations, particularly as treated in action theory, are not purely internal and self-sufficient, as it were, but involve expectations from others ("alters") – mutualities or complementarities in behavior. Hence men are likely to become disoriented and alienated when those with whom they interact become aliens to them, even if the alien ways involve, from abstract moral standpoints, a change for the better. The Polish peasant probably did not positively like to be beaten, but he *expected* to be, and he himself undoubtedly committed a good deal of institutionalized mayhem on anyone subordinated to his authority. A liberal aristocrat would appear to him not only to act strangely but arbitrarily, and, in a way, as a constant personal reproach.

To give still more support to the argument for behavioral theories there is the object lesson provided by the sad history of Marxist theory. Marxism singles out certain objective social conditions as underlying internal wars. It also singles out certain social groups as indispensable to the making of internal war. But Marxist revolutions themselves have been made neither under the social conditions nor by the groups emphasized in the theory. What is more, these revolutions have been made in a large variety of conditions, with a large variety of means, by organizations constituted in a large variety of ways. This is true even if one can show that the appeal of Marxism is greatest in transitional societies, for the term transition, in its very nature, denotes not a particular social state but a great many different points on whatever continuum social development may involve.

PARTICULAR CONDITIONS OR GENERAL PROCESSES?

This argument has a close bearing upon a third strategic choice to be made in analyzing the causes of internal war. Even if one emphasizes behavioral characteristics in theories of internal wars, one must, as I have said, always relate these characteristics to the social setting. The question is how to do this. Should one, in the manner of most of the hypotheses listed above, develop propositions emphasizing particular social conditions or, in the manner of a few of them, select propositions about general characteristics of social process?

In the first case, one would relate internal war to particular socio-economic changes, in the second to characteristics of the general phenomenon of social change itself, such as rapid change or erratic change in any sectors of society, or conditions that may result from any social change whatever, such as imbalances between social segments (e.g., between elites of wealth and elites of status) or incongruities among the authority patterns of a society.

The proper choice between these alternatives is already implied in the arguments of the previous section. If many particular social conditions may be connected with internal wars, then clearly one should stress broad propositions about social processes and balances that can comprehend a variety of such conditions. The same position results if disorientation is conceived, in large part, as a breakdown in mutualities and complementarities of behavior. Not least, there is overwhelming evidence to show that *"anomie"*, the feeling that one lacks guidelines to behavior, is increased by rapidity of change in any direction (for example, by rapid economic betterment no less than rapid economic deterioration) and that "strain", the feeling that one's roles make inconsistent demands, is aggravated by uneven or incongruent changes in different social sectors (for example, when the economic sector of society becomes significantly modern while the political remains largely traditional).

What has been said about economic conditions preceding internal wars fits the argument particularly well. It is not just that cases can be found to support both immiseration and improvement theories of revolution, hence the view that internal wars are related to economic changes as such, not to change in any particular direction; more suggestive still is the fact that internal wars most frequently follow an irregular – an anomalous – course of economic change, long-term trends being interrupted by abrupt and short-lived reversals. Such a course exhibits at least two of the general characteristics of social processes that would, upon earlier arguments, seem to be related to the occurrence of internal wars: rapidity of change and eccentricity of change.

From this standpoint it would be most interesting to investigate whether *any* rapid and eccentric course of economic development tends to be related to internal war, perhaps even one involving long-term stagnation or deterioration followed by abrupt short-term improvement. This idea is not as far-fetched as may seem; after all has not Durkheim fully documented the argument that *"fortunate crises*, the effect of which is abruptly to enhance a country's prosperity, affect suicide like *economic disasters"*?[25]

Undoubtedly there is a danger that broad formulations concerning general social processes will turn into empty and untestable generalizations, trivialities like the much-repeated proposition that political violence tends to accompany social or economic change. But this danger is avoidable; one can, after all, be specific and informative about general social processes as well as about their substantive content.

[25]  Emile Durkheim, *Suicide* (London, 1952), 243 (my italics).

## OBSTACLES TO INTERNAL WAR

So far I have tried to make two related points. The first is that one is most likely to gain understanding of the forces impelling societies toward internal war if one avoids preoccupation with the more visible precipitants of internal wars, including conspiracies, and directs one's efforts to the analysis of their preconditions, stressing disorientative general social processes and particularly taking into account elite behavior, performance, and cohesion. The second point is in a sense the converse of this: that existing etiologies of internal wars are chaotic and inadequate precisely because studies have so far concentrated on precipitants rather than preconditions, insurgents rather than incumbents, and particular aspects of social structure rather than the effects on orientations of general social processes.

An important point must now be added. Even if we had better knowledge of the forces which push societies toward political violence, a crucial problem relating to the etiology of internal wars would remain, one that is generally ignored in the studies available to us. This problem concerns forces that might countervail those previously discussed: "obstacles" to internal war, as against forces which propel societies toward violence.

In the real world of phenomena, events occur not only because forces leading toward them are strong, but also because forces tending to inhibit, or obstruct, them are weak or absent. An automobile may generate a great deal of force, but if driven up a steep incline is unlikely to go very fast. A government may have the desire and technical capacity for rapid industrialization, but if faced by the rapid growth of an already too great population may simply find it impossible to channel sufficient resources into capital goods to achieve a certain rate of development. So also internal wars may fail to occur solely or mainly because of certain hindrances to their occurrence.

Some of these hindrances may be absolute in character, in that wherever they exist internal war fails to materialize; hence their obverse may be considered "requisites" of internal war (necessary, but not sufficient, conditions). In the main, however, obstacles to internal war, like forces making for internal war, are better conceived as factors making such wars more or less likely, rather than either inevitable or impossible – their actual significance depending, at least in part, on the strength of forces pulling in a contrary direction. It certainly seems unlikely that we shall ever find a condition that makes internal war quite inevitable under any circumstances, and equally unlikely that we could discover conditions that always rule it out (except perhaps purely definitional ones: e.g., the absence of any perceived frustrations). In real life, internal war, like other concrete events, results from the interplay of forces and counterforces, from a balance of probabilities pulling toward internal war and internal peace.

*Repression.* The most obvious obstacle to internal war is, of course, the incumbent regime. It goes almost without saying that by using repression the established authorities can lessen the chances of violent attack upon themselves, or even reduce them to nil. Internal wars, after all, are not made by impersonal forces working in impersonal ways, but by men acting under the stress of external forces. This much at least there is in the conspiracy theory of revolution: wholly spontaneous riots by wholly unstructured and undirected mobs may occur, but hardly very frequently or with much effect. Actual cases of internal war generally contain some element of subversion, some structure for forming political will and acting upon decisions, however primitive and changeable. On this point, if no other, the great enemies of revolution (Burke, Chateaubriand, Taine) are at one with the great revolutionaries (Lenin, Trotsky); it is also this point, rather than some more subtle idea, which underlies Pareto's and Brinton's argument that revolutions are due to elites as much as non-elites. And anything with a structure can of course be detected and repressed, though not always very easily.

The matter, however, is not quite so simple. Repression can be a two-edged sword. Unless it is based upon extremely good intelligence, and unless its application is sensible, ruthless, and continuous, its effects may be quite opposite to those intended. Incompetent repression leads to a combination of disaffection and contempt for the elite. Also, repression may only make the enemies of a regime more competent in the arts of conspiracy; certainly it tends to make them more experienced in the skills of clandestine organization and *sub rosa* communication. No wonder that botched and bungled repression is often a characteristic of pre-revolutionary societies. The French *ancien régime*, for example, had a political censorship, but it only managed to make French writers into masters of the hidden meaning, and whet the appetite of the public for their subversive books. "In our country", a French aristocrat said, "authors compete with one another for the honors of the bonfire"; even the Queen seems to have spent many delicious evenings reading the forbidden Encyclopedia with her ladies.[26] Russia, under the later Czars, was practically a model of repressive bumbledom; her policy of exile, for example, created close-knit communities of revolutionaries more than it destroyed their cohesion.

The worst situation of all seems to arise when a regime, having driven its opponents underground, inflamed their enmity, heightened their contempt, and cemented their organization, suddenly relaxes its repression and attempts a liberal policy. The relaxation of authority is a part of the pre-revolutionary syndrome, no less than other forms of social amelioration; in that sense, repression in societies with high internal war potential is little more than a narcotic, intensifying the conditions it seeks to check and requiring ever larger doses to keep affairs in balance – if other things are equal. We can see this dynamic at work in the development of totalitarian rule, particularly if we

[26] For much information relevant to this point, see Hyppolite Taine, *Origines de la France contemporaine*, rev. ed., 12 vols. (Paris, 1899-1914), vol. 1.

remember that blood-letting, while certainly the ultimate in repression, is only one form that coercion can take.

From this standpoint, repression may be both an obstacle to and precipitant of internal war. Repression is of course least likely to prevent internal war in societies which, unlike totalitarian regimes, have a low capacity for coercion. In such societies, adjustive and diversionary mechanisms seem to check revolutionary potential far better. Indeed, they may in any society.[27]

*Diversions and Concessions.* Diversionary mechanisms are all those social patterns and practices which channel psychic energies away from revolutionary objectives – which provide other outlets for aggressions or otherwise absorb emotional tensions. If Elie Halévy's theory is correct, then English nonconformist evangelicalism, especially the Methodist movement, furnishes an excellent case in point.[28] Halévy, being French, was deeply puzzled by the fact that England did not have any serious revolution in the early nineteenth century, despite conditions which, on their face, seem to have contained very great revolutionary potential – conditions resulting from the industrial revolution and from the fact of endemic revolution throughout the Western world. His solution was that English evangelicalism, more than anything else, performed a series of functions which greatly lowered the revolutionary level of British politics. Among these functions were the provision of outlets for emotional expression and the inculcation of a philosophy which reconciled the lower classes to their condition, made that condition seem inevitable, and made patient submission to it a sacred obligation. In England, at least at the time in question, religion seems indeed to have been the opiate of the people, as Marx and Engels, no less than later and different-minded historians, seem to have realized.

England may have been spared major political violence since the seventeenth century for other reasons too: for example, because at least twice in English history, just when she seemed to be on the very brink of civil war, external war opportunely occurred, unifying the country as external wars will: at the time of the Napoleonic wars, and again in 1914 after the mutiny in the Curragh threatened to develop into something much more serious. Indeed, diverting popular attention from domestic troubles by starting foreign wars is one of the most venerable dodges of statecraft. This too, however, is a weapon that cuts two ways. Military adventures are excellent diversions, and military successes can marvellously cement disjoined societies, but military failure, on the evidence, can hardly fail to hasten revolution in such cases. Russia may well have entered the first World War to distract domestic unrest, but, if so, the outcome was revolution rather than the contrary.

---

[27] "Power", says Merriam, "is not strongest where it uses violence, but weakest. It is strongest where it employs the instruments of substitution and counter-attraction, of allurement, of participation..." C. E. Merriam, *Political Power* (New York, 1934), 179-80.
[28] Elie Halévy, *A History of the English People*, 6 vols. (London, 1960), vol. 1.

Orgiastic excitements – festivals and dances, parades and circuses, *Reichs-parteitäge* and mass gymnastics – also provide diversionary outlets for popular discontent. "If the late czardom," says Edwards, "instead of abolishing vodka, had made it more plentiful and very cheap – if, in addition, they had stimulated to the utmost those forms of religious frenzy and excitement to which the Russian populace appear to be so susceptible – then it is at least possible that the people would have been so exhausted mentally, emotionally, and financially by their alcoholic and religious orgies that they would not have had sufficient energy left to carry out a successful revolution."[29]

Totalitarian regimes seem to be shrewder about such matters, as well as being more coercive. The massive sports programs which are a feature of every totalitarian regime (German, Russian, or Chinese) may have a variety of purposes – physical fitness as preparation for war, or the inculcation of discipline – but one of them assuredly is to absorb the energies of the young and the interest of the not-so-young. No less than eschatological ideology, sport is the opiate of the masses in totalitarian countries, and not in these alone.

Adjustive mechanisms reduce, or manage, tensions, rather than providing for them surrogate outlets. Concessions are perhaps the most obvious of such mechanisms. It is banal, but probably true, to say that timely concessions have been the most effective weapons in the arsenal of the British ruling class, and one of Halévy's more cogent points about the pacific effects of evangelicalism on nineteenth-century England is that it made the elite extraordinarily willing to ameliorate the lot of the masses. It enjoined upon them philanthropy as a sacred duty and educated them in the trusteeship theory of wealth – remember Wesley's counsel "gain all you can, save all you can, give all you can" – at the same time as it made the masses extraordinarily willing to suffer their burdens in peace. (For this reason, we can of course regard all functioning institutions for adjusting conflict as barriers to internal war.) But concessions too may work in two directions, no less than repression and certain diversionary tactics. They may only lead to further and greater demands, further and greater expectations of success, and must therefore, like repression, be continuous, and continuously greater, to succeed. "There is no better way [than a conciliatory policy]" according to Clemenceau, "of making the opposite party ask for more and more. Every man or every power whose action consists solely in surrender can only finish by self-annihilation. Everything that lives resists..."[30]

*Facilities for Violence.* A final set of obstacles to internal war are conditions that affect the capacities of alienated groups to use violence at all, or, more often in real life, to use it with fair prospects of success. These conditions do not always prevent violence. But they can prevent its success. For this very

[29] Edwards, *The Natural History of Revolution*, 49.
[30] Quoted in G. Sorel, *Reflections on Violence* (New York, 1915), 71.

reason, they help determine the likelyhood of decisions to use violence at all. What are some of these conditions?

Perhaps the first to come to mind is terrain. While practically all kinds of terrain can be used, in different ways, for purposes of rebellion, not all can be used to equal advantage. The ideal, from the viewpoint of the insurgents, seems to be an area which is relatively isolated, mountainous, overgrown, criss-crossed by natural obstacles (hedges, ditches, etc.), and near the sea or other sources of external supply – terrain which affords secure bases to the insurgents in their own territory, gives them the advantage of familiarity with local conditions, and allows ready access to them of external supporters.[31]

The communications facilities of a society are another relevant condition. Marx, among many others, seems to have realized this when he argued that urbanization increases the likelihood of revolution, if only in that it makes men accessible to one another and thus makes revolutionary organization easier to achieve. "Since the collective revolutionary mentality is formed by conversation and propaganda," writes the French historian Lefebvre, "all means that bring men together favor it."[32] In this one case, a condition which may heighten the chances of successful internal war (bad communications) may also discourage its outbreak. There may be nothing more mysterious to the celebrated peaceability of peasants, as compared to city-dwellers, than the physical difficulty in rural life, especially if fairly primitive, to form a "collective revolutionary mentality"

Terrain and communications are physical obstacles to (or facilities for) internal war. There are human obstacles as well. For example, internal wars seem rarely to occur, even if other conditions favor them, if a regime's instruments of violence remain loyal. This applies above all to the armed forces. Trotsky for one, and Lenin for another, considered the attitude of the army absolutely decisive for any revolution;[33] so also did Le Bon.[34] Pettee, on the other hand, dissents, but for a rather subtle reason: not because he considers the attitude of the armed forces insignificant, but because he feels that armies never fail to join revolutions when all other causes of revolution are present, and that they never fail to oppose them when this is not the case.[35] We could enlarge this point to read that internal wars are unlikely wherever the cohesion of an elite is intact, for the simple reason that insurgent formations require leadership and other skills, and are unlikely to obtain them on a large scale

[31]   For examples of how such terrain benefits insurgents, see Peter Paret, *Internal War and Pacification: The Vendée, 1793-1796* (Princeton, 1961); W. E. D. Allen, *Guerrilla War in Abyssinia* (London, 1951), 19; Chalmers Johnson, "Civilian Loyalties and Guerrilla Conflict", *World Politics*, July 1962; and Ernesto Guevara, *Che Guevara on Guerrilla War* (New York, 1961) – among many others.
[32]   G. Lefebvre, "Foules Révolutionnaires", *Annales Historiques de la Révolution Française*, 1934, 23.
[33]   Trotsky, *The Russian Revolution*, 116.
[34]   Gustave Le Bon, *The Psychology of Revolution* (New York, 1913), 29.
[35]   G. S. Pettee, *The Process of Revolution*, 105.

without some significant break in the ranks of an elite. Even if elites do not always "cause" their own downfall by becoming rigid or foreign to their people, they can certainly hasten their own demise by being internally at odds. From this standpoint, if not from that of Mosca's theory, elite cohesion is a factor which should be classified among the obstacles to internal war, as well as among their causes.

A final human obstacle to internal war – perhaps the greatest of all – is lack of wide popular support for rebellion. It seems generally accepted among modern writers on internal war, indeed it is the chief dogma of modern revolutionaries, that without great popular support the insurgents in an internal war can hardly hope to win (and with it are hardly likely to lose) – unless by means of a *coup d'état*. So vital is this factor that some writers think that the distinctive characteristic of internal war is the combination of violent techniques with psychological warfare, the latter designed, of course, to win the active support of the non-combatants; this is asserted in the much repeated pseudo-formula of the French theorists of *guerre révolutionnaire*: revolutionary warfare = partisan war + psychological warfare.[36] To be sure, psychological warfare occurs nowadays also in international wars. Its role in these, however, is not nearly so crucial as in internal war; it is incidental in one case but seems to be decisive in the other.

One reason for this is that in internal wars, unlike international wars, there is generally a great disparity in capacity for military effort between the incumbents and insurgents. The former tend to be in a much stronger position – not always, of course, for this is where the loyalties of the established instrumentalities of violence enter the picture, but more often than not. The insurgents are therefore forced, in the normal case, to supplement their capabilities by taking what advantage they can of terrain and the cooperation of the non-combatant population. Like terrain itself, a well-disposed population affords a secure base of operations to rebels, as well as providing them with indispensable logistical support. Rebels who can count on popular support can lose themselves in the population (according to Mao "the populace is for revolutionaries what water is for fish"), count on the population for secrecy (in wars in which intelligence is practically the whole art of defense), and reconstitute their forces by easy recruitment; if they can do all of these things, they can be practically certain of victory, short of a resort to genocide by the incumbents.

Great popular support is necessary also because internal wars, precisely because the common disparity of forces rules out quick victory by the insurgents (except by *coup*), tend to be long drawn out wars of attrition – perhaps

---

[36] G. Bonnet, *Les guerres insurrectionelles* (Paris, 1958), 60. The point that in guerrilla warfare almost everything turns on popular support is argued in many sources, most strongly perhaps in C. A. Johnson, "Civilian Loyalties and Guerrilla Conflict", *World Politics*, July 1962.

better, either very prolonged or very quickly settled. In such wars, when victory always seems remote, when, at times, impasse is the best that can be hoped for, when the disruption of normal life is greater even than in external war, the morale of the revolutionaries, their ultimate trump card against their opponents, can hardly be sustained if they feel themselves isolated from their own people.

For all of these reasons, calculations about popular loyalties normally play a role in the decision to resort to political violence. The calculations may be mistaken but they are almost always made, sometimes, as in the case of the Algerian nationalist struggle, in ways approaching the survey research of social science.[37]

## TOWARD AN ETIOLOGY OF INTERNAL WARS

Needless to say, these arguments do not amount to anything like a finished etiology of internal wars. My concern here has been with preliminary, but fundamental and neglected, questions of strategy in theory-building, no more. Nevertheless, taking it all in all, this study does imply something more than that certain lines of inquiry are more promising than others in internal-war studies. When its arguments are added up, there emerges at least a considerable clue to the *form* that an adequate etiology of internal wars should take, even if little of a very specific nature can as yet be said about content. We have arrived at a paradigm, if not a fully-fledged theory.

Two points can serve as summary, as well as to spell out the nature of the paradigm I have in mind. One is that internal-war potential (the likelihood that internal war in some form will be precipitated)[38] should be conceived formally as a ratio between positive forces making for internal war and negative forces working against it – with the *possibility* that internal war of some kind may be fomented existing no matter what the overall potential, and the *probability* of its occurrence increasing as internal-war potential rises. This is certainly elementary, but it is in fact far more usual, in both general theories and specific interpretations of internal war, to speak of revolutionary or pacifying forces alone, and to depict rebelliousness as either absolutely present or absolutely lacking in societies. The other, and more important point, is that the forces involved should be conceived in both cases as functions of four factors. The positive forces are produced by the *inefficacy of elites* (lack of cohesion and of expected performance), *disorienting social processes* (delegiti-

---

[37] Interview with M. Chanderli, F. L. N. Observer at the United Nations, December, 1961.

[38] I stress internal-war *potential* because this is all one can assess if the actual occurrence of internal wars depends on precipitants beyond the scope of systematic analysis or even the predictive capacities engendered by practical wisdom. Needless to say, however, the actual occurrence of internal wars gives the best assurance that the societies concerned indeed had great internal-war potential.

mization), *subversion* (attempts deliberately to activate disorientation, to form new political orientations and to impede the efficacy of elites), and the *facilities* available to potential insurgents. Countervailing these factors are four others: the *facilities* of incumbents, *effective repression* (not any kind of repression), *adjustive concessions* and *diversionary mechanisms* – the first referring to the incumbents' perceived capacity to fight if internal war occurs, the others to preventative actions.

This summation provides at least the minimum that one expects from paradigms: a formal approach to study and a checklist of factors that should be particularly considered whether one is interpreting specific cases or constructing general theory. But a minimum is not much. It is necessary to go further, particularly in the direction of determining the relative values of the factors and their relations to one another. After being stated, the variables must be ordered. Consequently, to conclude, I should like to add some suggestions that indicate how one might proceed from the mere cataloguing of promising variables toward their systematization.

In the first place, it seems, from what has been said about possible obstacles to internal war, that the negative forces vary within a much smaller range than the positive ones, so that beyond a point, internal-war potential can be reduced only with geometrically decreasing effectiveness, if at all. Take, for example, adjustive concessions. These cannot be indefinitely increased, for, in the end, they would be tantamount to surrender, and long before that point, would only serve to increase the insurgents' capabilities (not to mention the probable effects on the insurgents' demands and the incumbents' cohesion). Repression is intrinsically limited as well, among other reasons because it requires repressors and because its use will tend to intensify alienation; as in the case of concessions there may be an optimum of repression, but a maximum of it is as bad as none at all. And one can doubt the efficacy of diversions where disorientation is very widespread and goes very deep; besides, intrinsic limitations operate in the case of this factor too, for a society that lives on diversions to the extent of, say, the Roman Empire is for that very reason in decay. The factors that make for internal-war potential clearly are less inherently circumscribed. More clearly still, certain of them, like the crucial facility of popular support, belong to the realm of zero-sums, so that an increase of forces on the positive side implies a concomitant decrease on the other. In this sense, the variables involved in internal-war potential have a certain hierarchical order (an order of "potency"): one set is more significant than the other.

Such an order seems to exist within each set as well. For example, no one rebels simply because he has appropriate facilities – otherwise, the military and police would be everywhere and constantly in rebellion. At the very least, internal war presupposes some degree of subversion as well as brute capabilities. Subversion in turn, however, presupposes something that can be subverted – disorientations to activate and to reshape toward new legitimizations. And much evidence suggests that, whatever forces may be at work in a society, in whatever fashion, disorientation and subversion are both unlikely where the elite performs well, is highly cohesive, and is deeply enough attuned to the general spirit of social life to provide the mutualities and complementarities that settled social orientations require – granted that certain social processes make this extremely improbable. Per contra, elite inefficacy in itself always invites challenge, from within or without, no matter what other forces may be at work in the non-elite; in one form (incohesion), it implies the likelihood of internecine elite conflict, in others the probability of alienation of the non-elite. If disorientation arising from other sources is added, the brew obviously becomes more lethal (and its explosion tends to take a different form), with or without much concerted subversion. The latter, and insurgent facilities, are essentially extra addatives, the more so since insurgents can hardly lack facilities on some scale where elite inefficacy and political disorientation are great; these factors may intensify internal-war potential, but do not create it.

The factors that reduce internal-war potential can be arranged (with rather more ambiguity, to be sure) in a similar order of potency. The essential criterion that establishes their weight is the extent to which they are intrinsically limited, either because they can become self-defeating or because they are zero-sums that do not allow increases on the positive side to be balanced by increases on the other. Diversions, while certainly not unlimited, are probably the most potent of the factors, for they can apparently be carried very far before they thoroughly devitalize societies. Repression and concessions seem to have a much lower optimum point. It is difficult at present to say which of them is the less potent; in all probability, however, it is repression – if only because concessions may increase the legitimation of authority among potential dissidents (that is, serve as surrogates for other kinds of elite "performance") while acts of repression, as well as being inherently self-denials of legitimacy, are well-tailored to cope only with the less potent factor of subversion. Incumbent facilities, finally, while being by all odds the most ambiguous factor, seem to belong somewhere between diversions on one hand and concessions on the other. The reasons for this are three: First, since the most vital of them are zero-sums, they can be, in a sense, either very weak or very potent, a decrease in them implying a corresponding increase in insurgent facilities and the reverse holding as well (a sort of inherent limitation different from that operating in the case of the other factors). Secondly, it seems, on the evidence, more difficult for incumbents to regain lost facilities (especially lost loyalties) than for insurgents to multiply their stock of them, even if "logical" reasons for this are not readily apparent. And thirdly, while an increase in incumbent facilities most clearly reduces one of the positive factors, that factor happens to be least potent of the four.

The catalogue of forces making for internal-war potentials thus takes on a certain preliminary order – even if this order is as yet far from precise.

A further element of order can be introduced into the list of variables by noting that, to an extent, they can be paired with one another, specific negative and positive forces being particularly closely related. This is manifest in the case of insurgent and incumbent facilities – clearest of all where the facilities in question are zero-sums. All else being equal, it is obviously not the absolute value of facilities on either side that matters, but the ratio of the facilities concerned. Just as obviously, as already stated, there is a special relation between subversion and repression. Disorientation or elite inefficacy can hardly be repressed; only subversion can.[39] Less manifestly, but pretty clearly still, adjustive concessions bear a particular relation to certain elite failures, particularly in performance, and diversions can, to an extent, provide gratifications that alleviate the psychic stresses of disorientation; but neither is likely to counteract anything else.

One final point that bears more indirectly upon the ordering of the variables listed above requires consideration. It is an appropriate theme on which to conclude, for it is the point with which we started. Throughout the discussion, no distinction has been made between types of internal war, and this not without reasons.[40] The fact remains, however, that internal wars, although in some ways similar, are in most respects greatly various. An adequate etiology of internal wars should therefore be able to tell one more than whether internal war in some form will occur in a society. It should also enable one to account for the specific forms internal wars take in different circumstances.

Any discussion of this matter is at present greatly handicapped by the lack of a settled, well-constructed typology of internal wars – and constructing such a typology is a task great enough to require another, and rather extensive, study. This much can be said, however, without settling on specific typological categories: Approaching the etiological study of internal wars in the manner suggested here makes it possible to deal with the many different phenomena covered by the term internal war within a single theoretical framework, yet in a way that yields quite different accounts of clearly disparate events. And this is surely desirable where phenomena that differ in many respects have also much in common.

The point is that two things can be done with the paradigm I have sketched. By weighing the general balance of positive and negative forces, one can arrive at an assessment of the overall degree of internal-war potential in a society. By considering the *particular* forces, combinations of forces, and ratios of forces that are strong or weak – the forces that are especially instrumental in determining the overall result – one can arrive at definite ideas of what kinds

[39]    To avoid misunderstanding, it should be clearly understood that repression here refers not to putting down rebels in internal wars but preventative actions by the incumbents.
[40]    See above, 133-136.

of internal war are likely to occur (quite apart from the possibility that the general degree of internal-war potential may itself set limits to the varieties that internal war can take). For example, where elite inefficacy, especially incohesion, greatly predominates among the positive forces, something like what many have called palace revolution is a very likely result. Where disorientation is very great but other positive factors are negligible, one might expect relatively unorganized, sporadic rioting as the normal response. Where subversion looms large relative to other factors, *coups*, *Putsches* or terrorism are more likely. Where incumbent and insurgent facilities are rather equally matched and elite cohesion is particularly tenuous, the stage is probably set for full-scale civil war. One could, in fact, contrive a useful, although very complex, typology of internal wars by working out probable results for the various possible constellations of factors included in the paradigm; and one could similarly take any typology otherwise worked out and produce for it a set of appropriately corresponding combinations of the factors.

The signal advantage of this procedure is that it avoids what defaces the whole corpus of historical studies of internal war available to us, the *ad hoc* piling up of unrelated theories, and prevents also the most conspicuous flaw of unhistorical, abstract models of revolutionary processes, the disregarding of special forces in particular cases. As well, the procedure I suggest can deal coherently with another eminently historical and theoretical matter, the transformation of many internal wars in the course of their development – the revolutionary "process". It can do so simply by applying typological theories dynamically. For the constellations of forces that provide initial impetus to internal wars are likely to undergo constant transformation in their course, much as such constellations may vary in the pre-revolutionary period. Subversion may become more intense, more purposeful; the balance of facilities may shift; incumbent elites may become more cohesive or disunited under fire; mild disorientation may become severe as authority is challenged and society disrupted by violence; the insurgents may win power, but at the cost of their own cohesion and without being able to provide effective new legitimations – and thus internal wars may proceed from stage to stage, from type to type, in unique or characteristic, continuous or spasmodic, dynamic patterns.

*Princeton University*

# 8.

## THE CONCEPT OF IDEOLOGY

### GEORGE LICHTHEIM

Few concepts play a larger part in present-day discussions of historical and political topics than does that of ideology, and yet it is not always clear what meaning is applied to the term by those who employ it. Even if one confines one's attention to the utterances of sociologists and historians, leaving out of account the terminological misuse seemingly inseparable from ordinary political discourse, it is apparent that different and conflicting meanings are intended by writers who casually refer to the "ideology" of this or that political movement.

From the vulgar misunderstanding inherent in the familiar phrase "we need a better ideology to fight the enemy", to the refinements of academic dispute over "the ideology of science", one encounters a terminological vagueness which appears to reflect some deeper uncertainty about the status of ideas in the genesis of historical movements.

It is here intended to clarify the theme by examining the different signifi-cations attached to the term "ideology", and the shifting status of the phenom-enor itself, granted that a propensity so widespread as the duplication and distortion of reality in thought lends itself to the historical approach. If this initial assumption is allowed to pass as a working hypothesis, it is hoped that the term "ideology" will be shown to possess both a definite meaning and a particu-lar historical status: the history of the concept serving as a guide to the actual interplay of "real" and "ideal" factors whose dialectic is obscurely intended in the formulation of the concept itself. The subject has recently been dealt with by, among others, Mr. Ben Halpern ("'Myth' and 'Ideology' in Modern Usage", *History and Theory*, I, 2, 1961, 129–149). In what follows it is not proposed to take issue with his analysis, but to pursue a line of thought suggested by the present author's concern with the manner in which the ideology concept relates to what is usually known as the "philosophy of history", notably in its Hegelian form.

### THE REVOLUTIONARY HERITAGE

Historically, the term "ideology" made its first appearance at the time of the French Revolution, its author, Antoine Destutt de Tracy, being one of the group of *savants* whom the Convention in 1795 entrusted with the management of the newly founded *Institut de France*.[1] During the brief period of its predominance – until Napoleon in 1801 made his peace with the Church, and concurrently turned against the liberal intellectuals who had helped him into the saddle – the *Institut* became associated in the public mind with an outlook which indeed pre-dated the Revolution, but was now made official and brought into relation with the practice of the new regime. In 1794, at the height of the Terror, the guiding ideas of the faith had been given their final expression, under the most dramatic circumstances possible, by Condorcet in his *Tableau historique des progrès de l'esprit humain*; but it was under the Directory, with moderate liberalism briefly in the saddle, that the "*idéologues*" of the *Institut* placed the official seal on his doctrine.[2] Their prestige flattered the vanity of Bonaparte, who in 1797 became an honorary member of the Institute. How much the distinction meant to him appears from the fact that during the Egyptian campaign of 1798–9 he signed his proclamations to the Army as "Général en chef, Membre de l'Institut". It was a justified appreciation of their influence over the educated middle class that in 1799, at the time of the *coup d'état de Brumaire*, induced him to seek the support of the "*idéologues*", who in turn helped to promote his accession to power.[3] It was likewise fear of their hold over public opinion which in January 1803 led him to cap his growing personal despotism (and his Concordat with Rome) by the virtual destruction of the Institute's core, the *classe des sciences morales et politiques*, from which liberal and republican ideas radiated throughout the educational "establishment". The story of Bonaparte's degeneration can be written in terms of his relations with the "*idéologues*": down to the day in December 1812 when – returned to Paris from the disaster in Russia – he blamed them, in an address to the *Conseil d'Etat*, for the catastrophe into which his own despotism had plunged the country.[4]

The "ideologists" of the Institute were liberals who regarded freedom of thought and expression as the principal conquest of the Revolution. Their attitude was "ideological" in the twofold sense of being concerned with ideas,

---

[1] Georges Lefebvre, *La révolution française* (Paris, 1957), 443. The creation of the Institute was part of an attempt to provide France with a nation-wide system of higher learning committed to the philosophy of the Enlightenment.

[2] Lefebvre, 578: "Destutt de Tracy se proposait de déterminer par l'observation comment se forment les idées: de là le nom de l'école."

[3] Lefebvre, 534: "Arrivé à Paris... il montrait une discrétion toute républicaine et fréquentait l'Institut, où il fraternisait avec les idéologues." Cf. A. Aulard, *Histoire politique de la révolution française* (Paris, 1926), 694, for the illusions of the liberal intellectuals, who firmly expected Bonaparte to inaugurate the enlightened commonwealth of their dreams.

[4] "C'est à l'idéologie, à cette ténébreuse métaphysique qui, en cherchant avec subtilité les causes premières, veut sur ces bases fonder la législation des peuples, au lieu d'approprier les lois à la connaissance du cœur humain et aux leçons de l'histoire, qu'il faut attribuer toutes les malheurs de notre belle France." Cited in Hans Barth, *Wahrheit und Ideologie* (Zürich, 1945), 30; cf. Taine, *Origines de la France contemporaine* (Paris, 1898), II, 219-220. On other occasions he put it more briefly, e.g., "Cannon killed feudalism. Ink will kill modern society." (Napoléon: *Pensées*; Paris, 1913; 43).

and of placing the satisfaction of *"ideal"* aims (their own) ahead of the "material" interests on which the post-revolutionary society rested. They could put up, at least temporarily, with an enlightened dictatorship which safeguarded the major gains of the Revolution, but not with a regime which visibly steered back towards an absolutism supported by established religion. Napoleon ignored them, though he defended the social foundations of the new order and in 1815, after his return from Elba, made a last attempt to win their support. Under the Bourbon Restauration they headed the liberal opposition. In 1830 the July Revolution, by introducing parliamentary government, at long last realized one of their chief aims, though in a somewhat prosaic form. Marx, from a different standpoint, shared Napoleon's disdain for them. In 1845, remarking upon the manner in which the bourgeois character of the Revolution had gradually disclosed itself, he commented ironically upon their illusions, having previously noted that "Robespierre, Saint Just and their party fell because they confused the realistic democratic commonwealth of antiquity, which rested on the basis of real slavery, with the modern spiritualist-democratic representative state based on the emancipated slavery of bourgeois society."[5] Yet the ideologists, whatever their political fancies, had another and tougher side to them: they were the forerunners of positivism. The *Institut* under their direction became a centre of experimental studies. While Destutt de Tracy turned his attention to the history of ideas, Cabanis pioneered experimental psychology, Pinel placed the treatment of mental illness on a new foundation, Dupuis (in his *Origine de tous les cultes*) treated the natural history of religion in an empirical manner; others extended the new viewpoint to the history of literature and art. This intellectual explosion was the counterpart of the better known and perhaps even more brilliant achievements of Lagrange, Laplace, Monge, Berthollet, Cuvier, Saint-Hilaire, and Lamarck in the natural sciences, which between 1790 and 1830 raised France's contribution in this field to a pinnacle of achievement never equalled before or since. When Comte around 1830 synthesized the new world-view (in the light of what he had learned from the far more original Saint-Simon), he was drawing upon the work of a generation of scholars who had already transformed the inherited eighteenth-century view by introducing the historical approach. If the ideologists continued the rationalist tradition, they also began the process of modifying it, though – unlike the German Romantics – they did not abandon its basic principles.[6]

---

[5]  *Die Heilige Familie* (1845 [reprinted Berlin, 1953]), 191; cf. *The Holy Family* (London, 1957), 164. "It was not the revolutionary movement as such that became Napoleon's prey on the 18th Brumaire... it was the *liberal bourgeoisie*... Napoleon was the last stand of revolutionary terrorism against the bourgeois society which had likewise been proclaimed by the Revolution... If he despotically suppressed the liberalism of bourgeois society – the political idealism of its daily practice – he showed no more concern for its essential material interests... whenever they conflicted with his political interests. His contempt for the industrial *hommes d'affaires* was the counterpart of his scorn for the ideologues." (*Ibid.*, tr. from 1953 German edition, 193-194).

[6]  Lefebvre (*op. cit.*, 578) includes Madame de Staël's *La littérature considérée dans ses*

The twofold character of the liberal "ideology", as a system of normative ideas and as an incipient critique of the very notion of absolute norms, makes its appearance already in the work of Destutt de Tracy from which the school derived its name. His *Eléments d'Idéologie* (1801–15) presents a "Science des idées" for which he cites the authority of Locke and Condillac.[7] They are praised for having inaugurated the "natural history of ideas" – that is, the scientific description of the human mind – though Condillac had qualified his naturalism by retaining the traditional religious emphasis upon the substantive reality of man's soul and the uniqueness of man compared with the animal creation.[8] For Destutt, who superimposed the materialism of Cabanis upon the Lockean sensationalism of Condillac, the study of "ideology" is part of zoology. What he means is that human psychology should be analyzed in biological terms; that is, without paying attention to religion. Moral problems are relegated to metaphysics, described as a realm of illusory fancies "destinés à nous satisfaire et non à nous instruire".[9] The true foundation of the sciences is rather to be found in a "Science des idées" which will describe the natural history of the mind, that is, the manner in which our thoughts are formed. There is no supersensible reality behind the individuals and their several "ideas" (sensations and notions).

Il est seulement à remarquer qu'il n'existe réellement que des individus et que nos idées ne sont point des êtres réels existant hors de nous, mais de pures créations de notre esprit, des manières de classer nos idées des individus.[10]

But this "materialist" theme is crossed by a normative purpose: the "Science des idées" is to yield true knowledge of human nature, and therewith the means of defining the general laws of sociability. The reduction of individual "ideas" to generally held notions is intended to lay bare the common ground of human needs and aspirations, thus providing the lawgiver with the means of furthering the common good. What is "natural" is also "social". Once human nature is properly understood, society will at last be able to arrange itself in a harmonious fashion. Reason is the guarantor of order and liberty.[11] As with Condorcet, Destutt's aim is pedagogical: it is to lay bare the guiding principles of republican citizenship. His theorizing has a practical, normative, purpose. The freeing of the human mind from ignorance and superstition is not undertaken for its own sake, but because only a mind delivered from error can perceive those universal

---

*rapports avec les institutions sociales* (1800) among the notable productions of the school.
[7]  A. Destutt de Tracy, *Eléments d'Idéologie* (2nd. ed., Brussels, 1826), I, 3; cf. Barth, *Wahrheit und Ideologie*, 16 f.
[8]  Condillac, *Oeuvres complètes* (Paris, 1798), III, 592.
[9]  *Eléments*, I, XIV.
[10]  *Eléments*, I, 301.
[11]  "Le perfectionnement des lois, des institutions publiques, suites des progrès des sciences, n'a-t-il point pour effet d'approcher, d'identifier l'intérêt commun de chaque homme avec l'intérêt commun de tous?" Condorcet, *Tableau historique* (Paris, 1822), 292.

laws which make it plain "que la nature lie par une chaîne indissoluble la
vérité, le bonheur et la vertu".[12] The pathos of the Enlightenment is retained
in the "Science des idées", for all its incipient naturalism. Reason progressively
discloses a true picture of humanity which constitutes the foundation of civic
virtue. Morality is anchored in nature. The best social order is that which
corresponds to the permanent needs of man.

The antecedents of this faith are Baconian and Cartesian. To Condillac, who
preceded the ideologues and the Revolution, it had already seemed plain that
Bacon's criticism of the "idols" must be the starting point of that reformation of
consciousness which was the principal aim of the Enlightenment.[13] Bacon's
*idolum* becomes Condillac's *préjugé*, a key term also in the writings of Holbach
and Helvétius. The idols are "prejudices" contrary to "reason". To remove
them by the relentless application of critical reasoning is to restore the "unpre-
judiced" understanding of nature. Holbach maintains that

l'homme n'est malheureux que parce qu'il méconnait la Nature... La raison guidée
par l'expérience doit enfin attaquer dans leur source des préjugés dont le genre humain
fût si longtemps le victime... La vérité est une; elle est nécessaire à l'homme... C'est
à l'erreur que sont dues les chaînes accablantes que les Tyrans et les Prêtres forgent
partout aux nations.[14]

Helvétius (a favourite of both Marx and Nietzsche) develops this notion in the
direction of a rudimentary sociology of knowledge: "Our ideas are the necessary
consequence of the societies in which we live."[15] Scepticism is held in check
by the rationalist faith inherited from Descartes: reason has the power of cor-
recting its own errors.[16]

For Helvétius, the idols (*préjugés*) are the necessary fruit of social constraint
and selfish interest, but he is convinced that they can be discredited by reason
and removed by education. "L'éducation peut tout."[17] The cure for popular
superstition is pedagogy on a national scale. This is the point where Marx later
introduced his criticism of the Enlightenment.[18] Helvétius in fact never succeeded

[12] Condorcet, *ibid.*, 10.
[13] "Personne n'a mieux connu que Bacon la cause de nos erreurs, car il a vu que les idées,
qui sont l'ouvrage de l'esprit, avaient été mal faites, et que par conséquent pour avancer dans
la recherche de la vérité il fallait les refaire." Condillac, *Essai sur l'origine des connaissances
humaines* (Oeuvres, I, 507); cf. the article on Bacon in the *Encyclopédie*, III, and d'Alembert's
"Discours préliminaire".
[14] Holbach, *Système de la Nature* (Paris, 1770), preface.
[15] *De L'Esprit*, (1758), 114; cited by Barth, *op. cit.*, 62. For Rousseau's share in the elaboration of this attitude cf. Iring Fetscher, *Rousseaus politische Philosophie* (Neuwied, 1960),
*passim.*
[16] "ce qu'on nomme le bons sens ou la raison, est naturellement égale en tous les hommes...
la diversité de nos opinions ne vient pas de ce que les uns sont plus raisonnables que les
autres, mais seulement de ce que nous conduisons nos pensées par diverses voies" (Descartes,
*Discours de la méthode*, cf. *Oeuvres*, ed. Pléiade, 1952, 126.)
[17] Helvétius, *De l'Homme* (1773), II, 332.
[18] Cf. *Theses on Feuerbach*: "The materialist doctrine that men are products of circumstances and upbringing... forgets that it is men who change circumstances and that the

in clarifying the relationship of "interest" to "education". Wandering off into cynicism, he anticipated Nietzsche by arguing that the sole motor of human action is self-love and the will to power.

Chacun veut commander parce que chacun veut accroître sa félicité... L'amour du pouvoir fondé sur celui du bonheur est donc l'objet commun de tous nos désirs... toutes les passions factices ne sont-elles en nous que l'amour du pouvoir déguisé sous ces noms différents:"[19]

A suggestion which greatly pleased Nietzsche when he came across it.[20]

The confusion in which Helvétius landed himself was inherent in a "materialism" which treated the mind as the passive receptacle of sense impressions. At the same time he retained enough of the rationalist faith to remain confident that "prejudices" could be shown up as such, and that interest psychology could be subordinated to an objective understanding of the real needs of society. The "justesse de l'esprit" displays itself in the discovery of general laws whose truth is demonstrable. Their application to social life is a political problem that is, a problem of power. Philosophy and politics have their common ground in education, whereby inherited prejudices (mainly religious) are overcome and replaced by insight into the true nature of man and his environment. The place of religion is taken by a secular morality, inherently social because man is a social being.

By and large – and allowing for disputes between deists, materialists, and agnostics – this was the faith which the "ideologues" of the Institute inherited from their pre-revolutionary ancestors and which eventually became the official doctrine of French democracy and indeed of the French Republic. The point here is that, for all the inherent scepticism with respect to shared beliefs, the power of rational thought was not seriously called in question. Almost a century later, Comte's positivism, notwithstanding its authoritarian features, was still rooted in the same confidence. His complacent certainty that the "philosophie positive" represented the "véritable état définitif de l'intelligence humaine"[21] may today strike one as humorous, bearing in mind the paucity of discoveries attributable to the new method; but there is no mistaking the rationalist pathos which rings through his pseudo-religious rigmarole. Compared with the older generation, the change lies in the hierarchical straitjacket imposed upon the social order by a theorist in whom the generous optimism of the Enlightenment had congealed into a worried concern with social stability.[22] For Comte the "development of the human mind" issues in the recognition

---

educator himself needs to be educated. Hence this doctrine necessarily divides society into two parts, of which one is superior to the other..."
[19] *De l'Homme*, I, 238-239.
[20] Cf. Barth, 316.
[21] *Cours de philosophie positive*, ed. Ch. Le Verrier (Paris, Garnier), I, 23.
[22] For this aspect of Comte cf. Herbert Marcuse, *Reason and Revolution* (London, 1955), 342 ff.

that all historical phenomena are subject to "invariable natural laws",[23] but this chilling thought somehow sustains reason's faith in itself. To anticipate Engels's later formulation (itself an amalgam of Comtean and Hegelian determinism), freedom is anchored in the recognition of necessity. *Science* enables us to bind these extremes together. The dogmatism of Comte does not subvert the conviction that the study of society yields the discovery of universal rational principles.


## THE HEGELIAN TRADITION

Although Comte on some points anticipates Marx (or at any rate the version of Marxism subsequently canonized by Engels and his successors), his critique of the "ideologists" cannot be regarded as the forerunner of Marx's onslaught on the "German ideology", which latter had evolved quite independently of the French variant. The two lines of development must not be confused just because Marx affected to believe that Feuerbach and the Young Hegelians were the legitimate heirs of the *idéologues* (whence the title of his bulky tract which was not published in full until 1932).[24] The officially sanctioned "German ideology" of the 1840's had come into being as a reaction against the theory and practice of the French Revolution. Its true originator was Hegel, who from his youthful Jacobinism[25] had gradually moved to an almost Burkean worship of continuity, without ever quite renouncing his faith in universal reason and the rule of law.[26] His radical critics retained the historical approach he had introduced, and at the same time restored the moral iconoclasm he had abandoned. Their target was the conservative "Christian-German" ideology then invested with a quasi-official function by the pre-1848 regime. In assailing it, Feuerbach, Bruno Bauer, and the left-wing Hegelians in general, inevitably went back to the ultimate source of their own faith: the French Englightenment and its naturalist critique of theology and metaphysics.[27] A few years later Marx was to claim that their criticism of the official ideology was itself ideological. The precise

---

[23]  Comte, *op. cit.*, 26.
[24]  For the following cf., *Die deutsche Ideologie: Kritik der neuesten deutschen Philosophie in ihren Repräsentanten, Feuerbach, B. Bauer und Stirner, und des deutschen Sozialismus in seinen verschiedenen Propheten, MEGA,* V (1932); and the various translations.
[25]  Cf. *Briefe von und an Hegel* (Leipzig, 1887); *Hegels theologische Jugendschriften* (Tübingen, 1907), *passim.*
[26]  Cf. *Philosophy of Right* (1821): "It is part of education, of thinking as the consciousness of the single in the form of universality, that the ego comes to be apprehended as a universal person in which all are identical. A man counts as a man in virtue of his manhood alone, not because he is a Jew, Catholic, Protestant, German, Italian etc. This is an assertion which thinking ratifies, and to be conscious of it is of infinite importance." (Tr. T. M. Knox, Oxford, 1942, para. 209; 134).
[27]  Cf. Bruno Bauer, *Das entdeckte Christentum. Eine Erinnerung an das achtzehnte Jahrhundert und ein Beitrag zur Kritik des neunzehnten* (1843). For the influence of Holbach, Helvétius, and the *Science des idées,* on Feuerbach, Bauer and Marx, cf. Barth, *op. cit.*, 73 ff.

significance he gave to this charge needs to be understood in the light of the philosophical situation then prevailing.

The belief that general concepts, though held by particular individuals, are of universal application, is common to all thinkers who can be described as rationalists. It was retained by Hegel, notwithstanding his disillusionment with the outcome of the French Revolution, in which he had originally seen the practical working of Reason. Kantian philosophy had already synthesized Cartesian rationalism and Lockean empiricism in a procedure which restored the primacy of mind over matter: general concepts, though rooted in experience, were held to be independent of experience, inasmuch as they organized the sense data into intelligible wholes. The imposition of order upon the chaos of sense impressions was the work of the mind, which was in possession of the true and universal forms of understanding, the categories. The dependence of the individual mind upon the material presented by the senses – that hobby-horse of empiricism, from Locke to Hume – was not disputed, but treated as a state of affairs which occupies merely the foreground of reasoning. The "given" experience present to the individual is not an assemblage of brute "facts", but an ordered whole. In extending this Kantian approach from the realm of nature to history, Hegel affirmed the governing principle of the idealist faith: matter is organized by mind. Experience – the shibboleth of the British school – ceased to be a final datum. The way to the attainment of universality lay in grasping the principles which held the sensible world together.

Seen from Hegel's standpoint, Kant had remained in a half-way position between empiricism and true universalism. The latter required the assumption that the mind recognizes a world independent of the subject, whereas the Kantian categories were merely the necessary forms of any singular subject's possible experience. They constituted a phenomenal world, one and the same for all experients, yet Kant never took the decisive step of acknowledging that the world can be common to all experients only if all finite minds are differentiations of a universal mind: he did not, that is, conceive Mind as a "concrete universal". Reason for him is not indeed passive, but the individual consciousness is not seen as transcending itself, and its activity is not viewed as the immanence of a universal reason working through finite minds. If Kant in consequence has "no philosophy of Nature, only a philosophy of natural science",[28] Hegel on the contrary has a philosophy of History precisely because for him Reason is at once general and particular: a concrete universal which differentiates itself into particular thinking minds. On this view, the problem for the individual thinker is to apprehend the movement of Reason, of which his own thinking is a reflex. What manifests itself to philosophic thought is the history of Mind – veiled by its embodiment in Matter, but still plainly discernible as the motive force of the universal process. When "stood on its feet" by materialism, this philosophy yields the conviction that the logic of history is deci-

[28] G. R. G. Mure, *An Introduction to Hegel* (Oxford, 1940), 105.

pherable through an understanding of Man's capacity to "produce" his own world. Beyond the recorded facts there lies the totality of history which men have made, and are therefore able to understand. It is worth stressing this continuity, so often obscured by emphasis upon the naturalist inversion effected by Feuerbach and Marx. Feuerbach indeed "saw through" Hegel's terminology to the theology of Spirit lying behind it, but his return to the naturalism of the French Enlightenment did not imply acceptance of the empiricist mode of reasoning. Nature is a universal for Feuerbach, as history is for Marx. This is not to say that either of them was uncritical of Hegel's manner of treating logical concepts. (It was left for Marx's less intelligent followers to personify History into an independent entity: a misunderstanding against which he had protested in advance.)[29]

We are here concerned with the concept of ideology, not with the truth of Hegel's philosophy. What needs to be retained is that on Hegel's assumption the problem of overcoming the particularity of thinking is not insoluble; nor does it follow that because philosophers – or for that matter ordinary men – are born and raised under particular circumstances, they cannot rise above them. Man is essentially a thinking being, and as such able to apprehend the concrete universality which is history. Our historical concepts possess true generality because they relate to a universal agent that unfolds through the histories of particular peoples and civilizations. This agent for Hegel is Mind, for Marx it is human activity, *praxis*: the practice of men struggling to subdue nature and to develop their own latent powers. The determinant in each case is conscious activity, though Marx protests that for Hegel the historical process tends to become an independent entity superior to the individuals who compose it.[30]

The problem of ideology (in the sense of "false consciousness" or "imperfect consciousness") arises for Hegel because in his view individuals, and even entire nations, are instruments of history, executors of a process whose meaning is concealed from them, and which becomes selfconscious only *post festum* in the philosopher who sums up the sense of the epoch.[31] Hegel was aware that history is set in motion by men's interests and passions. He did not question its rationality just because men commonly behaved in an irrational manner: the process

[29] "History, like truth, becomes a person apart, a metaphysical subject, of which the real individuals are merely the bearers." *Die Heilige Familie* (Berlin, 1953), 116.
[30] "Hegel's conception of history presupposes an abstract or absolute spirit which develops in such a way that humanity is nothing but a mass which more or less consciously bears it along. Within the framework of empirical exoteric history, Hegel introduces the operation of a speculative esoteric history. The history of humanity becomes the history of the abstract spirit of humanity, a spirit beyond the real man. Concurrently with this Hegelian doctrine, there developed in France the theory of the doctrinaires, who proclaimed the sovereignty of reason in opposition to the sovereignty of the people..." *Die Heilige Familie* (1953), 57; cf. *MEGA*, 1/3, 257; *The Holy Family* (London, 1957), 115.
[31] *Vorlesungen über die Geschichte der Philosophie*, ed. Lasson (Leipzig, 1930), I, 9 ff. 25 ff, 78 ff.; cf. *The Philosophy of History*, ed. C. J. Friedrich (New York, 1956), *Introduction* and *passim*; Marcuse, *Reason and Revolution*, 224 ff.

had its own logic, which was not that of the individuals. The "cunning of reason"[32] could be observed in the manner in which the Idea (the rationality of the whole) triumphed at the expense of its own agents. The individual's fate was swallowed up in the dialectic of the process. The youthful Marx rebelled against this world-view, which struck him as theological; he lived to see it reinstated (with his own silent acquiescence) by Engels, though it was only gradually that the wheel came full circle, with the determinist emphasis upon "general laws" governing the course of history: laws apparently general enough to conform to Hegel's "cunning of reason", and scientific enough to be acceptable to a generation raised on positivism.[33]

For Hegel the problem had been to justify the ways of God to man. He did not doubt that these ways could be understood, at any rate retrospectively. This understanding is the work of philosophy, which in every age makes its appearance when a particular phase of Spirit has come to a close. Philosophy does not change the world: it interprets it and thus reconciles the world to itself. Yet Hegel's own philosophy was to change the world – if only because, even on its most conservative interpretation, it was subversive of revealed religion.[34] On the other hand, his system – more particularly his teachings on Right and the State – appeared to his radical critics as the "ideology" of the political status quo: its intellectual projection and justification. From here it was only a step to the notion that speculative philosophy as such barred the way to that reconstruction of the world which was required to realize the aims of philosophy: liberty and rationality. This step was taken by Marx, with the help of Feuerbach who had taught him to regard speculative thinking as the ultimate barrier to the understanding of man's role in the world.

The Marxian concept of ideology thus fuses two different principles: Hegel's insight into the transitory character of the successive manifestations of Spirit, and Feuerbach's materialist inversion of Hegel, with its stress on the this-worldly character of natural existence. Separated from each other these concepts remained speculative; joined together they yielded an explosive mixture. The explosion, however, did not depend for its effect on the kind of scepticism which follows from the alleged discovery that abstract thinking does not yield access to universal truths. The despairing conclusions drawn by Kierkegaard from this conviction do not form part of the intellectual revolution underlying the new philosophy of history: they belong – with Nietzsche's

[32] *Vorlesungen*, I, 83; cf. *The Philosophy of History*, 33.

[33] Engels, *Ludwig Feuerbach and the Close of Classical German Philosophy, passim.* Cf. Engels to Mehring, July 14, 1893 (in Marx-Engels *Selected Correspondence*, Moscow, 1954, 541): "Ideology is a process accomplished by the so-called thinker consciously, it is true, but with a false consciousness. The real motive forces impelling him remain unknown to him; else it simply would not be an ideological process."

[34] Barth, 78 f. To Hegel's followers the matter presented itself in a somewhat different light: since his philosophy was the fulfilment of speculative thinking in general, its appearance plainly marked the end of European history; cf. K. Löwith, *Von Hegel zu Nietzsche* (Stuttgart, 1950), 44 ff. This may well have been Hegel's own view.

kindred writings – to the attack on rationalism which in our own age has given rise to the existentialist analysis of the lonely individual. Nietzsche and Kierkegaard – just because they are concerned with the individual's role in a world whose functioning is indifferently taken for granted – have nothing to say about the manner in which history operates. Their revolt against rationalist metaphysics issues in subjectivism. Among the first universals to be cast overboard by these influential critics of rationalism was the concept of humanity.[35]

## FROM HEGEL TO MARX

What Marx meant by "ideology" appears plainly enough from the *Theses on Feuerbach*, where the latter is blamed for not having carried through to the end his inversion of Hegel's system. He says, for example:

Feuerbach sets out from the fact of religious self-alienation, the duplication of the world into a religious and a secular one. His work consists in resolving the religious world into its secular basis. But the fact that the secular basis deserts its own sphere and establishes an independent realm in the clouds, can only be explained by the cleavage and self-contradiction within the secular basis.[36]

This radicalization of Feuerbach's naturalist starting-point (itself a continuation of a tradition rooted in antiquity) left intact the rationalist principle which Marx shared with Hegel: namely, the belief that cognition gives access to universal truths not present in immediate experience. The Marxian conception of world history as a process of human self-alienation draws on Feuerbach's impassioned protest against the sacrifice of nature and of real, living, human beings, whose activities and whose sufferings Hegel had obscured. But Marx retains the Hegelian conviction that in the final analysis "history makes sense". The historical process vindicates Reason because it can be understood. To this extent Marx always remained a Hegelian, for all the emphasis upon "the real

[35]  Kierkegaard still tried to find logical flaws in Hegel's system. With Schopenhauer's disciple Nietzsche, subjectivism and aestheticism have already reached the point where logic is consciously discarded. One cannot take seriously Nietzsche's so-called critique of traditional thought. When he says (*Jenseits von Gut und Böse*, in *Werke*, ed. K. Schlechta, Munich, 1960, II, 571) "It has gradually emerged that every great philosophy has hitherto been the confession of its author and a kind of unintended and unnoticed *mémoires*", he is being trivial in the Voltairean manner, which is caricatured throughout this overrated essay; cf., his similar observations (in *Werke*, I, 448) on the "hereditary fault of philosophy": "All philosophers share the fault of proceeding from the currently existing man (*vom gegenwärtigen Menschen*) and expecting to reach the goal through analyzing him. Insensibly they have an image of "Man" as an *aeterna veritas*… as a sure measure of all things. Yet everything said by the philosopher about Man at bottom only applies to the men of a very limited period. Lack of historical sense is the hereditary fault of all philosophers…" That this kind of thing should have been taken seriously *after Hegel* testifies to a state of affairs perhaps best described as the collapse of responsible thinking.
[36]  *Karl Marx: Selected Writings in Sociology and Social Philosophy*, ed. Bottomore and Rubel (London, 1956), 68.

history of real people" which occupies so prominent a place in his polemics against his former associates.[37]

Marx's conception of ideology as "false consciousness" leads back to the problem of establishing the true consciousness which will enable men to understand their role. There is only one truth about history, and only one criterion for judging the discrepancy between what men are and what they might become: this criterion is supplied by philosophy, specifically by its understanding of man as a rational being. Thus philosophy, as the norm of reality, entails an implicit critique of this reality. Yet Marx also held that the philosophy of every age is the "ideological reflex" of determinate social conditions. How then could it function as the source of normative judgments pointing beyond the existing state of affairs? The problem did not arise if human self-alienation was conceived in the manner of Fichte and Hegel, as a mere misfortune which could be rectified by opposing a true consciousness to a false one. This had been Marx's standpoint in 1843, when he was already a revolutionary, but not yet a materialist.[38]

It might seem that on the materialist assumptions Marx accepted as part of his conversion to socialism in 1844-5, he was bound to arrive at a radical historicism and relativism. But although in many places the language of the *Holy Family* and the *German Ideology* (not to mention the *Communist Manifesto*) seems to support this conclusion, he did not in fact do so. He took over from his French predecessors the critical demolition of traditional metaphysics, yet he also went on ascribing a rational content to history. The rationality was a hidden one and had to be discerned in the logic of the "material" process itself, not in the "ideological" reflex it left in the minds of the participants. Like Hegel, he distinguished between Reality and Appearance. The reality of the historical process for Hegel was alienated Mind coming to terms with itself; for Marx it was alienated human labor reflecting itself in an ideological cloud-cuckooland. What he was later (in *Das Kapital*) to describe as the "fetishism of commodities", appears in his early writings as human self-alienation, whereby man's creations acquire a status independent of their creator.

The Marxian concept of ideology takes shape in this context, and from the start has a meaning different from that which it had for his eighteenth-century predecessors. Interest psychology is replaced by a metaphysic of human nature

---

[37] *Deutsche Ideologie*, 28 ff. and *passim*. In 1844-5 Marx (then resident in Paris) had partly excerpted Destutt de Tracy's *Eléments d'Idéologie*, and his use of the term "ideology" reflects a clear awareness of the devaluation it had meanwhile undergone.

[38] Cf. *Ein Briefwechsel von 1843*, in *Der historische Materialismus*, ed. S. Landshut and J. P. Mayer (Leipzig, 1932), 226. "The reform of consciousness consists only in this, that one enables the world to become aware of its own consciousness, that one awakens it from its dream, that one *explains* its own actions to it. Our entire purpose, as with Feuerbach's critique of religion, can only consist in transforming the religious and political questions into the self-conscious human form... It will then appear that the world has long possessed the dream of something of which it need only possess the consciousness in order to have it in reality."

whose outline Hegel had developed in the *Phenomenology of Mind*. Alienated social activity is to Marx what alienated mental activity is to Hegel. For both, the distinction between Reality and Appearance is involved in the manner in which *real* processes are transformed into *apparently* fixed and stable characters. Reality is process, appearance has the form of isolated objects. The task of critical thinking is to grasp the relations which constitute these apparent objects.

This approach still left unsolved the problem of relating the social content of ideology to the rational meaning of the process, as it differentiates itself through its various concrete manifestations. The historical character of the Marxian dialectic, and with it the problem of ideology in the modern sense, is a consequence of the discovery that there is not – as Feuerbach had thought – a single universal human standpoint from which to judge the alienations imposed by history; there are only particular human standpoints, corresponding to forms of society which arise from the interplay of material conditions and (more or less) conscious attempts to organize the "productive forces". The dialectic of being and consciousness is worked out in history; not, as Hegel had implied, as a shadow-play reflecting a metaphysical process, but as the "real" play. The "actors" are individuals and groups whose changing circumstances are mirrored in varying modes of thought. These modes are "ideological" in that the participants fail to comprehend the situation in which they are involved. But even the most thorough clarification of their actual historical role cannot, it would seem, enable them to transcend the particularity of their standpoint, since this is bound up with the concrete needs of their time and place. The only difference between "objective" and "ideological" thinking appears to lie in the capacity of the critical intellect to comprehend the particular determinations which condition each successive phase of human activity.

The principle that "social being ... determines consciousness"[39] appears to imply that every social order (however defined) has forms of consciousness peculiar to it. Yet Marx also asserts that "mankind always sets itself only such tasks as it can solve",[40] thus placing a statement about the whole process within the framework of a doctrine intended to supersede the "pre-scientific" viewpoint. To invoke "mankind" is to make an assertion about the totality of history, however empirical and non-metaphysical the writer's intention. There is not in Marx a clear distinction between sociological statements relative to particular situations, and philosophical generalizations pertaining to history as a whole. How is the dilemma to be met?

The principle that social being determines consciousness must be understood as itself an historical one: it refers to a state of affairs which has characterized history from the very beginning, but which is due to disappear when a rational

---

[39] Marx, *A Contribution to the Critique of Political Economy*, preface. Cf. *Selected Works* (Moscow, 1958), I, 363.
[40] *Ibid.*

order has been created. For the attainment of such an order implies the conscious direction of social life, hence the emancipation of consciousness from blind, uncomprehended, necessity. Consciousness is ideological because it is powerless. When it becomes the determining factor, it sheds its blinkers along with its dependence on material circumstances. *A rational order is one in which thinking determines being.* Men will be free when they are able to *produce* their own circumstances. Historical materialism is valid only until it has brought about its own dialectical negation. When this stage has been reached, it will no longer be possible to speak of historical "laws", for history is subject to "laws" only in so far as it is unconscious, that is, in so far as it is *not*, properly speaking, human history at all. The mature consciousness which in retrospect comprehends the necessity of this lengthy process of "pre-history" will not be an ideological one: it will be shared by all men, and will mark mankind's understanding of its own past.

Marx preserved the original motive of his thinking (together with the conception of history he had inherited from Hegel) by refusing to recognize the dilemma inherent in the principle that modes of thought are to be understood as "expressions" of changing social circumstances. He took it for granted that, though consciousness is conditioned by existence, it can also rise above existence and become a means of transcending the alienation which sets the historical process in motion. The *truth* about man is one and the same for all stages of history, even though every stage produces its own *illusions*. This truth is likewise the criterion for the practical activity which seeks to overcome man's alienation from his "true" being. The concept of ideology illumines the historical circumstance that men are not in possession of the true consciousness which – if they had it – would enable them to understand the totality of the world and their own place in it. Marx regarded his theory as a step towards the attainment of such a consciousness. The unity of mankind, and the universality of truth, were as real to him as they were to Hegel, and it was left to his disciples to destroy the coherence of this thought by abandoning its unspoken assumptions and transforming his doctrine into a variant of positivism.


## FROM METAPHYSICS TO POSITIVISM

The second half of the nineteenth century witnessed the dissolution of rationalist metaphysics and the rise of positivism, which from a particular school of thought in France transformed itself into the general method of the natural and social sciences. In this atmosphere, sociology took shape as the application of positivist principles – themselves rooted in the world-view of the eighteenth-century Enlightenment – to the study of institutions. Comte's *philosophie positive* in part still reflected its founder's link with the early socialist critique of society.[41]

---

[41]  Marcuse, *Reason and Revolution*, 323 ff.

With Herbert Spencer this antagonism turned into its opposite, though the original motive broke through again in Spencer's rebellious ex-pupils who renounced his individualist approach and developed the Fabian amalgam of Benthamite utilitarianism and socialism.[42] With the Fabian school indeed, British sociology, after a lengthy interval of liberal individualism, returned to its positivist and quasi-socialist origins. In France a parallel development is associated with the name of Durkheim. In both cases the "objective" study of social institutions gradually transcended the individualist framework. If Comte (who had derived his basic ideas from Saint-Simon) converted socialism into sociology, his French and British pupils reverted to the "ideology" he had spurned. They then discovered in piecemeal fashion that the "laws" of history left room for conscious activity which, to be effective, had to be grounded in the study of institutions. The "religion of humanity", which for them increasingly took the place of the official religion, required active participation. This activism did not contradict the scientific credo, for it was held that society's growing complexity demanded public intervention. Such action, then, was justified not simply on humanitarian grounds – though crass poverty and misery furnished an adequate motive – but on the grounds of rational obligation.

Comte's positivism did indeed raise the problem of "value judgments", for science merely described the facts, leaving it to the individual to judge them in accordance with his moral standards. But precisely because "value judgments" were excluded from science, they were free. Comte's moral neutrality left the field open for action guided by the desire for improvement of a social order judged imperfect in terms of inherited (secular or religious) morality. It even contained a normative element in the idea of a universal order transcending national differences. His evolutionary doctrine, however determinist in retrospect (or in prospect), had room for the kind of humanitarian impulse that transformed itself into a critique of the established order when it encountered concrete social problems such as poverty or unemployment. British evolutionary socialism was able to merge with empirical sociology because both shared the conviction that the study of "objective facts" would enable society to overcome the latent irrationalities embedded in the established order. The problem of "ideology" was not experienced as such, since it was taken for granted that all reasonable people were agreed on fundamentals. Similarly the phenomenon of class was not seen as a theoretical problem, but rather as a practical obstacle to the attainment of a moral consensus. Classes were undesirable because they barred the way to a community in which personal values could be genuinely shared. In this respect the working class had no advantage: it too possessed no more than a limited perspective which stood in need of being transcended.

[42]  Cf. Beatrice Webb, *My Apprenticeship* (London and New York, 1926), 112 f, 123 ff. The study of Fabian origins in recent years has done much to clarify the manner in which the Comtean impulse reached these late Victorian intellectuals by way of J. S. Mill and the novels of George Eliot.

While society was split into classes – whether mutually antagonistic or merely indifferent to each other – it lacked that unity which would enable individuals to meet on a common human footing. Hence classes were immoral, as well as being historically outmoded, since their existence was no longer justifiable on grounds of necessity. Any sectional standpoint was in principle as undesirable as any other, though the working class might temporarily benefit from a favorable prejudice, on the grounds of having in the past been made to carry a burden which ought in future to be equitably shared. Insofar as there was a problem of "false consciousness", it arose from these historic limitations, which were shared by all. Scientific insight into this state of affairs was also the means of transcending it: to begin with in thought, and increasingly – through moral and political action – in practice.[43]

These attitudes ultimately went back to the Enlightenment view of human progress as intellectual progress. This had been the standpoint of the *idéologues* and their successors, notably the Saint-Simonians. If Comte had removed the socialist component from sociology, he had retained the notion that the growth of positive knowledge was beneficial because it enabled men to understand the "laws" of social evolution. From there it was a short step to the conclusion that knowledge of the laws would make it possible to refashion society in accordance with moral values. In France this step was taken by Durkheim, whose public posture could be regarded as an uneasy balance between the positivism of Comte and the socialism of Marx.[44] But what was the source of the moral values? According to Durkheim they came to the individual from society: not a mere natural totality, but the concrete embodiment of ideal norms. Then how had the norms become embodied in social conduct? If the question was an historical one, it led to an examination of the manner in which different societies had organized themselves at different times around certain regulative principles. But no investigation of this kind could get beyond the factual statement that particular obligations had at one time or another been accepted as binding. If a crisis arose because the moral consensus broke down, the individuals forming society were faced with the need to establish a new consensus, but it was not explained on what grounds they were to make a choice. Durkheim was no relativist, but he got out of the difficulty only by hypostatizing "society" into an entity superior to its members. When confronted with

---

[43] For the above cf. above all the writings of the Fabian school. The counterpart of this evolutionary socialism was an economic doctrine which – unlike the labour theory of value – proceeded from the marginal utility stress on the contribution made by each individual to the sum total of social wealth and wellbeing. Socialism is here defined as a state of affairs where – economic inequality having been eliminated – everyone will be recompensed in accordance with his freely chosen performance: in technical language, wages and prices will correspond to marginal utilities. Cf. Henry Smith, *The Economics of Socialism Reconsidered* (Oxford, 1962), *passim*.

[44] Emile Durkheim, *Socialism and Saint-Simon*, ed. Alvin W. Gouldner (London, 1959), x ff., 90 ff; cf. also Morris Ginsberg, *Essays in Sociology and Social Philosophy* (London, 1956), I, 41 ff.

the resulting difficulties he fell back on the notion of conscience. At this point he might have had to overstep the boundary of science and acknowledge the existence of a problem of moral conduct, which in turn involved the problem of philosophy in general. This, however, would have entailed an explicit recognition that the whole train of thought led beyond the area mapped out by the *philosophie positive*. In practice Durkheim was obliged to treat his own values as moral absolutes, though the paradoxity of this procedure seems to have worried him. The same may be said of Max Weber.[45]

## THE ROMANTIÇ REVOLT

Mention of Weber raises the question why positivism encountered so much more resistance in late nineteenth-century Germany than in the West. Although this is properly an historical topic, it leads back to philosophy, for what stood in the way of a more rapid assimilation of positivist concepts was the German metaphysical tradition. Since this had been given its final formulation by Hegel, it might have been supposed that the traditional philosophical standpoint would be championed by the Marxists, inasmuch as they considered themselves to be in the Hegelian succession. Marxism, however, had itself been given a positivist interpretation by Engels. In consequence there was no real confrontation at all. What happened rather was that – idealist metaphysics having been discarded – the heritage of classical philosophy was shared out between positivism and vitalism, with the Marxists *de facto* ranged on the positivist side. The romantic opposition, as in France, took up the cudgels against rationalism in general, though in the German setting a writer like Nietzsche exercised an influence to which there was no parallel in France. In principle the resulting cleavage was a general European phenomenon, but only in Germany was the anti-rational trend strong enough to impose itself temporarily as the dominant one; in the end it even succeeded in promoting a political upheaval.[46]

[45] Cf. Karl Löwith, "Max Weber und Karl Marx", in *Gesammelte Abhandlungen* (Stuttgart, 1960), especially 30 ff; so far as Weber ever clarified his standpoint he may be said to have done so in his "Der Sinn der Wertfreiheit", and "Wissenschaft als Beruf", both in *Gesammelte Aufsätze zur Wissenschaftslehre* (2nd ed., Tübingen, 1951), 475 ff. and 566 ff. Cf. also *From Max Weber: Essays in Sociology*, ed. H. H. Gerth and C. W. Mills (London, 1947), *passim*. For a more recent discussion see W. G. Runciman, "Karl Marx and Max Weber", in his *Social Science and Political Theory* (Cambridge, 1963).

[46] H. Stuart Hughes, *Consciousness and Society* (New York, 1958), *passim*. For Gerth and Mills (*op. cit.*, 61 ff) Weber represents a synthesis of the Marxian and the Nietzschean approach to the problem of ideology, i.e., the problem of relating ideas back to their (social or psychological) roots. This seems to credit Nietzsche with rather more intellectual penetration than he actually possessed. In any event the popularly effective counterpoint to his position was furnished by Engels and his successors. In political terms this corresponded to the polarization of German intellectual life into Social-Democratic and National-Socialist versions of post-liberal thinking.

It would be misleading to treat this situation in terms of a straight conflict between rationalism and irrationalism. The classical rationalist position had in fact been abandoned by the Marxists as much as by everyone else. Even for the academically influential neo-Kantians, philosophy figured merely as the "beyond" of science. What remained after this intellectual debacle was the clash between positivism and vitalism, and since philosophy no longer supplied any guiding ideas, the debate took place at the level of sociological, or psychological, deflation of general concepts. Nietzsche's vulgarization of Schopenhauer (who cannot be described as an irrationalist) had its counterpart in Engels's popularization of Hegel. Both were writing for the general public, but Nietzsche had the advantage of addressing himself to readers already predisposed by a century of literary romanticism to come down on the irrationalist side. In the struggle for influence over the educated public, which opened in the 1890's and came to a momentous climax in the 1930's, the Nietzscheans gained ground at the expense of the *soi-disant* Marxists in the degree to which they were able to pose as heirs and defenders of a peculiarly German tradition. Yet the extremes met over the issue of replacing religion by "religious atheism": both Engels and Nietzsche believed in "eternal recurrence". (For that matter, Engels had enough affection for the world of the Edda to satisfy the tastes of a whole army of Nordic enthusiasts.)[47]

If one abstracts from the not very successful neo-Kantian revival, which remained an academic affair, the situation briefly sketched here remained unchanged until the first faint stirrings of the neo-Hegelian renaissance on the eve of 1914. Around 1880 it really must have seemed to educated Germans that philosophy was dead. Not surprisingly this was the moment when the debunking of universal concepts attained its peak. So far as Nietzsche was concerned, this was largely a matter of radicalizing the thinking of Schopenhauer, who for all his scepticism about the role of the intellect had still left unchallenged the principle that true cognition of the world is possible. Schopenhauer retained the distinction between objective (that is, disinterested) and erroneous (because

---

[47] Nietzsche's elaboration of the concept of eternal recurrence is too well known to require citation. For Engels's surprisingly similar (though quite independently developed) attitude, see the Introduction to his *Dialektik der Natur*, *MEGA* (Moscow, 1935); cf. Marx-Engels *Selected Works* (Moscow, 1951), II, 57 ff. especially 72-73: "It is an eternal cycle in which matter moves, a cycle that certainly only completes its orbit in periods of time for which our terrestrial year is no adequate measure, a cycle in which the time of highest development, the time of organic life, and still more that of the life of beings conscious of themselves and of nature, is just as scantily meted out as the space in which life and self-consciousness come into operation; a cycle in which every finite mode of existence of matter... is equally transient, and wherein nothing is eternal but eternally changing, eternally moving matter... But however often, and however relentlessly, this cycle is completed in time and space, however many millions of suns and earths may come into being and go out of being... we have the certainty that matter remains eternally the same in all its transformations, that none of its attributes can ever be lost, and... that with the same iron necessity with which it will again exterminate on the earth its highest creation, the thinking mind, it must somewhere else and at another time once more engender it."

interested and subjective) thinking. His target was intellectual corruption, not the intellect as such. When he said that people's judgments were "mostly corrupt and merely an expression in favor of their party or class"[48] he was being cynical about his contemporaries, without therefore giving way to despair about the capacity of the mind to reach valid conclusions. This step was taken by Nietzsche who debased Schopenhauer's sceptical pessimism into a destructive nihilism. The essential coarseness of Nietzsche's mind is concealed by a style modelled on that of his master, and by a declamatory pathos that employs the phraseology of the Enlightenment for the purpose of wrecking the already shaken belief in reason.

We live only through illusions... The foundations of everything great and alive rest upon illusion. The pathos of truth leads to destruction.[49]

From this irrationalism it was only a short step to the biological vitalism of the Third Reich and its ideologists. Nietzsche's critique of religion – ostensibly a revival of the eighteenth-century tradition – issues in a subjectivism no less anthropocentric than theology itself. The characterization of the world as "senseless" merely inverts the theological claim that the universe exists for the purpose of manifesting a providential concern for man. Since Nietzsche has "seen through" this illusion, he appeals for a faith centered upon the "will to power" – a biological metaphor. The critique of ideology is reduced to the destruction of religious idols (and the fabrication of new ones). The residual link with the eighteenth-century tradition is retained only in externals, such as the French title of Nietzsche's *Götzendämmerung*: a work originally translated (at the suggestion of its author) as *Crépuscule des idoles*.[50] In all essential respects he turned his back on the rationalist tradition. The principal "idol" he set out to smash was the belief in reason.

If there can be no valid perception of universals it is pointless to inquire into the meaning of history. What remains is "the eternal flux of all things", "perpetual change": the trivial notion that everything has its moment in time. "There are no eternal facts, just as there are no absolute truths."[51] Here too Nietzsche encounters Engels.[52] The chief difference is that his tone is hysterical,

---

[48]	*Sämtliche Werke*, ed. Hübscher (Leipzig, 1937-41), V, 479; cf. Barth, 199.

[49]	*Gesammelte Werke* (Munich, 1923-29), VI, 17, 74.

[50]	*Friedrich Nietzsches Briefwechsel mit Franz Overbeck*, ed. Oehler and Bernoulli (Leipzig, 1916), 453.

[51]	*Werke*, XI, 154.

[52]	Cf. *Ludwig Feuerbach*, in *Selected Works* (Moscow, 1951), II, 351: "The great basic thought that the world is not to be comprehended as a complex of ready-made things, but as a complex of processes... this... thought has... so thoroughly permeated ordinary consciousness that... it is now scarcely ever contradicted... If... investigation always proceeds from this standpoint, the demand for final solutions and eternal truths ceases once for all... one no longer permits oneself to be imposed upon by the antitheses... between true and false, good and bad... necessary and accidental. One knows that these antitheses have only a relative validity." (This, however, does not prevent Engels from asserting in the very same passage

whereas that of Engels is complacent – a distant foreshadowing of political cleavages yet to come. Neither man was able to salvage the classical heritage invoked in their respective writings.

The critique of ideology, when delivered from such a standpoint, reduces itself to what is called *unmasking*. Nietzsche is tireless in stripping the "mask" from respectability, from bourgeois morality, from idealist metaphysics, and of course from Christianity. History for him is a masquerade: not in the Hegelian sense that its logic reveals itself through transitory events and personalities, but in the sense that men drape their "real" biological drives and goals in idealist costumes. All thought is ideological; its unconscious function is to serve the life process. In contrast to this cynicism, Engels – who unlike Nietzsche retained the rationalist vocabulary, along with a proper respect for the classical tradition (whose meaning he had forgotten) – holds that *almost* all thinking is ideological; he takes a cheerful view of the matter, in as much as historical causality can be understood and guided.

Men make their own history, whatever its outcome may be, in that each person follows his own consciously desired end, and it is precisely the resultant of these many wills operating in different directions... that constitutes history... The will is determined by passion or deliberation, but the levers which immediately determine passion or deliberation are of very different kinds.

... the philosophy of history, particularly as represented by Hegel, recognizes that the ostensible and also the really operating motives of men who act in history are by no means the ultimate causes of historical events; that behind these motives there are other motive powers which have to be discovered. But it does not seek these powers in history itself, it imports them rather from outside, from philosophical ideology, into history.[53]

Behind the historical shadow-play there is a realm of "real" causation which can be understood. It is thus possible to grasp the logic of the process, but since it rolls on endlessly, one cannot assign any ultimate meaning to it. Matter being eternal, and its endless motion the only "law" of which we can be certain, history is reduced to the status of a singularity within the domain of nature. "Dialectical materialism" and romantic vitalism concur in the belief that Reality is Process, though the former retains a hankering for the rationality which was once the principal theme of philosophy. This at least provides a criterion for distinguishing between "objective" and "ideological" thinking. For Nietzsche the distinction is meaningless: all thought is a species of poetry, and the real Being of the world remains irreducible to discursive reasoning.

---

that throughout all these relative processes "a progressive development asserts itself in the end".)
[53] *Ludwig Feuerbach, S. W.*, II, 354-5.

THE LOGIC OF SCIENCE

At this level a serious analysis of the problem of ideology was not possible. Its restatement around 1900 was due to Max Weber, who had benefited from the neo-Kantian revival. For Weber, who had assimilated the historical relativism of Dilthey, science was both autonomous and morally neutral. At the same time the implications of this standpoint were no longer veiled by metaphysical remnants. In particular it was not possible for Weber to be complacent about the overall progressive direction of history. As he saw it, there was no guarantee that the rationalization of existence would promote the aims traditionally enshrined in philosophy. Matters were, if anything, getting worse – at any rate from the standpoint of one who valued personal freedom. This pessimistic outlook made it possible for Weber to divorce normative judgments from factual statements in a more radical fashion than Dilthey had done. Positivism acquired a Stoical cast: it underpinned the "freely chosen" standpoint of a thinker who saw himself defending a lost cause.[54]

Weber is important for our theme because his approach involved a sharpened distinction between the two meanings of "ideology". The term – as has been shown – can signify both the consciousness of an epoch and the "false consciousness" of men unaware of their true role. What a culture thinks about itself may be "ideological" in one sense without being so in the other; thus for example if the Middle Ages developed thought-forms which "reflected" the feudal-hierarchical structure of society, the official ideology might nonetheless serve as an accurate guide to that particular reality, just because it was mirrored in the categories. This is the sense in which the term is commonly employed both by Marx (though not by the epigoni) and by Weber. Plainly on this assumption there need be no question of "unmasking" anyone or anything. On the other hand, thinking may be "ideological" in the narrower sense of distorting, rather than reflecting, the reality it describes. Thus for Marx economics was either "scientific" or "ideological", depending on whether or not it gave an objective account of the socio-economic process. Ricardo in his eyes was none the less scientific for being bourgeois. Marx, however, also retained the notion that thought-forms impose their own limitations, so that, for example, Ricardo (or any other economist employing his concepts) was limited by his inability to transcend the mental framework proper to the bourgeois epoch: social categories cannot be transcended in thought until they have (in principle at least) been questioned in practice. In tacitly retaining this approach, Weber fell heir to the problem of accounting for the role of "ideology": not as the conscious or unconscious distortion of reality in the interest of some group, but

---

[54] Löwith (*op. cit., passim*) develops this theme through an analysis of Weber's relationship both to the historical Marx and to the "vulgar Marxism" of the epigoni; cf. also Runciman, 43 ff. The subsequent development of Weber's critique of modern society and its ideologies is linked with the name of Schumpeter: cf. in particular the latter's *Capitalism, Socialism and Democracy* (London and New York, 1950).

as the intellectual reflex of determinate social processes. Unlike Marx, for whom history as a whole exemplified a hidden rationality, he relativized sociology by severing it from philosophy: every culture has its own norms and values which enter into the perception of what is called "reality". Its norms are binding only upon those who accept them, though this does not invalidate them, since it is their fate to be "objective" and "subjective" at the same time. There is no way of transcending this situation, for the growth of rationality leads only to an awareness that it is not possible to ground value judgments in a universally accepted doctrine of human nature.

At this point the critique of ideology – originally a philosophical theme – turns into relativism. History and sociology combine to make it appear that consciousness cannot transcend its time horizon, since the concepts imposed upon the raw material of experience are themselves historical. Something like this had been suggested by Hegel, and following him by Marx, but they were saved from relativism by the belief that both the nature of man and the logic of history can still be grasped in an act of intellectual intuition. With Dilthey and Weber, the subjectivism already inherent in the neo-Kantian interpretation of the categories as empty forms imposed upon an unknown and unknowable material leads away from the notion of truth as universal. Now that reason has lost its status as a concrete universal, history is no longer seen as an intelligible totality held together in the last resort by the fact that it is one and the same for all men. What remains when this faith has been discarded is the subjective freedom of each individual to act according to reason, *his* reason; a freedom necessarily limited by the right of all others to do the same. Men act from freely chosen standpoints which are ultimately incompatible, on the basis of convictions which in the final analysis cannot be rationally justified. In this perspective the "ideological" character of thinking ceases to be a problem. It is accepted as an aspect of a situation which – since it cannot be altered or transcended – must be stoically endured.


## THE SOCIOLOGY OF KNOWLEDGE

The preceding section was concerned with the manner in which the ideology problem was formulated between, roughly speaking, 1860 and 1920. The dates are not chosen at random, just as it is not a matter of accident that the earlier debate had run from the French Revolution to the 1848 upheaval.[55] In both cases we are dealing with a social transformation which found its intellectual counterpart in a distinctive manner of conceiving the role of ideas. This would

---

[55] Marx's *Zur Kritik der politischen Ökonomie*, with the well-known Preface stating the "materialist conception of history", appeared in 1859; Weber's lecture on "Wissenschaft als Beruf" was delivered in 1919: a date which may be regarded as the effective end of the historical epoch that had given rise to both positivism and "orthodox Marxism".

probably be agreed even by critics of "historicism", and for the rest it may be suggested that a statement such as the foregoing does not commit one to anything beyond the bare assertion that there must be *some* correspondence between the collective experience of a culture and the way in which this experience is generalized in thought. It does not follow that either Marxism or positivism are to be understood as the "ideological reflex" of their age, though on the trivialized interpretation of "historical materialism" which we owe to its orthodox exponents such a conclusion might seem to impose itself. From the standpoint here chosen the matter appears somewhat differently.

It has already been suggested that Weber did not really "turn Marx upside down" (e.g., in asserting that Protestantism was a key factor in the rise of capitalism), but rather developed a "bourgeois" counterpart to the Marxian theory of history. It is true that in one important respect he went beyond Marx, in that his sociology concerned "industrial society" as such; it thus became relevant, during the following generation, for capitalism and socialism alike. But while this topic is of the first importance for contemporary sociologists, it is somewhat tangential to our problem. In any case it is possible to share Weber's pessimism about the future of freedom in an increasingly rationalized and bureaucratized world, without therefore accepting the neo-Kantian divorce between factual and value judgments as an ultimate datum for the reflective consciousness. The same applies to his notion that all possible standpoints are relative, not merely to the position of their holder (hardly a shattering revelation), but to the rationale of the process (if it can be discovered) which has transformed the naive hopes and aspirations of the eighteenth-century Enlightenment into our current disenchantment. Talk of "process" involves the assumption that history does have a discernible logic, but since this was not denied by Weber we are not moving outside his frame of reference in asking how far the "sociology of knowledge" is able to clarify the ideology problem.

Although the step from *Wissenschaftslehre* to *Wissenssoziologie* was taken by Karl Mannheim, one is, I think, justified in treating Mannheim's work as an epilogue to that of Weber. It is no longer a secret that an important link between them was provided by George Lukács, notably in *History and Class-consciousness:* a work which for many years led an underground existence before being recognized as the influence it was. Here both Mannheim's derivation from Weber, and his dependence on the early Lukács, are taken for granted, and the question is asked how far the concept of ideology was clarified by this belated fusion of the Marxist and the positivist standpoint.[56]

---

[56] For the following cf. Georg Lukács, *Geschichte und Klassenbewusstsein: Studien über marxistische Dialektik* (Berlin, 1923); Karl Mannheim, *Ideology and Utopia* (London, 1936; 2nd ed. 1960); and *Essays on Sociology and Social Psychology*, ed. Kecskemeti (London, 1953); Karl R. Popper, *The Poverty of Historicism* (Boston, 1957). The last-mentioned work is virtually a critique of Mannheim, who appears in it as the incarnation of "holistic" thinking and "historicism", and it is questionable how far its generalizations are appropriate to other targets.

If Weber could be described as a "bourgeois Marx", Mannheim appeared to the *cognoscenti* (that is, to those aware of his background, and of the somewhat tenuous link between his circle and the Budapest Marxists who staffed the brief Soviet experiment in 1919) as a "bourgeois Lukács" – not perhaps quite fairly, since he regarded himself as a Socialist, and in his later writings even made something of a fetish of economic planning.[57] None of this concerns us here; our topic is furnished by the manner in which he and Lukács – starting from a parallel awareness of the dilemma raised by the radical historicism of Dilthey and the resigned relativism of Weber – conceived the problem of ideology. Mannheim's exposition of the subject in *Ideology and Utopia* (first published in 1929) may be taken as read. The same cannot be said of Lukács, notwithstanding his current prominence as a purveyor of more or less orthodox Marxism-Leninism.[58] In 1923, when *Geschichte und Klassenbewusstsein* appeared – to be promptly disowned by its author when it encountered the inevitable critical barrage from Moscow – it was rightly regarded as a challenge to "orthodox Marxism" and positivism alike. Lukács in fact had revived the Hegelian conception of history and fused it with Lenin's revolutionary activism into an explosive mixture – far more explosive than the authorized version to which Communism was already committed, for Lukács really went through with the notion that the proletariat was the "identical subject-object of the socio-historical process".[59] Not only was it the class destined to make an end of bourgeois society: its coming triumph signalled the *practical* resolution of *theoretical* problems insoluble from a bourgeois standpoint, including the Kantian problem.[60] And this conclusion was developed not in the usual philistine manner, which virtually negated the very existence of philosophy, but through an analysis of logical and epistemological concepts which sought to establish their essentially historical character. Lukács in 1923 not merely revived the Hegelian dialectic: in his own fashion he did what Hegel had done in the *Phenomenology* when he treated the categories as manifestations of Spirit.[61] With this intellectual *tour de force* – a unique achievement, whose level was never remotely recovered by its own author: in his later years a pedestrian exponent of Marxist-Leninist scholasticism – the "heritage of classical German philosophy", vainly invoked by Engels in his platitudinous essay on Feuerbach, seemed in fact to have been secured for the Marxist school.

---

[57] Cf. his *Mensch und Gesellschaft im Zeitalter des Umbaus* (Leiden, 1935); *Diagnosis of Our Time* (London, 1943).
[58] No reference is intended here to Lukács's writings on art, notably the two massive volumes on aesthetics (*Die Eigenart des Aesthetischen* [Neuwied, 1963]) recently published as part of the Collected Works now being edited in West Germany.
[59] *Op. cit.*, 64.
[60] *Op. cit.*, 134 ff.
[61] Unfortunately this cannot be demonstrated in detail. For the rest it must suffice to mention the evident influence of Lukács on the work of H. Marcuse.

## LUKÁCS AND MANNHEIM

From our present standpoint it is plain enough that this was a mirage, and not only because history refused to follow the road mapped out by the theorist. Writing almost a decade before the re-discovery of Marx's "*Paris Manuscripts*", Lukács had intuitively fixed upon the alienation and restitution of man as the pivotal point in the Marxian world-view.[62] This gave him the meta-historical standpoint he needed to gain a critical view of the whole process. But while he thus eluded the relativism inherent in the orthodox approach, he involved himself in a different dilemma: a standpoint outside empirical history is a metaphysical standpoint, and while this is no criticism of Hegelian (or any other) philosophy, it becomes problematic for a Marxist. Thus when confronted with orthodox indignation, Lukács was unable to maintain his position. To do so he would have had to acknowledge that the category of "totality", which played the key role in his thinking, transcended not merely the artificially fore-shortened positivist world-view, but any conceivable standpoint compatible with what is called science. Lukács had seen well enough that empiricism can never attain to an intellectual grasp of the "concrete totality" of history. What he failed to see – or shrank from admitting to himself when it was suggested to him – was that the empiricism of science is the only possible standpoint for a thinker who is determined to get on without the help of metaphysics. His own "wager" on the revolution – though in the circumstances of the day not an irrational one – contained an element of romantic subjectivism which he refused to acknowledge. From a purely theoretical viewpoint there was no particular reason why the proletariat – rather than the intelligentsia or some other group – should have been seen as the "identical subject-object" of history. In fact, if it was a question of establishing a standpoint transcending the class struggle (not that Lukács had any such intention), the intelligentsia had a better claim.

This, as we know, was Mannheim's solution, but before coming to it, let us see how the role of consciousness is to be understood on Lukács's assumptions. As he is the only Marxist to have written an entire book on the subject, it may be as well to consider what he has to say. Starting from the Hegelian-Marxian view of history as a concrete totality of seemingly unrelated circumstances, he begins by criticizing the manner in which empiricism has made a fetish of science as the correct description of those frozen structures that confront the individual as "social reality".[63] The dialectical method, which restores

---

[62] Cf. the lengthy essay "Die Verdinglichung und das Bewusstsein des Proletariats" (*op. cit.*, 94 ff.) which presents a critique of idealist philosophy in conceptual terms derived from Hegel (and incidentally dismisses Engels's criticism of Kant as the absurdity it is).

[63] *Op. cit.*, 22 ff. In addition to the sociological method oriented to Comte and Spencer, Lukács also condemns those Marxists who had gone back to Kant. For in doing so they had ignored the fact that "Marx's critique of Hegel is... the direct continuation and development of Hegel's own critique of Kant and Fichte" (31).

the intelligibility of the process, also discloses the ideological character of those pseudo-empirical and "scientific" forms of thought which present the typical antinomies of declining late-bourgeois culture – e.g., the conflict between the individual and society – as though they necessarily pertained to every stage of history. The Marxian dialectic is able to perform this role because (unlike Hegel's idealist dialectic, with its retrospective attention fixed upon the past) it transcends both the *status quo* and the categories which are its intellectual counterpart. These categories reflect a particular reality whose meaning is concealed from the individual by the bourgeois mode of thought, which latter finds its apotheosis in the cult of positive science. All the typical dilemmas of modern life – the cleavage between theory and practice, form and content, science and metaphysics, and so forth – arise from this situation. The sharpest conflict is that between the progressive rationalization of particular aspects of existence and the mounting irrationality of the whole. The overcoming of this split – not merely in theory but in practice – is the task of *consciousness*: specifically the consciousness that transcends the bourgeois era, namely Marxism. With history moving towards a climax involving the fate of mankind,[64] the growing antagonism between the ruling class and the proletariat (which latter is compelled, for the sake of self-preservation, to fight for the attainment of ends not necessarily present *as such* to each of its individual members) assumes the aspect of a race between "blind" necessity and conscious purpose. For the automatism of the historical process, on which "vulgar Marxism" before 1914 had relied for the attainment of its ends, is quite capable of promoting a universal catastrophe.[65] The transition from the "realm of necessity" to the "realm of freedom" is not itself a necessary step. On the contrary, it is precisely during this critical transitional period that the blind automatism of the existing reified structures takes on the character of a fateful drift which can only be stemmed by the revolt of the exploited class. The latter, for all its empirical shortcomings, is the historical incorporation of mankind's will to escape from self-destruction. Its consciousness, which transcends the fixed categories of a society in process of dissolution, coincides with the "true" consciousness of mankind. This self-awareness is not a "scientific one", for *science is itself an illusion* – the last and greatest of bourgeois illusions, and one which, if not overcome, must unfailingly promote the catastrophe of humanity. The conflict between bourgeoisie and proletariat thus involves the fate of mankind. But the empirical proletariat is itself subjected to the ideological confusions and crises typical of bourgeois society in the era of its decomposition, and therefore – here Lukács takes leave of classical Marxism and adopts the Leninist standpoint – it requires the leadership of a revolutionary *party* which incarnates the consciousness of the epoch.[66] In the end, therefore, the consciousness on

---

[64] *Op. cit.*, 82.
[65] *Ibid.*
[66] *Op. cit.*, 261 ff, 276 ff, 298 ff.

which literally everything depends is once more that of a group of individuals, for of course the party itself has to be *led*. In his later years Lukács showed himself ready to face the implications of this dialectic: if Reason could be located in a group, it could also find its temporary embodiment in an individual who had substituted himself for the group.

What made this analysis seem both convincing and overwhelmingly urgent was the author's intellectual distinction. In the early 'twenties, prophets of doom abounded in Central Europe; one more or less would have made no difference. What distinguished Lukács was the firmness with which he placed his message within the context of classical German philosophy. His analysis of Kantian and neo-Kantian thinking – lengthily developed[67] in the intricately allusive style he had adopted from his pre-war teachers in Heidelberg – employed the Hegelian-Marxist vocabulary with telling effect, to the end of demonstrating that the crisis of contemporary thought heralded the imminent catastrophe of the society which had given birth to this very philosophy. He had indeed guessed correctly, though he erred in supposing that "the revolution" would prove him right. What actually happened was that the European crisis gave rise to the rival totalitarianisms of Communism and Fascism. His own side, moreover, repudiated him, and this although he had worked out the appropriate philosophical rationale of Leninism. The apocalyptic vision of a crisis in which the fate of mankind was in the balance had its effect upon the intellectual élite of European Marxism; but it appalled the new Muscovite orthodoxy, already committed to its own brand of scientism, and it was useless as a means of promoting revolutionary optimism among the masses. It therefore remained an underground doctrine, and its author a licensed heretic who in the end repudiated his own insights in favour of a refurbished "dialectical materialism". This necessarily entailed a commonplace transcript theory of perception, in the place of the dialectical theory of cognition put forward in the 1923 work. With this return to orthodoxy, the problem of ideology once more assumed subordinate status: there was a true consciousness (that of the working class, or rather of "its" party) and a false one (that of the "class enemy"), but *both had the same structure*. It was simply a question of replacing "bourgeois science" by "socialist science", or – even more absurdly – "bourgeois ideology" by "proletarian ideology". That "science" itself represents an "ideological" manner of thinking which of its nature cannot yield an adequate report of the world – this truly startling and genuinely "revolutionary" notion, which Lukács had extracted from Hegel, disappeared from view. Its own author came to renounce it. It was after all a good deal easier to stick to the time-honoured notion that science tells us all we need to know, provided it is not distorted by "reactionary" class interests. This had been the message of orthodox Marxism, as formulated by Engels, Plekhanov, Kautsky, and Lenin himself (though Lenin's *practice* was

---

[67] *Ibid.*, 122 ff.

wildly at variance with it and demanded a wholly different theory of cognition). In returning to this tradition, Lukács was not merely playing safe, but in all probability also satisfying a deep-seated psychological craving for spiritual certainty: the heretic had found peace in the haven of a new secular church.[68]

In the light of the foregoing, Mannheim's work appears as, so to speak, the dialectical counterpart to Lukács's abortive break-out. *Ideology and Utopia* (1929) was the positivist's rejoinder to *History and Class-Consciousness* (1923). Mannheim (who in 1919 had steered clear of Lukács's political commitments) adapted what he could use for his own purpose, which was frankly "theoretical" in the contemplative sense condemned by Lukács, for whom theory was meaningless if not joined to a particular practice. *Ideology and Utopia* is full of passages which reflect its author's awareness of the issues Lukács had stirred up a few years earlier. In particular, Mannheim's analysis of the manner in which ideological notions are formed rests upon the philosophy of consciousness developed by Kant and his successors.[69] Thus for him too consciousness does not simply "reflect" the world of experience, but on the contrary helps to shape it.[70] The notion of "false consciousness" (ideology in the precise or narrow sense) is linked to the discussion of Kant and Hegel. The traditional Marxist standpoint is dismissed as untenable, in that it tries to exempt itself from the verdict inherent in its own approach: socialism too must be treated as an ideology.

With the emergence of the general formulation of the total conception of ideology, the simple theory of ideology develops into the sociology of knowledge. What was once the intellectual armament of a party is transformed into a method of research in social and intellectual history generally.[71]

As with Comte a century earlier, socialism turns into sociology, but this time the problem of relativism is frankly faced.

Once we recognize that all historical knowledge is relational knowledge, and can only be formulated with reference to the position of the observer, we are faced once more with the task of discriminating between what is true and what is false... The question then arises: which social standpoint *vis-à-vis* of history offers the best chance for reaching an optimum of truth?[72]

We are back with Max Weber. In fact Mannheim's position can be defined

---

[68]  Though in his quasi-philosophical writings he never quite managed to shake off his youthful concern with the role of the mind and the irreducible character of spiritual experience. Unfortunately this topic, which is of importance for an appreciation of Lukács's work on esthetics, cannot be developed here.

[69]  *Op. cit.*, 57 ff.

[70]  58. "This does not imply that the subject merely reflects the structural pattern of the external world, but rather that, in the course of his experience with the world, he spontaneously evolves the principles of organization that enable him to understand it."

[71]  *Ibid.*, 69.

[72]  *Ibid.*, 71.

very precisely as an amalgam (doubtless he regarded it as a synthesis) of Weber and Lukács. What was new and original was the answer he gave to his own question: the optimal standpoint is that occupied by the social group which specializes in forming general concepts – the intelligentsia.

By linking the sociology of knowledge to the position of a definite stratum in society, Mannheim had anchored the exercise of freedom in the group interest of the intellectuals.[73] This was a step beyond Weber, for whom the problem of cognition was bound up with the role of the lonely thinker confronting the world. Mannheim's concern with group thinking does not, however, meet the objection that only a particular "historic" class at a particular moment of time can reshape the historical situation. The world of the individual is always a "given" one, in that it is experienced as a totality which the critical intellect cannot significantly alter. A group is still made up of individuals whose minds are engaged with various aspects of experience and whose differing standpoints will probably cancel out. This play of opinion and mutual cancellation of "prejudices" is in fact regarded by Mannheim as essential to the emergence of an adequate scientific standpoint.

The task of a study of ideology which tries to be free from value-judgments is to understand the narrowness of each individual point of view and the interplay between these distinctive attitudes in the total social process.[74]

Yet the reference to the "total social process" seems to presuppose a different and more philosophical viewpoint. On the assumptions made by Mannheim *qua* sociologist, there is no good reason why he should casually invoke the totality of history when it suits him. In fact when he does so he is employing language which makes sense only on the (Hegelian) supposition that the Whole determines its parts, and that the logic of history must be understood before one can proceed to the business of empirical investigation.[75]

[73] *Op. cit.*, 143: "... the intellectuals are still able to arrive at a total orientation even when they have joined a party. Should the capacity to acquire a broader point of view be considered merely as a liability? Does it not rather present a mission? Only he who really has the choice has an interest in seeing the whole of the social and political structure. Only in that period of time and that stage of investigation which is dedicated to deliberation is the sociological and logical locus of the development of a synthetic perspective to be sought... We owe the possibility of mutual interpenetration and understanding of existing currents of thought to the presence of such a relatively unattached middle stratum..."

[74] *Op. cit.*, 72. Cf. also further on: "The prevailing philosophic view which cautiously admits that the content of conduct has been historically determined, but which at the same time insists upon the retention of eternal forms of value... is no longer tenable."

[75] *Op. cit.*, 83. "The study of intellectual history can and must be pursued in a manner which will see in the sequence and coexistence of phenomena more than mere accidental relationships, and will seek to discover in the totality of the historical complex the role, significance, and meaning of each component element." The inconsistency inherent in such utterances (for which Mannheim might indeed have invoked the authority of Dilthey and Troeltsch) exposed their author to the charge that, for all his sceptical airs, he was really an historicist at heart; cf. Popper, *op. cit.*, 80.

## THE PROBLEM OF CONSCIOUSNESS

The problem of history is the problem of consciousness. It was Hegel who first pointed this out, and his successors – including Marx, who inverted his logic but did not replace it by a radically different manner of thought – continued to pose the question he had raised: how could the rationality of history be perceived by the intellect, given the fact that men are both inside and outside the historical process? The subsidiary problem of "false consciousness" arose from the awareness that the various possible standpoints were inadequate as well as incompatible. Meantime the analysis of cognition had led to the search for the "identical subject-object" of history: a universal whose activity was synonymous with the disclosure of history's peculiar logic. The pursuit of this aim over the past two centuries is not simply to be understood as a dispassionate search for objective truth, though belief in a *ratio* common to all men was inherent in the attempt to discern an historical logic. The intellectual effort was itself a factor in that theoretical and practical unification of the world which is now proceeding under our eyes. The mounting concern over the phenomenon of "false consciousness" was an index to the awareness that the future of civilization – if not the existence of mankind – may come to depend on the attainment of a "true consciousness" in which individuals and groups belonging to the most varied societies and cultures can share. From the standpoint here chosen it may thus be suggested that the attempt to discern a logic of history was more than an idle play with concepts: it responded to a practical purpose which in our own age has become more urgent as the globe shrinks, and historically divergent and disparate cultures press against one another. Because these pressures are experienced as ideological conflicts among people holding different and incompatible aims in view, it remains the task of the critical intellect to evolve modes of thought which will enable men to recognize the common purpose underlying their divergencies.

In this perspective, the transformation undergone by the concept of ideology appears as an index to the tension between the actual historical process and a critical consciousness nourished by the traditions of classical rationalism. In its original eighteenth-century form, the concept represented an implicit critique of society from the standpoint of early liberalism: a standpoint which was itself "historical" in that it took for granted (and therefore treated as "natural") the social relations proper to a particular phase of European history.[76] This naive certainty disappeared during and after the French Revolution. The

---

[76] Jürgen Habermas, *Theorie und Praxis: Sozialphilosophische Studien* (Neuwied, 1963), *passim*. For a recent defence of the positivist standpoint cf. Arnold Gehlen, *Studien zur Anthropologie und Soziologie* (Neuwied, 1963), *passim*. For a critique of positivism from a neo-Hegelian viewpoint cf. H. Marcuse, *One-Dimensional Man* (Boston, 1964), *passim*. For a critical view of the neo-Marxist position cf. Morris Watnick, "Relativism and Class Consciousness: Georg Lukács", in *Revisionism: Essays on the History of Marxist Ideas* (London and New York, 1962), 142 ff.

latter marked a turning-point in that the critique of existing (traditional but decaying, hence plainly irrational) institutions could no longer be delivered in the name of apparently self-evident principles. For the new institutions, which claimed to be in accordance with reason, turned out to be rational only in terms of the particular historical purpose they served: the emancipation of the "third estate" could not forever be equated with the attainment of a natural order conceived as the embodiment of absolute reason. Hence the fleeting balance attained around 1800 gave way to a deepening scepticism about the very "ideology" whose original proponents had set out to trace the natural history of ideas. In Hegel's philosophy, which arose directly from the urge to comprehend the meaning of the Revolution, there already appears in germ the notion that forms of consciousness are relative to changing historical situations. The universality of the whole has to be reconstructed, as it were, from the entire sequence of historical fossils – the latter comprising *inter alia* the conscious (subjective) aims of the individuals who occupy the foreground. These aims now appear as unconscious means of realizing a hidden purpose; they have become "ideological" in a sense not intended by the original *idéologues*.

This is the concept of ideology which Marx inherited from Hegel. It served him as a means of discrediting the universal claims of the liberal ideology he encountered in his passage from philosophy to politics. At the same time he retained the rationalist faith in an objective logic of the historical process – now understood as the process of man's self-creation. To Marx, as to any Hegelian, the actual world of empirical perception was only an imperfect realization – at times indeed a caricature – of the real or rational world, in which man's essential nature (his rationality) will have overcome the reified existence he leads while the surrounding object-world is not perceived as the product of his own creativity. The attainment of this liberated state is the work of history, whose dialectic is not disclosed by empirical perception, but by critical (philosophical) reflection upon the totality of the process. An understanding fixed upon isolated aspects of this totality necessarily falls short of the goal of philosophical reason. It is *ideological* at a second remove, in that it mistakes the reified structures of immediate experience for permanent constituents of reality. It treats, for example, war, poverty, class distinctions, and so on, as permanent features of history, instead of viewing them as temporary objectivations of mankind's gradual and painfully slow emergence from the realm of nature. So understood the concept of ideology recovers its ancient pathos: it is now employed to demonstrate the transitoriness of those arrangements which – irrational in themselves – nonetheless serve the rationality of the whole.

It is only with the loss of this dimension that "ideology" ceases to denote *false consciousness*. It now becomes synonymous with any kind of consciousness that can relate itself to the ongoing activity of a class or group effective enough to make some sort of practical difference. This is the ideology concept of contemporary positivism. Its limited practical relevance ought not to veil its incompatibility with the intellectual tradition (ultimately rooted in classical metaphysics) that is intended when one speaks of the philosophy of history. This philosophy arose from a complex of theoretical and practical problems, of which the original *idéologues*, and their eighteenth-century forerunners, took note in sketching a rudimentary model of world history. Essentially what concerned them was the growth of rationality and the imposition of conscious control upon "natural" chaos. The pragmatic character of this enterprise was never wholly obscured by its theoretical language. It was from the first an attempt to impose an ideal order upon the world, by making an appeal to man's "nature". Its success or failure was and is bound up with the power of Reason to see through the veil of ideology to the enduring realities of human existence. An understanding of what is involved in the concept of ideology is thus at the same time an exercise in that historical imagination which enables us to see our predecessors as men engaged in an enterprise whose outcome still concerns us. In Hegelian language we may say that – the final category retaining and preserving within itself the content of all the previous ones – the unification and pacification of the world (if it can be achieved) will demonstrate that history is indeed a concrete universal. For it is only at this level that what is called world history becomes synonymous with mankind's collective emergence from the state of nature. Whatever their residual differences, this is a perspective which liberalism and Marxism have in common.

*Columbia University*

# 9.

## MAX WEBER ON AMERICA: THEORY AND EVIDENCE

### GABRIEL KOLKO

Max Weber, in his discussions of methodology in the social sciences, formulated the concept of "ideal-types" in a manner which suggests that evidence is often not of primary concern to the historian. We are asked to create substantive concepts which in their conceptual purity may not be empirically verifiable. A conventional hypothesis, in contrast to an ideal-type, must be tested, and we must have or discover means for its proof or disproof; if the hypothesis does not refer to ultimately verifiable, concrete, or experiential phenomena, basic communication is undermined, and virtually anything may be asserted or believed. The ideal-type, we are told, "is formed by the one-sided *accentuation* of one or more points of view and by the synthesis of a great many diffuse, discrete, more or less present and occasionally absent *concrete individual* phenomena, which are arranged according to those one-sidedly emphasized viewpoints into a unified *analytical* construct. In its conceptual purity, this mental construct cannot be found empirically anywhere in reality. It is *utopia*." The ideal-type "is not a *description* of reality but it aims to give unambiguous means of expression to such a description".[1] In the social structure the ideal-type creates a normative standard for action from which we can deductively analyze "factors of deviation from a conceptually pure type of rational action".[2]

Weber effectively utilized the ideal-type in his religious sociology by showing what he alleged to be the causal importance of Calvinism in the development of Western capitalism. And, using Calvinism as the comparative standard, Weber in his studies of Hindu, Jewish, and Chinese religion attempted to show why the absence of economic rationalization and development in the East illustrated the causal significance of Calvinism in the West.

Here I shall attempt to show that Weber's ideal-typology of the causal importance of Calvinism in the development of Western capitalism suffers

[1]   Max Weber, *The Methodology of the Social Sciences,* trans. and ed. Edward A. Shils and Henry A. Finch (Glencoe, Ill., 1949), 90; I have discussed the theoretical problems involved at greater length in "A Critique of Max Weber's Philosophy of History." *Ethics,* LXX (1959), 21–36.
[2]   Max Weber, *The Theory of Social and Economic Organization,* trans. A. R. Henderson and Talcott Parsons, and ed. Talcott Parsons (New York, 1947), 92.

from serious methodological ambiguities, and that Weber's substantive historical treatment of American colonial economic history illustrates the fundamental inadequacy of the ideal-typology and of his specific theory of the Protestant Ethic as a tool of historical analysis. When one examines Weber's substantive theory as a hypothesis and by conventional canons of proof it becomes indefensible.

Most of the criticisms of Weber's Protestant Ethic have been written primarily in terms of its European relevance or his one-sided interpretation of Calvinist doctrine to suit his conceptually pure, if exaggerated, model. But it is worth noting that perhaps his most important single proof, colonial America, has been largely ignored by Weber scholars. This is unfortunate, since Weber viewed America as "the field of [capitalism's] highest development". He wrote the second half of *The Protestant Ethic and the Spirit of Capitalism* in 1905, immediately after a tour of the United States which had a profound impact on him, and part of his research was done in the libraries of Haverford College and Columbia University.[3] Throughout *The Protestant Ethic* Weber continually referred to colonial American history to sustain his thesis, and thereby advanced large-scale generalizations on early American development.

Weber saw no medieval antecedents or complicating institutional heritage to mitigate the impact of the Protestant Ethic on American economic development. "Without doubt, in the country of Benjamin Franklin's birth (Massachusetts), the spirit of capitalism . . . was present before the capitalistic order . . . In this case the causal relation is certainly the reverse of that suggested by the materialistic standpoint."[4] In parts I and V, I shall examine whether Weber fully understood the economic implications of Puritan doctrine and the dimensions of Franklin's ideas and personality, because to Weber, as to Werner Sombart, Franklin was without equal as the personification of the capitalist spirit.

Weber quite erroneously contrasted the economic development of the New England colonies to that of the non-Calvinist Southern colonies, where he claimed that "capitalism remained far less developed . . . in spite of the fact that these latter were founded by large capitalists for business motives, while the New England colonies were founded by preachers and seminary graduates with the help of small bourgeois, craftsmen and yeomen, for religious reasons."[5] In part II, I shall examine the extent to which the two regions

---

[3] Max Weber, *The Protestant Ethic and the Spirit of Capitalism,* trans. Talcott Parsons with foreword by R. H. Tawney (New York, 1930), 182. The tour was reported in Marianne Weber, *Max Weber: Ein Lebensbild* (Heidelberg, 1950), 316–45. A selected translation of Weber's American letters can be found in Walter Henry Brann, "Max Weber and the United States", *Southwestern Social Science Quarterly,* XXV (1944), 18–30.

[4] Weber, *Protestant Ethic,* 55–56.

[5] *Ibid.*

differed on such matters as usury and a variety of economic controls Weber assumed conducive to capital accumulation, and whether economic realities, beyond those necessitated by climate, differed between Calvinist and non-Calvinist settlements. In the same context, in part III, I shall inquire whether the similarities in economic development in the Northern and Southern colonies suggest causal determinants, such as the frontier and common problems faced by all seeking to create a society in a wilderness, which were substantially more important than religious ideologies. In part IV, I shall examine whether the larger conditions of American life permitted the development of routine enterprise and a systematic, predictable trade (which Weber thought reflected the impact of Calvinism on economic life).

I conclude in my final section (VI) that the economic structure which emerged in colonial America, including New England, reflected the larger political and geographical realities which Weber did not even begin to appreciate, and that these factors tended to create a political capitalism in which economic success was determined far more by political and social connections than by any special religious motivations. Ultimately, we shall see, Weber's description of America was based more on deductions from a rigid thesis than a valid understanding of American history.

## I

Weber assumed that Calvinism provided an impetus for systematic economic behavior and laid the foundation for modern capitalism. This doctrinal stimulus purportedly found its expression in institutional changes and the creation of the necessary conditions for rationalized capitalism, but nowhere in Weber is there a consideration of the extent to which Calvinist or Puritan doctrine provided a hindrance to continuous rationalized economic behavior and capital accumulation. In its total context, however, Puritanism in America was both a help and a hindrance to systematic economic behavior, and this hindrance was not only a matter of specific regulations on economic activities, but of questions involving "the glory of God and one's own duty".[6]

It was, according to the Puritans, the obligation of man to follow a calling and to conscientiously cultivate his vineyard. The Covenant of Grace which God contracted with the faithful made salvation possible, but this involved more than simple faith, since it included the obligation of external behavior and works as well. The pattern of such behavior must not be understood as being merely economically oriented, although it was that too. Signs of salvation were reflected not in the actual achievements of material signs of grace, as Weber suggested, but in man's continuous efforts and intentions to

[6] *Ibid.*, 276.

fulfill the Covenant.[7] One thing which the Puritan oligarchy unequivocally condemned in economic activity was the notion, which Weber erroneously associated with Puritanism, that "Labour must . . . be performed as if it were an *absolute end in itself*."[8] To the Puritans, however, excessive concern with wealth resulted in vanity, ·the neglect of the public good, the undermining of scholarship, and, above all, a challenge to the dominance of the spiritual oligarchy in God's Commonwealth. "Neither riches nor poverty . . . but a meane between both", declared Thomas Morton.[9]

Weber not only misunderstood the demands of Puritan doctrine on economic behavior, but he was never conscious of the immediate economic and doctrinal tensions within the Puritan Commonwealth, between those desiring to live strictly by the prescriptions of Puritan ethics and those willing to deviate from them. Weber assumed that the attitude to economic behavior by the merchants could be deduced from the doctrines which he believed they held. The result was a failure to appreciate the conflict between ideas and economic reality. The Puritan oligarchy, drawn heavily from the traditionally anti-business minor English gentry, saw the tension· between religion and wealth. In Perry Miller's summary phrase: "At every point, economic life set up conflicts with ideology."[10]

This conflict found its first expression when the large majority of the merchants supported the Antinomian heresy of Ann Hutchinson, the wife of a merchant, just a few years after the founding of the Massachusetts colony. The Antinomian belief in faith and revelation as the sufficient assurance of election undermined the orthodox belief in probable grace manifested in an indispensable combination of faith and works, which Weber believed to be essential to systematic economic behavior. Although exile soon stamped out the leadership of the heresy, older Boston merchants remained ready to support the initiative of the newer merchants in the political conflicts with the Puritan oligarchy.[11]

[7] See Perry Miller, *The New England Mind: The Seventeenth Century* (Cambridge, 1954), 383 ff, 387–392; Perry Miller, *The New England Mind: From Colony to Province* (Cambridge, 1953), Chap III; Perry Miller, *Errand Into the Wilderness* (Cambridge, 1956), Chaps. III, V.

[8] Weber, *Protestant Ethic*, 62. My italics.

[9] Quoted in E. A. J. Johnson, *American Economic Thought in the Seventeenth Century* (London, 1932), 89; also 86–100 for an excellent summary of Puritan economic doctrine. Johnson concludes, in reference to Weber's Protestant Ethic, that "There is little significant evidence to support this thesis in the writings of the American Puritans . . . There is no more idealization of wealth accumulation than there is in the Catholic economic literature." (92). The American Puritan position was that "the care of the publique must oversway all private respects, by which not onely conscience, but meare Civill pollicy doth binde us; for it is a true rule that perticuler estates cannott subsist in the ruine of the publique". John Winthrop, "Model of Christian Charity", *The Puritans,* Perry Miller and Thomas H. Johnson, eds. (New York, 1938), 197.

[10] Miller, *From Colony to Province*, 51; Bernard Bailyn, "Kinship and Trade in Seventeenth-Century New England", *Explorations in Entrepreneurial Hist.*, VI (1954), 197–206.

[11] Bernard Bailyn, *The New England Merchants in the Seventeenth Century* (Cam-

Adherence to less rigorous theology marked another breach with Puritan doctrines, and the children of Calvinists tended to be assimilated into the larger merchant world where status was determined more by accumulated wealth than theological niceties. Intermarriage took place among the families of Boston merchants and in the process religion was a secondary consideration. This pattern was not only dominant in Massachusetts, where the conflict between Calvinism and the merchants was the greatest, but in other areas with large Calvinist communities. In South Carolina, the large Huguenot settlement experienced an "absorption into the Anglican church [which] was indirectly coercive, rapid and thorough".[12] In New York very few pure denominational lines remained by 1750.

In Massachusetts the connection between Puritan religion and economic interest might well be seen in the light of considerations which Weber ignored. The power of the oligarchy lasted only so long as the merchant class was unable to organize its latent power and political influence; until then, social unity could be maintained by the binding power of Puritan doctrine. This was only for a very brief period. The Puritans themselves thought it lasted, in something like its ideal state, for a decade. The Puritan religion could thus be viewed as ideology; not sustained by concrete class and economic interest, it proved a weak prop upon which to build a new political structure. Had the alliance between the religious conceptions of the Puritans and the merchant class been as real as Weber assumed it to be, the conflict might not have occurred so quickly. If the failure of Puritanism to maintain itself without larger class support tells against Weber, so does the converse; we find the merchants ready to turn to theologies capable of neutralizing or counteracting the alleged doctrinal superiority of the Puritan elite. When heresy failed to succeed, assimilation to less restrictive denominations served the purpose.

## II

Because of the multiple economic aspects of Puritanism, most of which Weber did not appreciate, the Puritan oligarchy attempted to create a state not unlike that which Weber described as the goal in China during the domination of the literati—a commonwealth that "had the character of a religious and utilitarian welfare-state, a character which is in line with so many other typical traits of patrimonial bureaucratic structures bearing

---

bridge, 1955), 40 ff.; see Miller, *The Seventeenth Century*, 370 ff., for a discussion of Antinomianism.

[12] Arthur Henry Hirsch, *The Huguenots of Colonial South Carolina* (Durham, N. C., 1928), 90. For Boston, see Bailyn, *New England Merchants*, 135–139; for New York, see Virginia D. Harrington, *The New York Merchants on the Eve of the Revolution* (New York, 1935), 17.

theocratic stamps".[13] It is a state of this character, rather than one basing its economic policy on pro-merchant beliefs, that might serve as a useful model as we turn to consider some exigent problems of the colonial economy.

On such matters as economic control, usury, and just price there was little difference between the colonies. The general need to prevent starvation placed certain limits on economic freedom, and the pervasive acceptance of much essentially mercantilist practice made active government intervention inevitable. In Massachusetts, contrary to what one might infer from the Calvinist position as presented in *The Protestant Ethic,* the Puritan oligarchy strictly regulated the conditions upon which usury might be practiced, and these conditions virtually eliminated any predictable chance for repayment. If a potential poor borrower could not repay a loan he was to be the object of charity and not commerce, and charity was as much a Christian obligation as was business. More important, if a debtor was unable to execute his obligation, the good Christian was to excuse the debt and refuse to take pledges of goods necessary to the daily life of the debtor. Although the merchants ignored the economic prescriptions of the Calvinist divines, they undoubtedly received no comfort from the assertion that they were acting against the laws of Christianity. The attitude toward usury in Massachusetts, in any event, merely confirms the criticisms of H. M. Robertson that Weber did not understand the entire Calvinist position on usury.[14]

The Southern colonies, no less than the Northern, attempted to control prices and prevent profiteering, and like the Northern colonies generally failed. Massachusetts, obeying necessity as much as following medieval precedent and religious conviction, fixed prices from 1633, but failure to maintain effective control forced it to decentralize much of the responsibility to the towns after 1641. Virginia, from its inception, established limits on profits, as did the Council of New Netherland after 1653. Boston controlled the import and export of wheat and the price of bread until the post-revolutionary period, and Charleston, South Carolina, maintained extensive control over the quality, price, and marketing of food until then as well. New York also regulated the price of basic foodstuffs for a significant period.[15] It was

[13] Max Weber, *The Religion of China,* trans. and ed. Hans H. Gerth (Glencoe, Ill., 1951), 136.

[14] H. M. Robertson, *Aspects of the Rise of Economic Individualism* (Cambridge, 1933), 115–117; also see Johnson, *American Economic Thought,* 213–223, for a discussion of usury and Puritanism. Throughout the colonial period, and in most colonies, interest was strictly regulated by law at low rates, and with the general provision that contracts in excess of the legal maximum were void. Massachusetts in 1641 restricted the rate of interest to eight percent so that there would not be "usury amongst us contrary to the law of God". (Quoted in J. B. C. Murray, *The History of Usury,* Philadelphia, 1866, 77.) In 1693 the rate was reduced to six percent.

[15] Richard B. Morris, *Government and Labor in Early America* (New York, 1946), 84–89; Leila Sellers, *Charleston Business on the Eve of the American Revolution* (Chapel Hill, 1934), 21–24; Joseph Dorfman, *The Economic Mind in American Civilization* (New York, 1946), I, 45–46; Johnson, *American Economic Thought,* 26–32; Harrington, *New*

assumed as a matter of course in the colonial period that one of the purposes of the state was to prevent the ruthless exploitation of the public's immediate and basic needs, or at least to make an effort in that direction. Survival in a frontier situation often made public control indispensable, and in Massachusetts Puritan concepts of just price merely reinforced the trend.

According to Weber, asceticism aids capital accumulation, and asceticism was a characteristic Puritan virtue—"the English, Dutch, and American Puritans were characterized by the exact opposite of the joy of living".[16] Yet in South Carolina the characteristic French *joie de vivre* was by no means absent from the large settlement of Huguenots, right from the beginning of their establishment in the latter part of the seventeenth century. In New York and Philadelphia as well, the merchant community, regardless of denomination, soon fell into a modish and socially exclusive pattern of life and consumption which diverted potential capital into non-productive activities, into the attempt to consolidate status on a level corresponding with their economic power. In Boston the pattern was no different.[17] Sumptuary legislation, established in Virginia as well as Massachusetts, broke down functionally several decades after its introduction.

The utilization of barter as the primary means of exchange in the West India trade created a situation in which New England not only failed to represent ascetic virtue, but spread moral ruin, or at least one of its preconditions, wherever it might. Rum and molasses became the basic staple of the crucial West India trade, and the ability of the New England merchant to exchange his produce, fish, wood, and goods for West Indian rum was contingent on the decidedly unascetic customs of the farmers, mechanics, and fishermen throughout the colonies. By 1720, the major New England manufacture was rum, about one-seventh of which was transported to Africa for the slave trade.[18] Some went to the Indians in the fur trade, but the bulk of it remained in the colonies or was sent up the Maine and Canadian coast in

*York Merchants*, 282–284; William B. Weeden, *Economic and Social History of New England 1620–1789* (Boston, 1890), II, 526; Harold C. Syrett, "Private Enterprise in New Amsterdam", *William and Mary Quarterly*, 3rd Ser., XI (1954), 536–550; see David J. Saposs, "Colonial and Federal Beginnings", *History of Labour in the United States*, John R. Commons, ed. (New York, 1918), I, 25–137, for the role of government not only as the protector of labor and controller of quality, wages, and prices, but as the subsidizer and promoter of economic activity.

[16] Weber, *Protestant Ethic*, 41; also see *China*, 245–246.

[17] For South Carolina, see Hirsch, *Huguenots*, 156, 170, 182–185; for New York, see Harrington, *New York Merchants*, 30ff.; for New England, see Weeden, *History of New England*, II, 742–744; Victor S. Clark, *History of Manufactures in the United States, 1607–1860* (Washington, D. C., 1916), I, 119; for Philadelphia, see Frederick B. Tolles, *Meeting House and Counting House: The Quaker Merchants of Colonial Philadelphia, 1682–1763* (Chapel Hill, 1948), Chap. VI; also Carl Bridenbaugh, *Cities in Revolt: Urban Life in America, 1743–1776* (New York, 1955), Chap. IX.

[18] Arthur Meier Schlesinger, *The Colonial Merchants and the American Revolution, 1763–1776* (New York, 1918), 25.

exchange for fish. "Throughout all the colonies drunkenness was a prevailing vice, as it was in England", writes James Truslow Adams, "and nearly every event, such as house raisings, harvestings, christenings, college commencements, funerals and even the ordination of ministers, was frequently made the occasion of scandalous intemperance." [19]

## III

For the American Colonies, the difference between the Puritan North, where, on account of ascetic compulsition to save, capital in search of investment was always available, from the conditions in the South has already been clearly brought out by Doyle....

The existence of iron-works (1643), weaving for the market (1659), and also the high development of the handicrafts in New England in the first generation after the foundation of the colonies are, from a purely economic view-point, astounding. They are in striking contrast to the conditions in the South, as well as in the non-Calvinistic Rhode Island with its complete freedom of conscience.... It can in fact hardly be doubted that the compulsion continually to reinvest savings, which the Puritan curtailment of consumption exercised, played a part. [20]

While these assertions may buttress Weber's thesis, they are incomplete or invalid historically. The stimulus to self-sufficiency existed in all colonies, not merely in Calvinist Massachusetts, and it was expected that, given the shortage of capital which was a problem in all the colonies, the colonial governments or towns would stimulate the creation of industries and crafts. In this respect Virginia was no different from Massachusetts. Discussions of religious ethics are extraneous to an accounting for the events that actually occurred. Indeed, insofar as Rhode Island, Virginia, and Maryland wished to foster social unity and avoid the religious conflict and bigotry characteristic of Massachusetts, they were in a more advantageous, rational economic position.

From its inception, the London Company had diverse motives for founding a colony in Virginia. Politically the settlement was to strengthen English power in the hemisphere *vis-à-vis* Spain and Portugal. Profits were to be limited, religious conflict avoided, and industry as well as agriculture fostered. [21] Small local mills and industries sprang up throughout the colonies as demand warranted and state and local bounties and grants made the means available. [22] Virginia's first brick kiln was set up in 1611, its first

[19] James Truslow Adams, *Provincial Society, 1690–1763* (New York, 1927), 160–161; also see 94-5, 311; Weeden, *History of New England*, I, 188.

[20] Weber, *Protestant Ethic*, 278.

[21] Wesley Frank Craven, *The Southern Colonies in the Seventeenth Century* (Baton Rouge, 1949), 69, 141–142, 228.

[22] Clark, *History of Manufactures*, 31–32, 70–71; Philip Alexander Bruce, *Economic History of Virginia in the Seventeenth Century* (New York, 1895), II, 486–491ff.

glass plant in 1621, and Virginia claimed the first two glass plants in America. Massachusetts' first glass works stopped operations in 1670 "for lack of capital".[23] In 1640, the Puritan oligarchy suggested the consideration of "what course may be taken for teaching the boys and girls in all towns the spinning of yarn", but in 1646 Virginia actually opened two public flax houses in Jamestown to teach the art of linen making, and in 1666 ordered each county to do the same. Maryland also founded such schools, and although it did lag behind Virginia, Massachusetts eventually followed suit.[24] Bounty laws and acts to maintain craft quality and stimulate production were common in all colonies but most effective in Pennsylvania, which later became the leading manufacturing colony.[25] Weber's citation of Massachusetts' weaving for the market is a misleading example. Its repeated measures in the 1640's and 1650's to create self-sufficiency and build the industry failed despite an ample supply of raw materials. Cloth production was for home use, of poor quality, and most fine cloth was imported throughout the better part of the colonial period. The situation was no different in Virginia, for local handicrafts sprang up by necessity among poor, isolated farmers wherever they might be.[26]

Success in early colonial manufacturing was due to tangible factors to which religious concepts cannot be said to have made much difference. The iron industry developed where the resources were most abundant and, as in the case of Pennsylvania, where the high cost of transportation for agricultural goods stimulated diversification.[27] The textile industry later developed in New England for similar reasons: water power, ports, proper humidity for production, and a surplus labor supply.[28]

The impression given by Weber was that the iron industry began in New England and centered there because of an initially religiously-motivated class of dynamic entrepreneurs. The assertion that an iron-works existed in Massachusetts in 1643 is, by itself, a meaningless fact. One of the reasons Virginia was founded was to supply iron to England, and in late 1621 a complete iron mill was finished at Falling Creek. In March 1622, when the mill was about to begin production, the entire population was massacred by Indians and most of the machinery thrown in the river.[29] The first Massachusetts iron mill began with substantial state bounties and considerable

---

[23]  Clark, *History of Manufactures*, 152; also 169; for Virginia, see Bruce, *Economic History of Virginia*, II, 135, 440–442, 486–491ff.
[24]  Clark, *History of Manufactures*, 67.
[25]  *Ibid.*, 70–71; Bruce, *Economic History of Virginia*, II, 412–413, 478–481ff.
[26]  Bailyn, *New England Merchants*, 71–74; Craven, *Southern Colonies*, 211–213; Clark, *History of Manufactures*, 169, 195–200.
[27]  Clark, *History of Manufactures*, 76–77, 88.
[28]  Caroline F. Ware, *The Early New England Cotton Manufacture* (Boston, 1931), *passim*.
[29]  Kathleen Bruce, *Virginia Iron Manufacture in the Slave Era* (New York, 1931), *passim*.

*English* capital, which eventualy grew to £ 15,000, but by 1652 it was so overwhelmed with debts that its production thereafter was sporadic.[30] When the colonial iron industry is established, it is in precisely the place where anyone committed to a belief in the nexus between Calvinism and industrial enterprise would expect not to find it. In 1715, Maryland was the largest colonial iron producer, but Pennsylvania became the leader in the field by 1750. Throughout the colonial period, however, Virginia and Maryland were far more important iron producers than New England, and in 1775 the colonies produced one-seventh of the world's total output.[31]

## IV

To Weber the essential quality of capitalism was its rationality, and it was the role of Puritanism in evoking a systematic "supramundane orientation" of works as a sign of probable salvation which made modern rational capitalism possible. Such an attitude toward the world was indispensable, and its expression would be found in predictable trade based on peaceful profits from exchange and freedom of mobility, trade, and occupational choice— "sober, strict legality and the harnessed rational energy of routine enterprise".[32] Man's salvation was in large measure in his own hands.

Rather than having "a horror of illegal, political, colonial, booty, and monopoly types of capitalism" and unpredictable economic chances, the American merchant lived with this form of commerce throughout the colonial period. These circumstances were quite beyond his control and had nothing to do with his own attitude toward the situation, to which he rather unreflectively accommodated himself. If one were to characterize succinctly the colonial economy, one would say that it lacked most, if not all, of the prerequisites for the creation of a rational capitalism in Weber's terms. And, as we shall see, the merchants lived with these conditions, thrived on them for at least a century, and eventually developed a vested interest in continuing certain of their political aspects.

Given the crucial importance of the West India trade to the merchants as a means of acquiring the credits for their English debts, it was inevitable that unpredictability characterize American commerce. A ship load of goods sent to one destination often found the market glutted, or no return cargo, and might have to wander throughout the Indies in search of a suitable exchange. Since, after 1700, the discretion of making a bargain was generally left to

---

[30] Arthur Cecil Bining, *British Regulation of the Colonial Iron Industry* (Philadelphia, 1933), 13ff.; for the abortive Massachusetts iron-mill, see Bailyn, *New England Merchants*, 62–71.
[31] Bining, *British Regulation*, 15–19, 122, 129–134.
[32] Weber, *China*, 247; also see 242–249, and *Protestant Ethic*, 17–18.

the ship's captain, the merchant was always unsure of the results. Combined with this insecurity was frequent unreliability among factors and the bills of credit of West Indian planters. Frequent colonial wars increased the danger of losses in the hands of privateers. In addition, there was the general unpredictability in the quality of goods one might receive from a West Indian planter or American merchant when ordering goods sight unseen.[33]

Far more important in creating uncertain and illegal economic conditions was the conscious mercantilist policy of Great Britain from 1660 on. Although no concerted attempt was made to enforce mercantile restrictions until 1763, the colonial merchants nevertheless were compelled to conduct the better part of their trade in a technically illegal fashion. This might take the simple form of false bills of lading to avoid taxation, or running goods ashore illegally. It might also involve privateering, direct trading with European nations or, in wartime, lucrative trade with the Dutch, French, and Spanish enemies of England. This illicit trade resulted in "debauched public sentiment and corrupt official practice", declared no less loyal a son of New England than Weeden.[34] According to Schlesinger: "Smuggling was almost exclusively a practice of merchants of the commercial provinces [New England]." [35]

Because of the desire to facilitate smuggling, and because it was necessary to have the cooperation of the official authorities to build illegal slitting mills or produce beaver hats, it was vital for colonial merchants to "dissuade" the proper authorities from performing their duties effectively. The means utilized were all illegal, some more than others. Many of the colonial governors had their own investments in illegal operations and were naturally sympathetic to the merchants. In several instances governors were bought out, and others were too dependent on colonial legislatures for their incomes, or without means of enforcement, to protest effectively. When unfriendly, governors were generally isolated. As a matter of procedure, however, most of the vice-admiralty was controlled by the smuggling merchants, and many of the best lawyers were retained to represent the merchants. The result was that most illegal slitting mills and similar establishments were freely built and never reported by the governors to the Board of Trade in London.[36]

In his discussion of China, Weber declared that "wealth, and especially landed wealth, was not primarily a matter of rational profit-making".[37] Much

---

[33] Harrington, New York Merchants, 78 ff., describes the problems of purchasing sight unseen. For the West Indies trade, see Richard Pares, Yankees and Creoles (Cambridge, 1956), passim.

[34] History of New England, II, 661.

[35] Colonial Merchants, 40.

[36] Ibid., 46; Clark, History of Manufactures, 200–205; Bining, British Regulation, 86–92; Hirsch, Huguenots, 151–152; for a general survey, see Charles M. Andrews, The Colonial Period of American History [England's Commercial and Colonial Policy] (New Haven, 1936), IV.

[37] China, 86.

of this land was acquired through the political accumulation of capital, which purportedly characterized the Chinese economy as a whole and represented a diversion of capital which might otherwise have been spent in rational economic activity. Given the traditional status of land in England, the general lack of other transferable property within the colonies, and the unpredictability of trade, currency, and investments, it is not surprising that much of the capital within the colonies soon found its way into land-holdings and, eventually, land speculation. In this respect, and often in the means of acquiring land, there was little difference in principle between colonial Massachusetts, South Carolina or China.

Exact economic calculation, according to Weber, was possible only with free labor, and since this was a precondition of rational capitalism he expected the Puritans to naturally favor it. He held that "the early history of the North American Colonies is dominated by the sharp contrast of the adventurers, who wanted to set up plantations with the labour of indentured servants, and live as feudal lords, and the specifically middle-class outlook of the Puritans".[38]

The New England Puritan, however, merely conformed to the accepted colonial principles for securing and utilizing labor, and apparently nothing in Puritan doctrine changed that fact. At least half of the total white population in the Thirteen Colonies arrived as indentured labor, and Massachusetts received its fair share. Indentured servants entering the colonies because of their criminal records were generally received in the South and Pennsylvania, but those voluntarily emigrating were distributed throughout the colonies. Massachusetts established laws governing indentured servants from the inception of the colony, strictly enforced their obligations to their masters, and fixed the length of their service at seven years, which was the general average in the early colonial period. When the supply lagged, bounties were offered. In 1710, the Massachusetts Legislature offered 40 shillings a head to any ship captain bringing in male servants between the ages of eight to twenty-five. Prisoners captured by the English in their wars were often sent to the colonies, and part of the labor force of Massachusetts' first iron-mill consisted of captured Scottish soldiers.[39]

The first Negro was brought to Virginia in 1619 by the Dutch, but slavery assumed no real importance in Virginia, and did not even become legally enforceable, until the end of the century and the rise of the West Indies trade. It was never the plan of the Virginia "adventurers" to establish slavery, and until the middle of the seventeenth century indentured servants automatically became landed freeholders. In 1700, sixty percent of Virginia's

[38] *Protestant Ethic*, 173–174.
[39] Morris, *Government and Labor*, 372–373, 393, 402, 416–419, 437–441, 463–476, 506; for bounties, see Adams, *Provincial Society*, 98; for war captives, see Bailyn, *New England Merchants*, 68, and Bruce, *Economic History of Virginia*, I, 608–610.

free whites had neither slaves nor indentured servants. When slavery did grow in the South, the Southern Calvinists showed no hesitancy in owning them, and more "Cavaliers" descended from English merchants than from any other group.[40]

## V

Weber saw in Benjamin Franklin's ideas the quintessence of the Protestant Ethic. Franklin's *Advice to a Young Tradesman* was considered, as Weber's wife tells it, as "the characteristic document of the capitalist spirit", and Weber quoted it at great length in *The Protestant Ethic*. "That it is the spirit of capitalism which here speaks in characteristic fashion, no one will doubt, however little we may wish to claim that everything which could be understood as pertaining to that spirit is contained in it." [41] And: "the *summum bonum* of this ethic, the earning of more and more money, combined with the strict avoidance of all spontaneous enjoyment of life, is above all completely devoid of any eudaemonistic, not to say hedonistic, admixture." [42]

After reading Franklin's *Autobiography* Weber saw in the man the personal fulfillment of the influence of the Protestant Ethic as well. In an important sense Franklin was the fulfillment of what is most characteristic of the typical bourgeois, but the reasons for this were hardly appreciated by Weber. Seeing economic action as a consistent reflection of doctrinal beliefs and influence, Weber was unaware of the element of paradox, conflict, and hypocrisy in the typical American bourgeois. Franklin, in reality, was much more like the Chinese mandarin who purportedly made capitalism impossible than Weber's stereotyped Puritan ascetic.

Franklin's economic ideology was much more involved than Weber presented it or could have known after a brief and selective reading of his more popular works. Influenced by the Physiocrats in his later life, Franklin accepted free trade, saw agriculture as the source of all productive wealth, and on this basis viewed manufacturers, merchants, professionals, and mechanics as little more than useless in the economic process. As far as he was concerned, "there seem to be but three ways for a nation to acquire wealth. The first was by *war,* as the Romans did, in plundering their conquered neighbours. This is *robbery*. The second by *commerce,* which is generally *cheating*. The third by *agriculture,* the only *honest way*." [43] Franklin

---

[40] Craven, *Southern Colonies*, 214; Bruce, *Economic History of Virginia*, I, 594, II, 81; Hirsch, *Huguenots*, 170–171. For merchant origins of large landowners see Thomas J. Wertenbaker, *The Shaping of Colonial Virginia: Patrician and Plebian in Virginia* (Charlottsville, 1910). On slavery, see Oscar and Mary F. Handlin, "Origins of the Southern Labor System", *William and Mary Quarterly*, VII (1950), 199–222.

[41] *Protestant Ethic*, 51ff.; Marianne Weber, *Lebensbild*, 387–390.

[42] *Protestant Ethic*, 53.

[43] Quoted in Lewis J. Carey, *Franklin's Economic Views* (New York, 1928), 150; also 140–142. Franklin was also something of a plagiarist. His concepts of value and

believed in interest, however, and in this respect differed from most Physiocrats.

Franklin accepted most of the vices of man and himself by no means refrained from them any more than he refrained from the vices of economic life. Upon travelling to London at the age of twenty to learn the printing trade, Franklin did not save his money like a true Puritan but rather spent evenings at such notably unascetic activities as theaters, sports, drink, and women. He returned to America with an illegitimate son who eventually fathered another who in turn did the same. In Philadelphia Franklin set to work determined to make something of himself, living a well scheduled life which included only eight hours a day for work. Franklin was a wise promoter, however, and his newspaper tried many things, from discussions of hypothetical adultery to Poor Richard's Almanac, to increase circulation.[44]

Franklin was never a prude and never became one. He retired from business at what is still the ripe young age of forty-two in order to escape "the little cares and fatigues of business".[45] His letter on how to choose a mistress is relevant to his asceticism, and while serving as American ambassador to France, Franklin in his old age left his wife at home and carried on several amorous affairs. In addition to women, Franklin indulged in good food and excellent wine. According to Weber, however, "transition to a pure, hygenically oriented utilitarianism had already taken place in Franklin, who took approximately the ethical standpoint of modern physicians, who understand by chastity the restriction of sexual intercourse to the amount desirable for health".[46]

Franklin not only appreciated the value of good health and food, but also the value of political connections in achieving wealth (Poor Richard had nothing to say on the matter, which is one reason why he, unlike Franklin, never became rich). He used his position in the political caucus of the Junto and wrote a tract advocating the "Necessity of a Paper Currency", in order to get the contract to print money, and eventually much of Pennsylvania's printing work, for his own firm. Franklin was the public printer of Penn-

---

interest were printed, almost verbatim, from William Petty. The *Almanac* was, predictably, primarily a collection of English proverbs, written mainly by Anglicans, suitably doctored by Franklin. See Robert H. Newcomb, "The Sources of Benjamin Franklin's Sayings of Poor Richard", Unpublished Ph. D. thesis, University of Maryland, 1957; also Carey, Chap. II.

[44] Bernard Fay, *Franklin, The Apostle of Modern Times* (Boston, 1929), 96–114, 136–140, 155–161.

[45] Carl Van Doren, ed., *Benjamin Franklin's Autobiographical Writings* (New York, 1945), 54–56.

[46] *Protestant Ethic*, 263; Fay, *Franklin*, 454–456, 461–469; see his letter on mistresses in L. Lincoln Schuster, ed., *A Treasury of the World's Great Letters* (New York, 1940), 160–162. Colonial sexual habits, in general, fail to sustain Weber's assertion on Puritanism and sex. See Edmund S. Morgan, "The Puritans and Sex", *New England Quarterly*, XV (1942), 591–607; and Adams, *Provincial Society*, 158–161.

sylvania until 1764, and it is commonly agreed that his advocacy of paper money was motivated to an important extent by that fact.[47] His political influence was too great to stop at mere printing contracts, for Franklin became involved with some of his Philadelphia associates in an attempt to form two new colonies on an enormous tract of 1,200,000 acres they obtained in the West on the basis of a flimsy and probably illegal purchase from Indians. Franklin's task was to convince the royal government to authorize the project, a matter to which he actively but unsuccessfully gave his efforts in 1766–67.[48]

## VI

In China, wrote Weber, a class of prebends accumulated land and property through the unpredictable exploitation of political offices. Modern industrial capitalism cannot grow in such a politically irrational environment, and *The Religion of China* was devoted to the question of why the Chinese social structure never created the rational political conditions essential to capitalism. Weber believed the answer could be found by examining Chinese religious ethos.[49]

In the American colonial period we can discern a pattern of development in which the role of political capitalism, as in China, is decisive in the economic process. The relationship of the state to the economy, and the impossibility of pursuing economic action without regard to it, was made inevitable by English mercantilist practice, by the insufficiency of private capital, and by precedent.[50] The basic political history of Massachusetts in the seventeenth century is centered around the struggle between the Puritan oligarchy and merchants who wished to control the state for their own interests. The control or bribery of the imperial bureaucracy, itself filled with men seeking their own fortunes, was necessary from the moment the attempt to implement mercantilist controls occurred. The everyday lives of the merchants were unpredictable, and circumstances and lack of knowledge hindered rationalization and predictability in economic life. In early American economic development the advantages of political capitalism were exploited by the merchants and large landowners within each colonial government at the same time that the imperial government was ignored or opposed within the larger mercantilist system when it failed to work to their benefit and

---

[47] Carey, *Franklin's Economic Views*, 6–7, 15–16; Dorfman, *Economic Mind in America*, I, 179.

[48] Fay, *Franklin*, 330–331, 348–350; Dorfman, *Economic Mind in America*, I, 187; Shaw Livermore, *Early American Land Companies* (New York, 1939), 113ff.; Clarence Walworth Alvord, *The Mississippi Valley in British Politics* (Cleveland, 1916), I, 321ff.

[49] *China*, 86, 103.

[50] Clark, *History of Manufactures*, 71.

profit. In this context the existence of the Protestant or any other ethic was immaterial.

As long as promising economic opportunities could be exploited within the framework of mercantilist restrictions, the merchants could be satisfied. The result was illegality and corresponding unpredictability, but the merchants simply adjusted to this fact. Only when England wished to end illegality, a basic conflict between the merchants and the imperial system arose. Until that time the merchants supported or opposed policies and actions only to benefit themselves.[51] The closing of the trans-Appalachian lands by the Quebec Act of 1774 aided the belief by many merchants that the direct control of the state was a necessary precondition for the exploitation of existing economic opportunities. The revolution was not a measure against the role of the state in the economy, at least insofar as the revolutionary merchants were concerned, but an attempt by merchants and land speculators fully to utilize the state for their own economic operations.

In the immediate post-revolutionary period the internal class discord between frontier debtors and coastal planters and merchants crystallized a conflict which had begun in the colonial period. The state, especially in New England, became a prize not only because of the economic advantages it actually and potentially afforded, but to preserve the power of the economic elite against democratic encroachments and to enforce its debt claims.[52] But it is the utilization of the state for its economic advantages that interests us here. And it was land which became the primary object of the efforts of Boston merchants and Virginia planters.

The utilization of political contacts to acquire desirable economic goals was, of course, nothing new prior to the revolutionary period. Indeed, political office or personal political contacts were among the comparatively sure ways to economic success for ambitious governors and merchants alike. When the Massachusetts Legislature began the legal distribution of land for primarily speculative purposes in the 1720's, it was the town merchants with influential political connections who acquired it. In addition, "the chartered trading companies had by 1750 come to be regarded purely as semi-political 'vested interests' ".[53] In the colonial period, however, the legal definition of

---

[51] Livermore, *Early Land Companies,* 38. Also see Oliver M. Dickerson, *The Navigation Acts and the American Revolution* (Philadelphia, 1951), Chap. 11, for this point and merchant support for government economic regulation.

[52] For Vermont debt riots, see Chilton Williamson, *Vermont in Quandry, 1763–1825* (Montpelier, 1949), 19–20; for New Hampshire, see Jeremy Belknap, *The History of New-Hampshire* (Dover, 1831), I, 396–403; for the Massachusetts crisis, see Oscar and Mary Handlin, *Commonwealth: A Study of the Role of Government in the American Economy* (New York, 1947), Chap. 2; for the general scene, see Merrill Jensen, *The New Nation, 1781–1789* (New York, 1950); for earlier conflicts, see Curtis P. Nettels, *The Roots of American Civilization* (New York, 1938), Chap. 13.

[53] Livermore, *Early Land Companies,* 67; also 80; Adams, *Provincial Society,* 244–247; Alvord, *Mississippi Valley in British Politics,* Chap. XI. Land, and the possibilities of

the charter was vague, and served primarily as a political guarantee of economic monopoly or special privilege—an instrument of political capitalism such as that obtained by the Chinese prebend. The revolution only served to intensify the importance of political and personal contacts in obtaining land and government privileges. It was a conventional and accepted manner of getting what one desired, and on this question there was no difference between the Massachusetts merchants and Virginia planters.[54]

Most American historians concerned with colonial history, especially that of the seventeenth century, would question the priority of causal factors in Weber's explanation. Even ignoring the disparity between religious concepts and economic behavior, and the impossibility of predicting economic development by deduction from theologically-grounded attitudes, we are left with Weber's misunderstanding of the nature of Puritanism and his sharp exaggeration of its differences with Anglicanism as a means of social control and economic stimulus. Weber ignored the impact of the frontier in creating the major preconditions of economic activity in all sections. He also ignored the degree to which geographic and climatic circumstances generally explain the important differences between the regions which were to develop in the eighteenth century—by which time theology was in rapid flux throughout the colonies and had become far less powerful in New England. In this context, Weber's utilization of the Protestant Ethic as the explanation of American colonial history is a classic example of the dictum that correlation is often confused with causation.

Some of the implications of this study for historical theory in general may be worth noting. I have attempted to disprove the causal role of the Protestant Ethic in its early American context, primarily by an appraisal of his-

---

fortunes based on it, was the key factor in attracting the colonial bureaucracy to the colonies in the 17th century. See Edward Channing, *A History of the United States* (New York, 1905), I, Chap. 17 and *passim*. Examples of the exploitation of politics to accumulate offices, and their fees, can be found in Ellen E. Brennan, *Plural Office-Holding in Massachusetts, 1760–1780* (Chapel Hill, 1945), 32–35, 110–116; and, to 1750, Evarts B. Greene, *The Provincial Governor* (Cambridge, 1898), Chap. III, 112–124, 157–159. Also see W. T. Baxter, *The House of Hancock: Business in Boston, 1724–1775* (Cambridge, 1945), 95–110, 120–123, Chap. IX; Bernard Bailyn, "Politics and Social Structure in Virginia", *Seventeenth-Century America*, James M. Smith, ed. (Chapel Hill, 1959), 90–115.

[54] Livermore, *Early Land Companies*, 134, 139, 155–156, 162–164; Robert A. East, "The Business Entrepreneur in a Changing Colonial Economy", *Journal of Economic History*, Supplement VI (1946), 19; Robert A. East, *Business Enterprise in the American Revolutionary Era* (New York, 1938), *passim;* Oscar Handlin, "Laissez-Faire Thought in Massachusetts, 1790–1880", *Journal of Economic History* Supplement III (1943) 55–65; Louis Hartz, "Laissez-Faire Thought in Pennsylvania, 1776–1860", *Journal of Economic History*, Supplement III (1943), 66–77; Joseph S. Davis, *Essays in the Earlier History of American Corporations* (Cambridge, 1917), II, 328ff. The role of the state in the distribution of public land is exhaustively discussed by Alfred N. Chandler, *Land Title Origins* (New York, 1945).

torical facts that can be independently established but were ignored by Weber or unknown to him. Weber's theory is not disproven by pitting other theories against his, thus leaving us with a multiplicity of conflicting historical interpretations, but by an attempt to solve the debate, so to speak, empirically. If our specific historical facts are valid, historical theories which ignore them can be refuted as mere substitutes for historical enquiry, often quite easily. This is a different business, in principle at least, from attempting the disproof of the validity of one kind of historical explanation out of arbitrary preference for another.

My attempt to refute Weber's arguments does not imply a desire to impugn the objectivity or validity of contingent historical hypotheses, those based to a much greater extent on established historical facts than Weber's theory was. The multiplicity of such hypotheses and the controversies over their merit, relative to one another or to concepts like those employed by Weber, lend superficial support to the relativist's claim of the "subjectivity" of historical knowledge. In fact, however, they often lead to new hypotheses and concepts of a higher degree of independent validity. Ironically perhaps, refutation of the Protestant Ethic, as Weber understood it, also leads to a validation of the concept of political capitalism, which Weber limited to China, as a central element in any analysis of early American history.

As an ideal-typology, as an analytical construct rather than a hypothesis contingent on facts, the concept of the Protestant Ethic in America may perhaps be defended. But the question remains to what extent a useful fiction in the form of an ideal-typology is any more fruitful in the social sciences than a hypothesis that is verifiable.

*Harvard University*

# 10.

## MAX WEBER ON CHINA

### OTTO B. VAN DER SPRENKEL

### I

That Max Weber made a fundamental contribution to Sinology, and in particular to the study of Chinese society and social institutions, is indisputable. The paradox is that he was able to do this despite a serious methodological flaw in his approach to the subject; despite having to work with a severely limited range of sources, available to him only in translation and often in versions that were faulty and sometimes even grossly misleading; [1] and despite the fact that his writings on China abound in errors of detail, while some of his generalizations are as dogmatically wrong-headed as they are sweeping. This is a discouraging catalogue, but there is more. The determined reader still has to face the difficulties of Weber's style and the disorganized presentation he gave to his ideas. As his wife wrote of him: "He attached no importance whatever to the form in which his wealth of ideas was presented. So many things came flooding out of the storehouse of his mind... that time and again he found it impossible to force them into a lucid sentence structure." [2]

What Weber wrote about China is to be found partly in his long essay *Konfuzianismus und Taoismus* (*KuT*); and, for the rest, in short passages and fragmentary utterances scattered through a number of his other works. [3]

---

[1] Weber was well aware of these problems. He wrote: "The non-expert is sadly handicapped by the fact that only the tiniest fraction of the documentary sources and inscriptions have been translated. Unfortunately, no sinologist was at my side to check the translations. It was therefore only after much painful reflection and with the greatest reservations that I decided to allow this part of my work to be printed." *KuT*, 278n.

[2] Marianne Weber, *Max Weber, Ein Lebensbild* (Tübingen, 1926; reprinted Heidelberg, 1950), 350.

[3] *KuT*, begun just half a century ago in 1913, was published in 1915 in vol. 41 of the *Archiv für Sozialforschung;* and re-issued as part of vol. 1 of the *Gesammelte Aufsätze zur Religionssoziologie* (Tübingen, 1920), 276-536. In judging the work in detail it must be remembered that fifty years, during which research monographs and authoritative translations of Chinese sources have appeared in ever increasing numbers, have elapsed

It is necessarily a difficult task, both for the general sociologist (who is moreover as a rule unable to control the evidence behind Weber's statements) and for the sinologist, to disentangle and bring together the guiding ideas that underlie his "construct" of Chinese society.[4] But the effort is rewarding: even Weber's mistakes are apt to be more stimulating, and to open up more fertile lines of inquiry, than most other people's target-centered truths.

However, before going on to consider Weber's analysis of Chinese society, a brief comment is needed on what I have already referred to as the "serious methodological flaw" in his approach: I mean his use of historical materials taken from widely different periods of Chinese history, ranging from the Shang-Yin and Chou kingdoms of the second and first millennia B.C. to the early decades of the twentieth century when he himself was writing, with utter disregard for the chronological sequence of events. Bendix has sought to defend and excuse Weber's procedure, though he succeeds only in bringing out the nature of the offense and in making explicit the unstated assumption on which its commission rests. He writes: "Weber confined himself by and large to the early period of Chinese history . . . the emphasis on the early period was not exclusive, however. Weber freely cited data up to

---

since Weber wrote. A not altogether satisfactory English translation by Hans H. Gerth was published by the Free Press, Glencoe in 1951 under the title *The Religion of China.* See the present writer's review-article "Chinese Religion" in *The British Journal of Sociology,* 5 (1954), 272-75. This is Weber's only work devoted exclusively to *China,* but there are many passages concerned with Chinese society and institutions in his monumental *Wirtschaft und Gesellschaft (WuG),* first published (Tübingen, 1922) as the third volume of the *Grundriss der Sozialökonomik* sponsored by the publishing house of Mohr (Siebeck). The most important of the longer references to China is on pages 707-12. Substantial portions of *WuG* have been translated into English (not including this passage) and a useful list is given in the excellent book by R. Bendix, *Max Weber, An Intellectual Portrait* (London, 1960), 11-12. Perspicuous remarks on the Chinese city will be found in sections 1 and 2 of *Die Stadt,* an essay that first appeared in vol. 47 of the *Archiv für Sozialwissenschaft und Sozialpolitik* in 1921 and was later incorporated as ch. 8 of Part II in *WuG,* 513-600. An English translation, *The City,* by Martindale and Neuwirth, was published in Glencoe (1958) and London (1960).

[4] Sinologists, with one or two notable exceptions, have profited little from Weber's insights into their own domain. The labor of refining sinological metal from Weber's massive seams of low-bearing ore has proved too onerous. The "Bibliography on Max Weber" prepared by Hans and H. I. Gerth (*Social Research,* 16 [1949], 70-89) lists 466 books and articles provoked by his writings, of which only one (by von Rosthorn) is directly concerned with his work on China. Additional minor, though real, irritations that bear particularly on the sinologist are the inconsistent and often outlandish romanizations of Chinese names, titles, and phrases, which Weber takes as they stand from the older literature in different European languages (without, it seems, always knowing to whom or to what they refer), and the very inadequate references he gives to the sources from which he quotes (e.g., "the Annals"). The understanding, and hence the use that should properly be made, of Weber's work, particularly in some of the highly specialized fields into which he entered, would be greatly facilitated by critical annotated editions (or translations) in which these obstacles to comprehension were tidied away, and some guidance given to the results of more recent scholarship. Max Rheinstein's *Max Weber on Law in Economy and Society* (Harvard University Press, Cambridge, 1954) is a model of how this should be done.

the beginning of the twentieth century and in so doing ignored chronology. While this aspect of his work has often been criticized, it is sufficient for our purpose to point out that it had a rationale. *Certain aspects* of the Chinese social structure had remained *relatively unchanged* – at any rate up to the fall of the Manchu dynasty in 1911 – and the various possibilities inherent in that structure therefore could be elucidated by reference to events from different periods." [5] What this line of reasoning assumes is the old myth of an "unchanging China". Unconscious acceptance of this myth by a German scholar who received his formative training in the last quarter of the nineteenth century is explainable in terms of the ruling German historical tradition of that time, which, when it took note of the existence of the Asian civilizations at all, did so only to dismiss them as "static", as making no contribution to the movement of world history, and therefore of no interest to the historian. Dynamism in history was the exclusive attribute of the West. [6]

It should be counted as a merit to Weber that in his inquiry into the sociology of religions he concerned himself also with the "Wirtschaftsethik" of the religions of East and South Asia. In so doing he widened the horizon of socio-economic and institutional investigation beyond what had hitherto been its customary limits in Western scholarship. [7] As regards China, it would have been asking too much to expect a developmental treatment. Not only had Western historical writing on China (which Weber had perforce to consult) reached its nadir in the late nineteenth century, but Weber's way of approaching his subject inhibited him from looking in the first place for change and the causes of change. His preferred analytical tool is the ideal-type. This is not a description of reality but a normative and classificatory construct built up by aggregating concrete individual phenomena which may or may not be present, or may be present in greater or lesser degree, in any

---

[5]  R. Bendix, *Max Weber*, 117. The italicized phrases "hedge" the argument somewhat, and so weaken it. My point could hardly be better expressed than in the following comment by Alvin W. Gouldner, "On Weber's Analysis of Bureaucratic Rules", in R. K. Merton, ed., *Reader in Bureaucracy* (Glencoe, 1952), namely, that Weber's theories are "relatively innocent of spatio-temporal cautions" (48).

[6]  Compare Leopold von Ranke's description of the Asian peoples as *"Völker des ewigen Stillstandes"*. Japan's self-modernization and her defeat of Russia struck the first blow at this idea; and the revolution of 1911 should have done as much for China. But historiography, of its nature, must lag behind the event. In any case, the real point was not that Japan and China were capable of change in the nineteenth and twentieth centuries (and under the impact of the West at that) but that there had been "development" in the histories of both countries from the beginning. The latter view, as regards China at least, began to win acceptance only with the publication of Otto Franke's *Geschichte des chinesischen Reiches,* the first volume of which appeared as recently as 1930. See the present writer's article, "Franke's Geschichte", in *Bulletin of the School of Oriental and African Studies*, 18 (1956), 312-32.

[7]  This is not to overlook or detract from the worth of E. T. C. Werner's (Spencerian) *Descriptive Sociology: Chinese* (London, 1910), a pioneer compilation that deserves to be better known.

given example of historical reality. Weber's ideal-types, as Bendix well puts it, are "artifacts of the researcher based on historical materials",[8] and, although no ideal-type ever exactly mirrors an historical situation as it actually existed or exists, nevertheless it "must be at least in the realm of probability and not merely possible; that is, there must be found somewhere at least a close empirical approximation. Thus, the construction of an ideal-type can also be regarded as a working hypothesis".[9]

Weber seeks to attain clarity in the analysis of actual institutions and social behavior patterns by collecting as much observational data as possible and then classifying the picture so obtained in accordance with its degree of deviation from, or approximation to, one or more of the thematically relevant ideal-types he has set up. His method, in other words, is one of "positioning" the various situations he is examining on a sort of spectroscope whose bands are demarcated by ideal-types. Adoption of this technique no doubt accounts for Weber's predilection for the comparative method, which indeed he uses with great effect. On the other hand, he is not overly concerned with transitions from one type to another. The only developmental process which he discusses in any detail is the one he calls "the routinization of charisma"; and in general there is little emphasis in Weber's work on the dynamics of change.

This judgment may appear to need modification in the light of certain passages in *KuT,* especially earlier in the second chapter, "The Feudal and Prebendal State", which both describe and suggest reasons for the transition from Chou feudalism to what Weber calls the "patrimonial" empire of the Ch'in-Han.[10] He refers to the *Chou Ritual* which, as he says, "already portrays a highly schematized form of state organization, with irrigation works, specialized crop cultivation (e.g., sericulture), call-up registers for the army, statistics, and grain stores, all supervised by a rationalized bureaucracy. That such a system really existed," he adds, "is very problematical, since, according to the historical records, rational state administrations first appeared as a product of the competitive struggles of the Warring States." He continues with these perceptive sentences: "There are grounds for believing that a patriarchal epoch,[11] similar to that of the 'Old Kingdom' in Egypt, preceded

---

[8] Bendix, *Max Weber*, 281. Cf. also Karl Jaspers, *Max Weber, Politiker, Forscher, Philosoph (Munich, 1958), 53.

[9] Max Weber, *Basic Concepts in Sociology*, transl. with an introduction by H. P. Secher (New York, 1962), 14. For a different view see G. Kolko, "Max Weber on America", in *History and Theory*, I, 3 (1961), 243.

[10] See 318-29 of the German text; 37-45 of Gerth's translation. The applicability of the term "patrimonial" is discussed below.

[11] Weber is referring here not to "Sultanism" (a system of personal despotism backed in the last instance by military force) but to a patriarchalism resting on hereditary charisma inhering in the sib of the priest-king. In earliest times, so the legends of the canonical books would suggest, charisma could be conveyed by designation, as Yao named Shun as his successor, and Shun, Yü; though with the latter, the reputed founder of the Hsia dynasty, the hereditary principle became operative.

the feudal period. For there is no doubt that in China, as in Egypt, the bureaucracy entrusted with water-control and construction works goes back to high antiquity, and was developed from among the ruler's personal retainers. The presence of this officialdom from the outset tempered the nature of feudalism in the age of the Warring States, and constantly directed the thoughts of the literati to questions of administrative technique and a bureaucratic organization that could serve the useful ends of the state." [12]

Notable here are (1) Weber's correct assignment of the beginnings of "rational" policies in internal administration, military organization and the like, to the Warring States period; (2) the importance he gives to water-control as the factor mainly responsible for the growth of centralized political authority; [13] and (3) his unerring identification of the "literati" as the key status group in Chinese society, and of the bureaucracy as its creation and creature.

History, for Weber, is always the handmaiden of sociology, and it was no part of his plan or purpose in studying the "economic ethic" of Confucianism to describe or account for China's transition from feudalism to the "patrimonial-bureaucratic" empire. Nor do his scattered remarks, often no more than hints, offer a sufficient substitute for such a description and explanation. In this sense the judgment made above must be confirmed: namely, that Weber's main interest lies in the morphological understanding of societies, their institutions and the patterns of behavior that characterize them; and in answering the question: why is this what it is and not something else, how does it work, what gives it stability (or instability)? This it not to say that Weber refuses to concern himself with problems of genesis and mutation where these arise naturally in the course of his inquiry, but only that he normally regards such questions as secondary, and is content to throw out suggestions which, however fruitful they may prove themselves in stimulating the work of others, he does not feel obliged to follow up himself. [14]

---

[12]  *KuT*, 318-19. Cf. Gerth, *Religion*, 37.

[13]  Weber makes this point most forcefully in *KuT*, 298-9, where he writes: "The need for water-control, both in China and in Egypt, as the prerequisite for any rational conduct of economic life, was decisive for the emergence of a centralized authority together with its patrimonial officialdom." See also his *General Economic History* (Collier Books ed., New York, 1961), 237. The important monograph by Chi Ch'ao-ting, *Key Economic Areas in Chinese History as Revealed in the Development of Public Works for Water-control* (London, 1936), is, in part, a brilliant and balanced working out of this idea. The early work of K. A. Wittfogel, *Wirtschaft und Gesellschaft Chinas* (Leipzig, 1931), should also be consulted, especially the sections entitled: "Too much or too little water — a fateful question for Chinese agriculture" and "China's hydraulic system" (189-300). In his later writings, especially *Oriental Despotism* (New Haven, 1957), Wittfogel seriously overplays his theme, loading so much on to the back of the "hydraulic hypothesis" that it breaks under the strain. Cf. the excellent review of this book by S. N. Eisenstadt in *The Journal of Asian Studies*, 17, 3 (May 1958), 435-46.

[14]  For instance, no account with pretensions to thoroughness of China's transition from feudalism to centralized state control could fail to note the importance of the creation of centrally-administered local government areas (*hsien*) out of territories held on

## II.

In the remainder of this paper I shall examine (and on a number of points disagree with) the picture that Weber presents of Chinese society as it functioned in the two thousand years covered by the Empire.[15] In so doing, it will be necessary to simplify, and concentrate attention on what appear to be the major strands in his analysis.

One of the features of Chinese society that most impressed Weber was its enduring stability. This was in his opinion the result of a delicate balance between two opposing forces: on the one hand the Emperor, representing the central government, who with his patrimonial bureaucracy as instrument was able to spread a net of centrally-directed administration over the Empire; on the other, recalcitrant to this administrative network and stubbornly pursuing its own infinitely divided interests, the local lineages and the gilds. The power relations between these two social forces were complex, but they lie at the very heart of Weber's picture of traditional Chinese society. The product of their millennial confrontation was in fact an inherently unstable balance, but one in which the two antagonists were so evenly matched, with each in the last analysis able to limit the activities of the other, and with neither willing to risk a conflict à outrance for fear of bringing to light internal weaknesses, that a continuing situation of "stalemate" resulted which had all the surface appearance of stability.[16]

We may begin with the central power, whose embodiment is the Son of Heaven, and whose agent is the bureaucracy. The Chinese bureaucracy, in all periods from the Han to the Manchus, is invariably qualified by Weber as "patrimonial", and further as strongly marked by "irrational" features.[17]

---

feudal tenure which for one reason or another escheated to the crown, or out of lands newly conquered from neighboring states or from frontier barbarians. There is no obvious reason why such lands, freely at the disposal of the ruler, should not have been granted as feudal holdings. In the event they were not; and from the seventh century B.C. *hsien* existed side by side with feudal domains. Their effect was at once to strengthen the fiscal and military power of the ruler and weaken the barony. For a full discussion see D. Bodde, *China's First Unifier* (Leiden, 1938), 133-46 and *Appendix* on "The Rise of the *hsien* and *chün* System in Ancient China", 238-46.

[15] From 221 B.C. to A.D. 1911. In spite of the wealth of material Weber adduces from the early sources (and notwithstanding the opinion expressed by Bendix in the passage quoted earlier — see note 5 above) the Empire is his real subject. Almost nothing of what he has to say either about the bureaucracy, the examination system, Confucianism as a "status ethic", the local lineage, the gild or the city can be intelligibly related to the period before the unification of 221 B.C.; though almost all of it has relevance to an understanding of the imperial age.

[16] Less polite words than "stability" are also in order. Weber somewhere in his writings speaks of the "chinesische Erstarrung des Geisteslebens". Here something more like *rigor mortis* is suggested.

[17] In a long footnote to his passage cited above on the *Chou Ritual* Weber briefly resumes the government organization of the Han, basing himself on Ed. Chavannes, *Mémoires historiques de Se-ma Ts'ien*, 2 (Paris, 1897), App. I, 513-33 (cited by Weber

We have already noted his view that a movement towards rational administration was clearly discernible in the period of the Warring States in the fifth to third centuries B.C. Rational elements must therefore have been present and, one would think, to an even greater extent, in the administration of the unified Empire under the Han (206 B.C.–A.D. 220) and later. The requirements of Weber's system lead him to minimize their importance. According to his typology of authoritarian modes, the patrimonial is one variant, among several, of patriarchal authority. But "it is characteristic of patriarchal authority (and of the patrimonial sub-class that belongs to it) that, besides the system of inviolable sacred norms whose infraction results in magical or religious disaster, it also acknowledges a sphere in which the arbitrary decision of the ruler has free play, an area in which decisions are taken, in principle, on personal rather than on functionally appropriate grounds. In this sense patriarchal authority is irrational".[18] Hence the government organization of the Han, and indeed of later dynasties too, because they are classed as patrimonial, is necessarily "irrational" since all patrimonial domination is by definition "irrational".

No sinologist would be disposed to quarrel with the view that there were irrational elements (in the Weberian sense) in Chinese government, nor would he dispute that possession of the imperial office often conferred wide powers of arbitrary decision on its holder. Nevertheless certain modifying factors should be noted: namely (1) that a great deal depended on the personality and caliber of the Emperor; rulers of forceful character and strong purpose like Wu Ti of the Han, T'ai-tsung and Empress Wu of the T'ang, or the K'ang-hsi Emperor of the Ch'ing, by their vigorous action enlarged the scope of the office, while other lesser incumbents allowed it to dwindle almost to insignificance;[19] (2) that there was no doctrine of divine right in China. The Mandate of Heaven to rule had to be merited by performance. It was not granted in perpetuity to any ruler or ruling house, and could be forfeited by bad behavior. This doctrine, which implied a contingent right of rebellion

---

as *App.* II, and the error repeated by Gerth, *Religion*, 263). After listing the principal Han offices he writes: "It will be seen that this list exhibits, in sharp contrast to the rational and hence historically less credible constructions of the *Chou Li*, all the irrational features of a patrimonial officialdom which has grown out of the management of the ruler's household, the ordering of his ritual functions and the organization of the army, and to which has been added offices required for the administration of justice, the water-control economy and for other more purely political reasons" (*KuT*, 318n3; cf. Gerth, *Religion*, 264).

[18] "Die Wirtschaftsethik der Weltreligionen: Einleitung", *GAzRS*, 1, 269-70; cf. translation in H. H. Gerth and C. Wright Mills, *From Max Weber: Essays in Sociology* (New York, 1946), 296.

[19] A similar observation has been made about another, and less obviously "irrational", executive post: that of President of the United States. It is clear that this was a very different office when Jackson, Lincoln, and the second Roosevelt were in the White House from what it was under Polk, Fillmore, and Arthur.

in the subject, certainly acted as a check on arbitrary rule; (3) that in state matters the Emperor was normally expected to act in accordance with the advice of his chief ministers.[20] In theory of course their appointment and dismissal were exclusively his decision; in practice they often enjoyed long tenures of office.[21]

The central government of imperial China was not, as it is today, monolithic, but *composite*. The Chinese themselves distinguished between what they called the "inner court" (*nei t'ing*) and "outer court" (*wai t'ing*). The former comprised the Emperor and various groups that revolved around him as their center. These groups, whose relative strength varied in different periods of China's history, normally included some or all of the following: (1) the Emperor's consort and influential members of her clan, (2) members of the clan of the Emperor's mother, the Empress Dowager, (3) the Heir Apparent, where one had been designated, and his supporters, (4) the palace eunuchs, often comprising several factions in alliance with other groups, (5) military notabilities, and (6) civil officials who were the close advisers of the Emperor: in some periods a Chief Minister, in others a collegium. Decisions in general had a collective background but were finally taken either by the Emperor, by the persons who controlled one or more of these groups, or by both together. Whether a particular Emperor measured up to his task or not, whether he ruled or only reigned, the imperial office still remained theoretically the fount of honor and the ultimate source of all authority. Its control, especially when the incumbent was weak, incompetent or a minor, was the great prize of inner court politics.

The *wai t'ing* or outer court consisted essentially of the bureaucracy, and while the political maneuvers of the *nei t'ing* were played out for the most part in the palaces and courts of the Forbidden City, the theater of operations of the *wai t'ing* embraced not only the central ministries of the capital but extended over the whole territory of the Empire.[22] What precisely was the nature of this bureaucratic apparatus? It was in the first place a hierar-

---

[20]  Cf. *Sources of Chinese Tradition*, ed. W. T. de Bary, Wing-tsit Chan, and B. Watson (New York, 1960), 172-3. Note Eberhard's view that Ch'in Shih Huang-ti "is the only Chinese ruler who could be called a despot", *Conquerors and Rulers* (Leiden, 1952), 12, n.4. He also writes: "Emperor Wu of the Han dynasty apparently tried again to become an absolute ruler, but he did not succeed. In the following periods we see that the emperor was always an instrument or an exponent of different cliques of great and powerful gentry families. They determined his decisions and his policy" (*op. cit.*, 27). Eberhard's point, though perhaps too dogmatically expressed, is a sound one, even if we do not follow him all the way in attributing decisive power to the "great gentry families."

[21]  No detailed study covering all the major dynasties has to my knowledge been made of this question; but for long tenures in the Ming (1368-1644) see my article "High Officials of the Ming" in *Bulletin of the School of Oriental and African Studies*, 14 (1953), 87-114, especially 91-3 and Table V; and Tilemann Grimm, "Das Neiko der Ming-Zeit von den Anfängen bis 1506" in *Oriens Extremus*, 1 (1954), 139-77.

[22]  Weber seems to have been under the impression that a clearly drawn line divided the services of the capital from those of the provinces. This was not so. The normal

chically-ordered élite of administrators recruited almost exclusively from the ranks of the educated gentry.[23] Within the service promotion was largely by merit, as revealed by fitness reports drawn up by the subject's immediate superior and furnished at regular intervals to the authorities at the capital with whom decisions as to promotion or demotion lay. Its members, from the sixth century on, were increasingly selected by public competitive examination.[24] They constituted, to use Weber's formula, "a status group of certified claimants to office prebends".[25] They were, finally, a cohesive body imbued with a strong esprit de corps and a lively sense of the social distance which separated them, the "twice born", from the ordinary people, the *min*.

Paralleling the tensions already noted as operative within the inner court there was also a fundamental, if often latent, contradiction within the bureaucracy, the outer court: namely, that between the official in his rôle as an official, as a servant of the state, and in his capacity as a gentry-member with loyalties to his social group and, in particular, to the members of his own lineage.

Moreover there were also and inevitably differences of interest and outlook between the inner and outer courts themselves: between, on the one hand, the Palace and all it included and stood for; and, on the other, the elaborately structured bureaucracy whose members were immersed at all levels in problems of day-to-day administration as well as participating, at the higher levels at least, in the formulation and testing of policy.[26] This conflict

---

official career would include a number of provincial postings, interspersed with terms of duty in the ministries and bureaus of the central government. This constant movement between the center and the periphery applied to even the highest officials.

[23] In earlier periods it was mainly the preserve of the upper gentry. From Sung times on (10th-11th centuries), with the spread of printing and the consequent increased availability of books needed for acquiring a classical training, the social reservoir from which the officials were drawn was gradually expanded to include the middle and even lower levels of the gentry group.

[24] Weber's account of the rôle played by the examination system is considered below. For the system as it operated under different dynasties see: R. des Rotours, *Traité des examens* (Paris, 1932); E. A. Kracke, *Civil Service in Early Sung China* (Cambridge Mass., 1953); and Etienne Zi, *Pratique des examens littéraires* (Shanghai, 1894). The first of these works relates to the T'ang, and the third to the Ch'ing.

[25] *KuT*, 404, "eine Schicht diplomierter Pfründenanwärter". Cf. Gerth, *Religion*, 115.

[26] To complicate the picture further, there was also a certain "spilling over" of sections of the bureaucracy from the outer court, its own proper province, into the more restricted circles and rarified atmosphere of the inner court. Here we must distinguish between the Chief Ministers who formed the apex of the bureaucratic pyramid and whose interests were broadly the same as those that motivated the mandarinate as a whole, and the more specialized officials who were the Emperor's personal assistants. The latter are well exemplified by the Grand Secretaries (*Ta Hsüeh Shih*) of the Ming. In the beginning these officials had been seconded mainly to give secretarial assistance to the Emperor but by the early decades of the fifteenth century they already formed a sort of "cabinet" (the *Nei Ko*) and had taken over the leading executive rôle in the government. It was the practice that those who passed highest in the examinations were appointed immediately to the Han-lin Academy, and it was from their number that the Grand Secretaries were chosen. A recent writer on Ming government has this

was important, and Weber was right in drawing attention to it, though his interpretation of it was, as we shall see, mistaken. Hucker's illuminating comment that "in an ideological sense, it might be called a tension between Legalistic principles and Confucian principles of government" is nearer the mark.[27]

Weber is inclined to discount the efficacy of the Chinese civil service in part on the ground that it was technically impossible for so small an establishment [28] to control effectively an empire so vast and so lacking in means of communication.[29] He writes: "As the territory of the Empire was so im-

---

to say: "The association of the Grand Secretaries with the Han-lin Academy embarrassed them in their relations with the administrative hierarchy. The men who served as functioning Ministers or Vice-Ministers in the Ministries were normally men of long administrative experience, not only in the capital, but in the Provinces as well. But the men selected to be Grand Secretaries almost invariably rose through a succession of Han-lin posts, broken if at all by an appointment in some service or ceremonial agency such as the Ministry of Rites ... To officials of the administrative hierarchy, this meant that the Grand Secretaries were representatives and spokesmen of the inner court, not of the outer court with which they themselves were identified. That is, the Grand Secretariat was considered an instrument of imperial authority, not of ministerial or bureaucratic authority. Grand Secretaries, in consequence, often found themselves in the uneasy rôles of mediators trusted by neither the Emperors whom they served nor the officialdom which they aspired to lead." See Charles O. Hucker, "Governmental Organization of the Ming Dynasty", *Harvard Journal of Asian Studies*, 21 (1958), 1-66, esp. 29-31. Cf. T. Grimm's article on the *Nei Ko* already cited.

[27] Hucker, *op. cit.*, 21. "Legalism" here refers to the authoritarian teachings of the *Fa chia*, the School of Laws and Punishments (or as Waley has it, the "Realists"), teachings that were naturally attractive to the ruler. The literati on the other hand were the natural guardians of the Confucian ideology, which commended itself to them on many grounds, not the least being that it underwrote their privileged position in society. On the relations of emperor and bureaucracy see also H. Maspero, "Comment tombe une dynastie chinoise: la chute des Ming", *Mélanges posthumes* III, *Etudes historiques* (Paris, 1950), 211-27, esp. 215-6.

[28] In absolute numbers the established civil service was never very large. The highest figure for the Northern Sung (960-1126), which may include military as well as civil officials, is given by a modern Chinese historian as 34,000 (see Y. C. Chang, "Wang Shou-jên as a Statesman" in *Chinese Social and Political Science Review*, 22 (1939), 167). A contemporary Ming source, the *Hsü wen-hsien t'ung-k'ao* compiled toward the end of the sixteenth century by Wang Ch'i, gives a total of 24,683 officials, of whom 1,416 served in Peking, 558 in Nanking, and the remaining 22,709 in the provinces.

[29] In fact, almost to the end of the eighteenth century the Chinese were far in advance of the rest of the world in matters of administrative organization. Moreover, China's road and canal systems and courier service, under the major dynasties at least, were models of efficiency. Her extensive geographical literature and great achievements in cartography (maps were often associated with itineraries) are here to the point. See J. Needham, *Science and Civilization in China*, vol. 3, "Geography and Cartography", 497-590. It is certainly difficult for a European to realize how long-established in China were practices that in the West we associate mainly with the modern age. Writing of the end of the eighteenth century, E. J. Hobsbawm remarks that "outside the colonies the official nominated by his central government and sent to a succession of provincial posts was only just coming into existence" (*The Age of Revolution: Europe from 1789 to 1848* [London, 1962], 10). Similar arrangements had existed in China for two thousand years.

mense and the number of officials in proportion to the total population so small, the Chinese government was not only extensive in character but, under rulers of merely average ability, it even failed to function as a centralized government. Directives coming from the center were often accepted by subordinate officials less as binding instructions than as advice which they could follow or not as they chose. Here, as in other parts of the world where similar conditions prevailed, the officialdom found itself compelled to take account of and come to terms with the counter-vailing forces of traditionalism, in the persons of the lineage elders and gild leaders, in order to be able to operate at all." [30]

Weber is beginning here to sound the theme which underlies his whole analysis of the structure of Chinese society. The central government, facing the task of imposing its will on the innumerable if disunited centers of local self-rule that existed in every county of the empire, had at its disposal the instrument of the bureaucracy. But this instrument possessed only a limited effectiveness, and moreover itself represented a potential threat to the continuing authority of the Emperor. Its efficiency could certainly be improved, but only at the risk of making this potential threat actual; for unless the bureaucracy was kept weak and disunited, and its effectiveness checked by various institutional devices, its members would succeed in "appropriating their benefices" and transforming them into "hereditary office-domains". Such a process of refeudalization would inevitably end in reducing the imperial institution to a nullity.

In support of his view that refeudalization was a real and pressing danger Weber urges one general theorem and several particular "theories". The theorem, which receives its fullest statement in the chapter "Bürokratie" in Part III of *Wirtschaft und Gesellschaft*, is that "the development of a money economy, permitting the payment of officials in cash, is the primary social and economic condition of bureaucracy in its modern form ... A money economy developed to a certain level is the antecedent condition, if not for the emergence, then for the persistence without attenuating changes, of a pure bureaucratic administration. History shows that in the absence of a money economy it is hardly possible that a bureaucratic structure could avoid undergoing substantial internal modification, or even transformation into something quite different. The allocation to officials of fixed allowances paid in kind from stocks in the store-houses of the ruler or out of his current receipts of tax-goods – a type of payment which for thousands of years was the rule in Egypt and China, and which played a significant rôle in the late Roman monarchy and elsewhere – means easily a first step towards the appropriation of the sources of taxation by the official and their exploitation as private property." [31]

[30]  *WuG*, Part II, ch. 7, "Patrimonialismus", 708.
[31]  *WuG*, Part III, ch. 6, 655. Cf. Gerth and Mills, *From Max Weber*, 204-5.

This picture of "the appropriation of prebends" by mandarins who thus transform themselves into an hereditary quasi-feudal territorial nobility is quite implausible to the student of Chinese history. Weber is writing about imperial China and his argument should properly apply first and foremost to those periods in which a major dynasty, having united the country under a single sway, employed a fully-fledged bureaucracy to administer its empire. But it wat precisely in such periods, notably the Sung, Ming and Ch'ing -- roughly the last thousand years, from 960 to 1911 with a brief interruption during the rule of the Yüan between 1280 and 1367 – that the mandarinate achieved its most "rational" (in Weber's sense) organization under the close direction of relatively strong centralizing governments. No hereditary nobility existed during these centuries, nor were there any discernible signs of a process of refeudalization.[32] The position was somewhat different in the T'ang period, which however was also the one that saw the beginnings of the selection of officials by open competitive examination and of the bureaucracy in its modern form. Under the T'ang the great landed families were still a strong force; but, as Balazs remarks, "the necessity of passing examinations in order to enter upon the official career soon brought into existence a counter-weight to the influence of the hereditary nobility, who then still possessed great power." [33] This puts the mandarinate in a different, one might almost say an opposite, light to that in which Weber sees it.

The classical period of Chinese feudalism was the Western Chou (c. 1050-770 B.C.). Its characteristic institutions, as Weber correctly noted, were challenged and in part subverted in the time of the Warring States; though the decisive destruction of the territorial bases of feudal power was the work of the Ch'in. Feudalism was replaced by a unitary and bureaucratically-administered empire, a political arrangement to which the Chinese world became habituated, and which it came to regard as part of the natural order of things, during the four centuries of the Former and Later Han (206 B.C.–A.D. 220). It was in the subsequent age of disunion which began with the collapse and disintegration of the Han and lasted until the Sui reunification in 589 that a form of feudalism again emerged to master large areas of the former empire. The breakdown of all public order meant that both rich and poor had to look to their own protection and safety as best they might. The rich turned their domains into fortresses and armed themselves, their tenants

[32]   The granting of noble rank (often bestowed posthumously) to elder statesmen, and of titles and estate-revenues to princes of the imperial house (which was particularly important under the Ming), present no ground for modifying this statement. Such ranks were automatically diminished by one grade with every generation so that the remote posterity of the original holder of a title reverted to the status of commoner. Episodes such as the so-called "War of the Three Feudatories" (San fan chih luan) of 1673-81, which was a bid for imperial power on the part of Wu San-kuei, cannot be brought under the rubric of "refeudalization".

[33]   E. Balazs, "Les T'ang", in Aspects de la Chine, I (Publications de Musée Guimet, Bibl. de Diffusion, t. LXIII, Paris, 1959), 78.

and slaves for the better defense of their property. The poor either sought to flee the troubled countryside or offered themselves as "clients" to the rich. "By the beginning of the third century", writes Maspero, "five-sixths of the population thus found themselves under the protection of the other one-sixth." [34] An unsuccessful attempt to check or limit this development was made by the Western Chin (265-316), but fratricidal struggles in the ruling house and barbarian invasions which expelled the dynasty from north China to the Yangtse frustrated their efforts. In the event the Chinese countryside from the fourth to the end of the sixth centuries was dominated by the great landed families. They, and not the members of the former bureaucracy, were the carriers and beneficiaries of the renascent feudalism of the Six Dynasties period. These wealthy families, powerful by reason of the number of their clients and the strength of their private armies, formed a rural nobility (the *kao mên* or "high gates") which wielded well-nigh absolute power within their own domains and on occasion intervened with decisive effect in dynastic politics. The rulers of the Eastern Chin (317-419) preferred to rely on commoners to fill the highest ministerial offices, seeking in these men, whose advancement was due to personal quality and imperial favor and not to noble birth, a counter-weight to the aristocracy. But the latter resolutely closed their ranks against such upstarts whom they called *han jên* ("cold men"). The middle echelons of the bureaucracy, and in particular those who served in the provinces, presented little problem to the dominant rural nobility. The examination system, still in its earliest stage of development under the Han, did not survive the decline of the empire. It was replaced, apparently on the initiative of Ts'ao Ts'ao the founder of the Wei (220-264), by the so-called "Nine Categories", according to which aspirants to office were graded in respect to their virtues and abilities by functionaries of the central government known as the "Impartial and Just". This arrangement, which was intended to strengthen the position of the ruler as against the rich nobles of the provinces, was soon subverted by them and in their hands became a weapon which enabled them to control the officialdom. By the beginning of the fourth century, writes the author of the most recent study of the "Nine Category" system, "the highest grades had become hereditary and were awarded after consulting the tables of genealogy ... nominations and promotions were made by a scribe in the Bureau of Civil Office on the basis of the registers of nobility. In fact, to the historian, the main interest of the system of the 'Nine Categories' is that it allowed the great families of the Wei and Chin to arrogate to themselves the power of selecting the personnel of the bureaucracy ... Although the original purpose of the system had been to withdraw this power from the provincial nobility and return it to the central government, in practice it proved to be one of the main factors

---

[34]  H. Maspero, *Les institutions de la Chine* (Paris, 1952), 74.

MAX WEBER ON CHINA

promoting the decentralization that marked the succeeding centuries: the system conferred on the rich aristocrats a legal means of dividing up the administration among themselves and so of establishing the type of feudalism that characterized the Chinese Middle Ages." [35]

We have turned back from the bureaucratic empire that was beginning to create its typical institutions in the T'ang, and achieved its full development in the Sung, to glance at earlier periods: those of high feudalism and of feudalism in decline in the Western Chou and Warring States respectively; that of the destruction of feudalism and the creation of the first centralized and bureaucratically administered empire in the Ch'in-Han; and that of the re-emergence of a form of feudalism in the Age of Division that followed the dismemberment of the empire. In the last of these periods China again experienced the rise to power of an aristocracy. The most highly regarded of the noble families were those whose founders had won land, wealth and clients in the civil wars that testified to the break-up of the Han. These were the "Old Families" or *chiu mên*. Next to them in prestige were the so-called "Secondary Families" or *tz'u mên,* and then the "Later Families" or *hou mên.* These comprised the lesser nobility. Following them in the social hierarchy, but at an appreciable distance, came the *hsün mên*, families who owed their titles of nobility to the meritorious services, usually military, of their founders. They too were carefully graded, and families who had enjoyed their titles for two or more generations outranked *hsün mên* of the first generation. This was a stratified society in which distinctions of class and rank were prized and well guarded. The intermarriage of persons of different rank was strongly discouraged and in some instances forbidden by law. There was probably less social mobility in China at this time than at any other. [36]

This summary picture of the ordering of society during the Six Dynasties period [37] suggests conclusions as to the place of the bureaucracy in the process

[35] The quotation is from the admirable study by Donald Holzman, "Les débuts du système médiéval de choix et de classement des fonctionnaires", in *Mélanges publiés par L'Institut des Hautes Etudes Chinoises,* vol. 1 (Paris, 1957), 414.

[36] E. Balazs is to the point when he suggests that "to understand the Chinese middle ages it is necessary to read Saint-Simon, with his persons of quality, of birth, of distinguished birth, of the first quality, of lesser quality, and with his 'extended and precise knowledge of houses, births and alliances'", *Traité économique du Souei-chou* (Leiden, 1953), 12, n.3. Birth was indeed of first importance, and it is no accident that the compilation of family genealogies, then known as *p'u tieh* (the ancestors of the later *tsung p'u*) should date from this period. According to the historian Chao Yi (1727-1814) the keeping of such records broadly coincides with the introduction by the Wei of the "Nine Categories" system discussed above (see his *Kai-yü ts'ung-k'ao,* ch. 17, 6a-9a). Hsiao Kung-ch'üan, to whom I owe the above reference, writes: "During the Six Dynasties, when the line between 'high' families and commoners became quite rigidly drawn, acquaintance with the *p'u tieh* (genealogical records) attained the dignity of an independent branch of 'learning'", *Rural China: Imperial Control in the Nineteenth Century* (Seattle, 1960), 665, n.59.

[37] What has been written above refers mainly of course to the Chinese dynasties that from the fourth to the sixth centuries ruled the South from Nanking. A similar type

of refeudalization rather different from those arrived at by Weber. In the only period of Chinese history in which such a process occurred, its protagonists were not the old officialdom of the Han but the great families who carved positions of local power for themselves by seizing the opportunities offered by the breakdown of public order. Some of these families stemmed from men who had achieved wealth as provincial governors under the Later Han; others from successful military leaders; while others again owed their influence to the prior possession of landed estates which they were able in the confusion of war and civil upheaval to transform into semi-autonomous domains. A general explanation of refeudalization in terms of "appropriation of prebends" is quite unacceptable.

This, however, is precisely the danger that Weber saw as threatening the authority of the emperor in later and more settled periods – when the bureaucracy, far from being the tool of a local *noblesse,* was the obedient instrument of a central government that not only controlled the selection and indoctrination of its members through the examination system but also habitually exercized powers of appointment, promotion, demotion and removal over every part of the civil service establishment. It is hard to avoid the conclusion that Weber was led to judge as he did, not by the evidence, but by his concept of what "patrimonial bureaucracy", as an ideal-type, entailed. This notion of Weber's that the eventual aim of the official was to appropriate his prebend and transmute it into an hereditary benefice colors his whole view of the bureaucracy, suggests reasons to him for a number of the institutional devices that were part of its structure, and underlies his explanation of why the Chinese bureaucracy failed to progress from patrimonialism to full rationality. Though Weber regards the mandarinate as patrimonial in the sense that it developed from the ruler's own household and never completely emancipated itself from this inheritance, and also in the sense that it was an extension of and emanation from the ruler's own authority and subject to his arbitrary will or whim, he is convinced nevertheless that between the emperor and his patrimonial staff of administrators there existed a basic opposition of interests which, if sometimes latent, was yet always present. Here he was certainly right, though not perhaps entirely so about the interests involved.

In the following important passage Weber, while conceding a certain measure of rationality to the Chinese bureaucracy, gives his own reasons for the presence of some of the features which in his view prevented it from

---

of feudalism also characterized the "barbarian" northern dynasties though there, in addition to factors present in the South, the phenomenon of "ethnic super-stratification" also played a significant rôle. In the North the Turco-Mongol conquerors little by little found themselves compelled to share their power with the Chinese noble families who had chosen to remain, and who on the whole succeeded in preserving their local status and privileges intact. On this point see the interesting material on the Northern Wei (386-550) brought together by W. Eberhard in *Das Toba-Reich Nordchinas* (Leiden, 1949), ch. 5, "Die Lehen", 84-96, esp. 86-7 and Table 10.

either developing normally or degenerating. In the event it was forced to remain a stunted growth.

He writes: "To defend itself against the constantly renewed threat of the appropriation of offices, to inhibit the building up by officials of a client-following based on patronage, and to prevent official posts from coming under the control of monopolistic groups of local notabilities, the patrimonial government of the emperor, besides relying on such usual expedients as short-tenure appointments, the exclusion of officials from posts in districts where their own clan members were resident, and surveillance by spies (the so-called Censors), introduced a further device – which here appears for the first time anywhere in the world – namely the system of qualifying examinations and certificates of conduct for office-holding. A man's suitability for office, and for a particular rank in the hierarchy, was decided, in theory exclusively and pretty much in practice as well, by the number of examinations he had passed. The nomination of officials to their posts, their promotion to higher offices or demotion to lower ones, was carried out on the basis of conduct reports ... In terms of formal structure this represented the most thorough-going approach that could have been made to civil service objectivity, and in this sense the Chinese was a radical departure from the true type of patrimonial bureaucracy, in which official position primarily depends on grace and favor. And if personal patronage and the purchase of benefices continued to exist – which was only to be expected – then nevertheless neither feudalization, nor the appropriation of benefices, nor the formation of client groups, was allowed to happen. These tendencies were checked by the action of both negative and positive factors: among the former was the intensive competition and mutual distrust which divided the officialdom against itself; among the latter was the extreme value which Chinese society placed on certificates of education acquired by passing the examinations. As a result the status conventions of the officialdom took on certain characteristic traits which marked with an indelible stamp the whole of Chinese life. These conventions were of a specifically bureaucratic type, were oriented to practical ends, and were the creation of an educated élite which, trained in the classics, regarded dignity and poise as highest among the virtues." [38]

[38] *WuG,* 708-9. Cf. the partial paraphrase in Bendix, *Max Weber,* 353. In the paragraph that follows the passage quoted above Weber gives another reason why China never developed a modern-style bureaucracy, namely that no provision was made for the specialization of functions. Any tendency in that direction was indeed officially discouraged. Hence little attention was given to that specialized training which Weber regarded as a necessary feature of all rational bureaucracy. He refers to English experience, but misses the point completely that a classical education was seen in England (and to some extent is still so seen) as a test of character and a measure of general ability, and therefore as a good practical criterion for the selection of upper bureaucrats. English thinking on this point seems to run parallel to Chinese. Weber contrasts the Confucian ideal, summed up in the saying that "the superior man is not a utensil" (*Anal.* II, 12), with Western insistence on specialized technical training. But the weight

This passage, like all of Weber's high-density writing, raises a number of points simultaneously. The most important is clearly his interpretation of the rôle played by the examination system. The Chinese were well aware that no imperial government with a vast territory to administer could exist without an efficiently functioning bureaucracy; and that therefore the quality and training, and above all the method of selection, of its officials were matters of the greatest moment. The examination system was the end result of a millennial preoccupation with these problems. At its best it tested directly the scholarship of the candidate, particularly his mastery of the Classics and Histories, and his ability to express himself, clearly and elegantly if still in conventional form, as to their meaning and the lessons to be drawn from them; and indirectly it was also a test of character, for the preparation required was a long and arduous one. This is not the place for a detailed analysis of the system. It is enough to note here that Weber systematically neglects the main purpose of the examinations, and regards them instead as the central government's principal weapon *against* the bureaucracy. By him the emphasis is placed on the use of the examination technique to divide and so weaken the officialdom, which otherwise would form a threat to the power of the ruler. He writes, for example, that by stimulating "a competitive struggle for offices on the part of the seekers after prebends, and so preventing them from joining together to become a feudal office-holding nobility, the system thoroughly achieved its aim".[39] And again: "The examination system, which was fully operative from the end of the seventh century, was one of the instruments by means of which the patrimonial ruler was able to prevent the formation of a closed Estate which, in contradistinction to himself, and in the manner of feudal lords and office nobles, would have monopolized all claims to official prebends."[40]

To write in this way is completely to misconceive the purpose served, and the results produced, by the examinations. They were, as is well known, in theory at least open to all, and were certainly competitive. The competition indeed was severe, as only a very small proportion of those who sat for an examination could expect to pass. But it is illegitimate to conclude from this that the competitive struggle was carried over with the same intensity from the examinations themselves into the official career to which they gave en-

---

of the argument is by no means all on one side. Specialization can lead, not to greater efficiency, but to what Robert K. Merton calls "dysfunctions" in the bureaucracy. Compare Veblen's concept of "trained incapacity", glossed by Merton as "that state of affairs in which one's abilities function as inadequacies or blind spots". See his *Social Theory and Social Structure* (Glencoe, 1949), 153. A gain in expertise might be more than offset by a loss in flexibility. It is relevant here that the Chinese mandarin was regarded as an "all-purposes" official. A District Magistrate, for example, was expected to administer his territory, see to its economic prosperity, preside over the district court and, if need be, take personal control of local military operations.

[39]  *KuT*, 408. Cf. Gerth, *Religion*, 119.
[40]  *KuT*, 405. Cf. Gerth, *Religion*, 116.

trance. On the contrary, the fact of having passed the examination transformed the successful candidate from an ordinary person into a member of a restricted élite enjoying immense social prestige and power.[41] To win admission to this influential and privileged group was the goal of every ambitious gentry-member; but once in, it was to the interest of the newly certificated *chü jên* or *chin shih* (Master or Doctor) so to conduct himself as to maintain and reinforce the privileged status of the group to which he now belonged. This is not to say that there were no rivalries or factions in the Chinese civil service, which in these respects was no different from other similar institutions, but rather to insist that status solidarity and not internal struggle was the feature by which it was most strongly marked.

It was suggested above that members of the Chinese bureaucracy, because they were recruited almost exclusively from the gentry class, were subject to the pull of divided, and on occasion conflicting, allegiances. On the one hand, their loyalty was demanded by the service whose functionaries they were; on the other, they had obligations to their social class and, more particularly, to their sib members. It must at the same time be borne in mind that the privileged gentry, as a group, had an overriding interest in the preservation of the social order which underlay and guaranteed their privileged position. It was to their advantage to support any and all forces making for political and social stability,[42] and this imposed certain limits on the distance they were prepared to go in pursuit of their private goals whenever such action seemed likely to weaken unduly the authority of the régime. The presence of a divided loyalty among the members of the bureaucracy remains all the same an important fact, and one with which the central government had to reckon. Hence the "other usual devices" referred to by Weber in the passage quoted above. The rule limiting office-tenures to three years was

---

[41] The term "twice-born" applied earlier in this paper to members of the bureaucracy is hardly an exaggeration. The change of personal status which came with success in the examinations must indeed have seemed the beginning of a new life. It is significant that in the biographical chapters of the Standard Histories the year of the subject's birth is seldom if ever given, but only the year in which he passed the examination to become *chü jên* or *chin shih*. A good account which brings out vividly the excitement which attended the notification of an examination success will be found in the opening chapter of the late Ch'ing novel by Wên Kang, the *Erh nü ying hsiung chuan;* translated by Franz Kuhn under the title *Die Schwarze Reiterin* (Zürich, 1954).

[42] The gentry were at no time a revolutionary force. Nevertheless they were always ready to abandon a *de jure* government which had shown itself incapable of maintaining order, and transfer their support to a revolutionary authority which had seized power and was wielding it effectively. By associating themselves with the new order the educated gentry had little to lose, while if they succeeded in penetrating and influencing it, they had everything to gain. The disorders preceding the establishment of the Ming offer a good example of this pattern of gentry behavior. The movement headed by Chu Yüan-chang began as a social war; but its character changed rapidly as more and more gentry elements, foreseeing its success, and despairing that the Yüan would ever be able to restore the country to peaceful and orderly conditions, infiltrated its ranks and gave it their support.

rigorously enforced for provincial appointments but, understandably, was largely ignored for posts in the bureaus and ministries of the capital, where longer tenures had some advantage and the particular dangers against which the rule was intended to guard were absent. The regulation against officials serving in their native province was again inspired by the desire of the central government to see that its servants would not be unduly exposed to pressures from their own sib members and influential neighbors. Neither these nor other measures of a like kind need to be explained by the fear of a patrimonial ruler that his officials would seek to appropriate their benefices and convert them into hereditary prebends. The gentry origin of the mandarinate is sufficient explanation.

Weber's argument may be summarized as follows: (1) the Chinese bureaucracy, while incorporating certain rational features, was patrimonial in origin and remained essentially so in character down to the end of the imperial era; (2) the fact that it functioned in a society whose economy was predominantly natural, and was never more than partially monetized, meant that there existed an ever-present danger that the sources of taxation would be appropriated by officials and exploited as private property; (3) the most important of the measures introduced by the central government to prevent such a development taking place was the state examination system: this system institutionalized a competitive struggle for prebends among office-seekers, excited mutual distrust among officials, and so divided and weakened the bureaucracy; (4) this, together with the fact that the bureaucracy was of necessity extensive rather than intensive, owing to the smallness of its numbers and the size and imperfect communications of the empire it administered, meant that it was never able fully to master the forces of local traditionalism that dominated the countryside. It is to these that we must now turn.

The last remaining tension of those which Weber emphasized in his analysis of Chinese society was that between the government as a whole, comprising both the inner and outer courts, and the countless, though geographically dispersed, representatives of traditional self-rule in the provinces, the sib elders and leaders of gilds and other professional groups.

Weber deserves the highest praise for his recognition of the lineage as a main key to an understanding of rural China. At the time that he wrote very little attention had been given to this most important institution, and sinologists have only recently begun to appreciate its significance and subject it to detailed study.[43]

---

[43] The pioneering work by D. H. Kulp, *Country Life in South China, The Sociology of Familism* (New York), was published only in 1925. Outstanding in the more recent literature devoted to this subject are: Hu Hsien-chin, *The Common Descent Group in China and Its Functions* (New York, 1948); Maurice Freedman, *Lineage Organization in Southeastern China* (London, 1958); Hsiao Kung-ch'üan, *Rural China, Imperial Control in the Nineteenth Century* (Seattle, 1960). Also useful, despite its semi-

The rôle which Weber assigns to lineage organizations emerges clearly from the following quotations. "The sib, which had in the West as good as lost every particle of its meaning by the Middle Ages, was fully preserved in China; developing to a degree which finds no parallel elsewhere, even in India; and playing a part both in the local administration of even the smallest units and in the life of economic associations. The patrimonial government, exercising its rule from above, clashed with strongly organized lineage institutions whose power sprang from below." [44] Again: "In practice the patrimonial bureaucracy found itself facing a considerable measure of local self-government, usurped or conceded. On the one hand there were the lineages; on the other the organizations of the rural poor. Bureaucratic rationality was confronted by a determined traditionalist power which, on balance and in the long run, proved stronger than itself, both because it possessed continuity and because it was the expression of close-knit personal relationships." [45] And finally: "It was the tremendous power of the lineage, under its strictly patriarchal leadership, that in actual fact made China's so-called 'democracy' possible. But this 'democracy', which has been so much written about, had *nothing whatever* in common with 'modern' democracy. On the contrary, it owed its existence to (1) the abolition of feudal class relations, (2) the fact that the patrimonial bureaucratic administration was so thinly spread over the country, and (3) the structural solidarity and all-embracing authority of the patriarchal sib." [46]

Recent studies of the Chinese lineage suggest that this picture is somewhat overdrawn. The evidence shows that lineage organizations were more numerous, better organized and more influential in South China than in the North.[47] This may be partly due to southward population movements of the Han Chinese under "barbarian" pressure. Such internal migrations were important as early as the Six Dynasties period, and notably after the fall of the Northern Sung and during the Mongol conquest. There are also strong grounds for associating developed lineage structures with local prosperity. The areas of fertile soil, productive agriculture, and dense population, conditions which are found predominantly in the southern and south-eastern provinces, are also those where clan organization is most frequently met

---

fictional form, is Lin Yüeh-hua, *The Golden Wing, A Sociological Study of Chinese Familism* (London, 1948).

[44] *KuT*, 375. Cf. Gerth, *Religion*, 86.

[45] *KuT*, 386. Cf. Gerth, *Religion*, 95. The point about continuity is an important one. The short tenures of officials serving in the provinces, particularly of District Magistrates, made continuity in the carrying out of government policies extremely difficult. Time was generally on the side of the local notabilities.

[46] *KuT*, 386. Cf. Gerth, *Religion*, 96. The italics and quotation marks are Weber's own.

[47] See the present writer's article, "The Geographical Background of the Ming Civil Service" in *Journal of the Economic and Social History of the Orient*, 4 (1961), 302-36, esp. 327-9 and Table V.

with. What forms of social organization, then, took its place in the north and northwest? As often happens, Weber's broad generalizations, which are signpost directions for future and fruitful investigations, are shown to need modification by the very research they provoke.

Weber's view, explained above, that the bureaucracy was deliberately subjected to institutional disabilities by the patrimonial ruler in order to weaken it as a potential threat to his own power, goes hand in hand with an overestimation of the patriarchal forces of local self-rule by which the bureaucracy was confronted. On the one hand we have the officialdom which, by the use of various devices, is "frozen" at a relatively inefficient level, and prevented either from degenerating into an openly feudal system with hereditary offices, or from throwing off its patrimonial nature and progressively growing into a fully rational system; on the other we have the patriarchal clans, nourished at the grass-roots level by the principle of filial piety, whose great local strength and gentry leadership make them a match, and even more than a match, for the officials who briefly sojourn among them. It is no surprise to find Weber writing that "the Chinese official was regularly quite powerless against the local associations, lineages and gilds, whenever these made common cause on particular issues. If they put up a serious and united opposition the mandarin would certainly lose his post".[48] In so depicting the power relationship between central government officials and the local associations Weber is ascribing far too much influence to the latter. A significant measure of local self-government existed in rural China but, to use his own phraseology, it owed its existence more to "concession" from above than to "usurpation" from below. It is to these manifestations of rural self-rule that Wittfogel has applied the term "beggars' democracies".[49]

It is of some interest to note that Wittfogel's account of Chinese society, which in the last analysis is presented as a monolithic despotism, is the exact opposite of that given by Weber. Both scholars can be accused of taking extreme positions. Wittfogel, however, operates with a single major concept: that of the hydraulic society "from which all curses flow"; and while not completely ignoring such factors as internal contradictions within the court, or the conflict between ruler and bureaucracy, or that between the government as such and the local associations, he either dismisses them as irrelevant to the realities of the power struggle or assigns them a minor and secondary rôle. In spite of the mass of detail which he brings together, his picture is essentially monochrome and simplist. In pursuing to the point of

[48]  *WuG*, 524. Cf. Martindale and Neuwirth, *The City*, 83.
[49]  See his *Oriental Despotism*, 108-26. Wittfogel explains these areas of social action, in which certain "politically irrelevant freedoms" are allowed to exist, in terms of the operation of a "law of diminishing administrative returns". After a point has been reached where additional "administrative endeavours cost more than they yield", the central power will allow its measures of control to taper off.

exhaustion his theme of the hydraulic society Wittfogel himself falls victim to a "law of diminishing returns" in yet another guise.

Returning to the question of central versus local power, it must be said that, while "beggars' democracy" is a graphic enough phrase, it conceals more of the truth than it reveals. Traditional Chinese government had its own "style"; and it was one that, wherever feasible, preferred under- to over-administration. The devolution of powers and responsibilities to extra-legal and even informal, as well as to officially constituted, bodies, was a recognized and widely used practice. To write of all local liberties as "politically irrelevant", as Wittfogel does, is misleading. Their political significance, and the areas of social life into which they entered, inevitably varied from time to time and place to place. Some spheres of action were traditionally regarded as mainly the business of the family, the lineage, and the craft and merchant gilds; and here the central government intervened only as a regulator of last resort, and often on the appeal of the local organizations themselves. In this way the lineages and gilds dealt with a wide variety of their internal affairs through their own arbitrational and disciplinary organs, the government remaining in the background. Other activities were equally recognized as falling properly within the competence of government. Among them, naturally, were certain matters, such as the assessment and collection of taxes, which the central government held to be vital to its authority and continued existence; and in these "sensitive" areas it brooked no opposition from local interests. In the last analysis, the emergence of such opposition in an organized form would be classed as rebellion and treated accordingly. Between these two extremes lay an extensive range of local affairs which were carried on in collaboration between the two parties, with the initiative coming now from one, now from the other. The partnership might run smoothly, or not; but the exigencies of the situation and the generally *pianissimo* style of Chinese government demanded that it should be continuous. Compromises were of its essence; and the question as to who, in a given instance, would hold the upper hand, was decided partly by the importance which government attached to getting its own way on some particular point, and partly by the tightness of the local organization and the vigor of its leadership.[50]

If what is written above approaches a true picture, it can be said that Weber, who was writing a full generation before Wittfogel, and was moreover no sinologist, offers an analysis that much more nearly matches the complexity of the subject, and identifies its elements, than the one given in

---

[50] This complicated balance between closely related and sometimes even inter-penetrating forces is not easily described in simple terms. Useful material for its study, particularly in the nineteenth century, is presented in Hsiao's *Rural China* (see note 43 above), esp. chs. 7-10, 261-500. Also important are the two books by Chang Chung-li: *The Chinese Gentry, Studies on Their Role in Nineteenth-Century Chinese Society* (Seattle, 1955); and *The Income of the Chinese Gentry* (Seattle, 1962).

*Oriental Despotism.* Some of Weber's evidence is insecurely founded. Some of his judgments are wrong. He can be convicted of errors of emphasis and stress. He was also a conceptualizer of genius, and on occasion was the prisoner of his concepts. Nevertheless, his success in breaking open a way to a much more searching and profound understanding of the structure of Chinese society and the forces operative in it, is little short of amazing. The account he gives of the bureaucracy well exemplifies the merits and disadvantages of his work. Taken *en gros*, it incorporates basically incorrect, or at any rate one-sided, judgments as to the social rôle, authority, and effectiveness of the officialdom. As against this, everything is gone into; every issue is raised and every important question asked. With his exceptional insight and flair, and with the great wealth of illustrative comparisons his wide reading enabled him to bring to bear on every aspect of his subject, Weber is continually throwing out ideas that have served, and can still serve, to initiate innumerable and always productive new lines of inquiry. A balance struck between the negative and positive sides of his achievement comes out magnificently in Weber's favor.

*Australian National University*

Revised February 1966

# harper ✦ torchbooks

## HUMANITIES AND SOCIAL SCIENCES

### American Studies: General

THOMAS C. COCHRAN: The Inner Revolution: *Essays on the Social Sciences in History* TB/1140

EDWARD S. CORWIN: American Constitutional History. *Essays edited by Alpheus T. Mason and Gerald Garvey* TB/1136

CARL N. DEGLER, Ed.: Pivotal Interpretations of American History TB/1240, TB/1241

A. HUNTER DUPREE: Science in the Federal Government: *A History of Policies and Activities to 1940* TB/573

OSCAR HANDLIN, Ed.: This Was America: *As Recorded by European Travelers in the Eighteenth, Nineteenth and Twentieth Centuries. Illus.* TB/1119

MARCUS LEE HANSEN: The Atlantic Migration: 1607-1860. *Edited by Arthur M. Schlesinger. Introduction by Oscar Handlin* TB/1052

MARCUS LEE HANSEN: The Immigrant in American History. *Edited with a Foreword by Arthur M. Schlesinger* TB/1120

JOHN HIGHAM, Ed.: The Reconstruction of American History TB/1068

ROBERT H. JACKSON: The Supreme Court in the American System of Government TB/1106

JOHN F. KENNEDY: A Nation of Immigrants. *Illus. Revised and Enlarged. Introduction by Robert F. Kennedy* TB/1118

RALPH BARTON PERRY: Puritanism and Democracy TB/1138

ARNOLD ROSE: The Negro in America: *The Condensed Version of Gunnar Myrdal's An American Dilemma* TB/3048

MAURICE R. STEIN: The Eclipse of Community: *An Interpretation of American Studies* TB/1128

W. LLOYD WARNER and Associates: Democracy in Jonesville: *A Study in Quality and Inequality* || TB/1129

W. LLOYD WARNER: Social Class in America: *The Evaluation of Status* TB/1013

### American Studies: Colonial

BERNARD BAILYN, Ed.: The Apologia of Robert Keayne: *Self-Portrait of a Puritan Merchant* TB/1201

BERNARD BAILYN: The New England Merchants in the Seventeenth Century TB/1149

JOSEPH CHARLES: The Origins of the American Party System TB/1049

LAWRENCE HENRY GIPSON: The Coming of the Revolution: 1763-1775. † *Illus.* TB/3007

LEONARD W. LEVY: Freedom of Speech and Press in Early American History: *Legacy of Suppression* TB/1109

PERRY MILLER: Errand Into the Wilderness TB/1139

PERRY MILLER & T. H. JOHNSON, Eds.: The Puritans: *A Sourcebook of Their Writings*
Vol. I TB/1093; Vol. II TB/1094

EDMUND S. MORGAN, Ed.: The Diary of Michael Wigglesworth, 1653-1657: *The Conscience of a Puritan*

EDMUND S. MORGAN: The Puritan Family: *Religion and Domestic Relations in Seventeenth-Century New England* TB/1227

RICHARD B. MORRIS: Government and Labor in Early America TB/1244

KENNETH B. MURDOCK: Literature and Theology in Colonial New England TB/99

WALLACE NOTESTEIN: The English People on the Eve of Colonization: 1603-1630. † *Illus.* TB/3006

LOUIS B. WRIGHT: The Cultural Life of the American Colonies: 1607-1763. † *Illus.* TB/3005

### American Studies: From the Revolution to 1860

JOHN R. ALDEN: The American Revolution: 1775-1783. † *Illus.* TB/3011

MAX BELOFF, Ed.: The Debate on the American Revolution, 1761-1783: *A Sourcebook* TB/1225

RAY A. BILLINGTON: The Far Western Frontier: 1830-1860. † *Illus.* TB/3012

EDMUND BURKE: On the American Revolution: *Selected Speeches and Letters.* ‡ *Edited by Elliott Robert Barkan* TB/3068

WHITNEY R. CROSS: The Burned-Over District: *The Social and Intellectual History of Enthusiastic Religion in Western New York, 1800-1850* TB/1242

GEORGE DANGERFIELD: The Awakening of American Nationalism: 1815-1828. † *Illus.* TB/3061

CLEMENT EATON: The Freedom-of-Thought Struggle in the Old South. *Revised and Enlarged. Illus.* TB/1150

CLEMENT EATON: The Growth of Southern Civilization: 1790-1860. † *Illus.* TB/3040

LOUIS FILLER: The Crusade Against Slavery: 1830-1860. † *Illus.* TB/3029

DIXON RYAN FOX: The Decline of Aristocracy in the Politics of New York: 1801-1840. ‡ *Edited by Robert V. Remini* TB/3064

FELIX GILBERT: The Beginnings of American Foreign Policy: *To the Farewell Address* TB/1200

FRANCIS J. GRUND: Aristocracy in America: *Social Class in the Formative Years of the New Nation* TB/1001

ALEXANDER HAMILTON: The Reports of Alexander Hamilton. ‡ *Edited by Jacob E. Cooke* TB/3060

THOMAS JEFFERSON: Notes on the State of Virginia. ‡ *Edited by Thomas P. Abernethy* TB/3052

JAMES MADISON: The Forging of American Federalism: *Selected Writings of James Madison. Edited by Saul K. Padover* TB/1226

---

† The New American Nation Series, edited by Henry Steele Commager and Richard B. Morris.

‡ American Perspectives series, edited by Bernard Wishy and William E. Leuchtenburg.

* The Rise of Modern Europe series, edited by William L. Langer.

|| Researches in the Social, Cultural, and Behavioral Sciences, edited by Benjamin Nelson.

§ The Library of Religion and Culture, edited by Benjamin Nelson.

Σ Harper Modern Science Series, edited by James R. Newman.

° Not for sale in Canada.

BERNARD MAYO: Myths and Men: *Patrick Henry, George Washington, Thomas Jefferson*                    TB/1108
JOHN C. MILLER: Alexander Hamilton and the Growth of the New Nation                                  TB/3057
RICHARD B. MORRIS, Ed.: The Era of the American Revolution                                            ̄TB/1180
R. B. NYE: The Cultural Life of the New Nation: 1776-1801. † *Illus.*                                  TB/3026
FRANCIS S. PHILBRICK: The Rise of the West, 1754-1830. † *Illus.*                                     TB/3067
TIMOTHY L. SMITH: Revivalism and Social Reform: *Protestantism on the Eve of the Civil War*          TB/1229
FRANK THISTLETHWAITE: America and the Atlantic Community: *Anglo-American Aspects, 1790-1850*  TB/1107
A. F. TYLER: Freedom's Ferment: *Phases of American Social History from the Revolution to the Outbreak of the Civil War. 31 illus.*                                                                               TB/1074
GLYNDON G. VAN DEUSEN: The Jacksonian Era: 1828-1848. † *Illus.*                                      TB/3028
LOUIS B. WRIGHT: Culture on the Moving Frontier          TB/1053

## American Studies: The Civil War to 1900

THOMAS C. COCHRAN & WILLIAM MILLER: The Age of Enterprise: *A Social History of Industrial America* TB/1054
W. A. DUNNING: Essays on the Civil War and Reconstruction. *Introduction by David Donald*             TB/1181
W. A. DUNNING: Reconstruction, Political and Economic: 1865-1877                                      TB/1073
HAROLD U. FAULKNER: Politics, Reform and Expansion: 1890-1900. † *Illus.*                             TB/3020
HELEN HUNT JACKSON: A Century of Dishonor: *The Early Crusade for Indian Reform. ‡ Edited by Andrew F. Rolle*                                                                                                      TB/3063
ALBERT D. KIRWAN: Revolt of the Rednecks: *Mississippi Politics, 1876-1925*                           TB/1199
ROBERT GREEN MC CLOSKEY: American Conservatism in the Age of Enterprise: 1865-1910                    TB/1137
WHITELAW REID: After the War: *A Tour of the Southern States, 1865-1866. ‡ Edited by C. Vann Woodward*                                                                                                              TB/3066
CHARLES H. SHINN: Mining Camps: *A Study in American Frontier Government. ‡ Edited by Rodman W. Paul*                                                                                                                TB/3062
VERNON LANE WHARTON: The Negro in Mississippi: 1865-1890                                              TB/1178

## American Studies: 1900 to the Present

RAY STANNARD BAKER: Following the Color Line: *American Negro Citizenship in Progressive Era. ‡ Illus. Edited by Dewey W. Grantham, Jr.*                                                                            TB/3053
RANDOLPH S. BOURNE: War and the Intellectuals: *Collected Essays, 1915-1919. ‡ Ed. by Carl Resek* TB/3043
A. RUSSELL BUCHANAN: The United States and World War II. † *Illus.*     Vol. I  TB/3044;  Vol. II  TB/3045
ABRAHAM CAHAN: The Rise of David Levinsky: *a documentary novel of social mobility in early twentieth century America. Intro. by John Higham*          TB/1028
THOMAS C. COCHRAN: The American Business System: *A Historical Perspective, 1900-1955*               TB/1080
FOSTER RHEA DULLES: America's Rise to World Power: 1898-1954. † *Illus.*                              TB/3021
JOHN D. HICKS: Republican Ascendancy: 1921-1933. † *Illus.*                                           TB/3041
SIDNEY HOOK: Reason, Social Myths, and Democracy     TB/1237
ROBERT HUNTER: Poverty: *Social Conscience in the Progressive Era. ‡ Edited by Peter d'A. Jones* TB/3065
WILLIAM L. LANGER & S. EVERETT GLEASON: The Challenge to Isolation: *The World Crisis of 1937-1940 and American Foreign Policy*     Vol. I  TB/3054;  Vol. II  TB/3055
WILLIAM E. LEUCHTENBURG: Franklin D. Roosevelt and the New Deal: 1932-1940. † *Illus.*               TB/3025

ARTHUR S. LINK: Woodrow Wilson and the Progressive Era: 1910-1917. † *Illus.*                         TB/3023
GEORGE E. MOWRY: The Era of Theodore Roosevelt and the Birth of Modern America: 1900-1912. † *Illus.*                                                                                                               TB/3022
RUSSEL B. NYE: Midwestern Progressive Politics: *A Historical Study of its Origins and Development, 1870-1958*                                                                                                        TB/1202
WALTER RAUSCHENBUSCH: Christianity and the Social Crisis. ‡ *Edited by Robert D. Cross*              TB/3059
PHILIP SELZNICK: TVA and the Grass Roots: *A Study in the Sociology of Formal Organization*          TB/1230
GEORGE B. TINDALL, Ed.: A Populist Reader ‡           TB/3069
TWELVE SOUTHERNERS: I'll Take My Stand: *The South and the Agrarian Tradition. Intro. by Louis D. Rubin, Jr. Biographical Essays by Virginia Rock*   TB/1072
WALTER E. WEYL: The New Democracy: *An Essay on Certain Political Tendencies in the United States. ‡ Edited by Charles B. Forcey*                                                                                       TB/3042

## Anthropology

JACQUES BARZUN: Race: *A Study in Superstition. Revised Edition*                                      TB/1172
JOSEPH B. CASAGRANDE, Ed.: In the Company of Man: *Twenty Portraits of Anthropological Informants. Illus.*                                                                                                           TB/3047
W. E. LE GROS CLARK: The Antecedents of Man: *Intro. to Evolution of the Primates.* º *Illus.*       TB/559
CORA DU BOIS: The People of Alor. *New Preface by the author. Illus.*     Vol. I  TB/1042;  Vol. II  TB/1043
RAYMOND FIRTH, Ed.: Man and Culture: *An Evaluation of the Work of Bronislaw Malinowski* ‖ º         TB/1133
DAVID LANDY: Tropical Childhood: *Cultural Transmission and Learning in a Rural Puerto Rican Village* ‖                                                                                                             TB/1235
L. S. B. LEAKEY: Adam's Ancestors: *The Evolution of Man and His Culture. Illus.*                    TB/1019
ROBERT H. LOWIE: Primitive Society. *Introduction by Fred Eggan*                                      TB/1056
EDWARD BURNETT TYLOR: The Origins of Culture. *Part I of "Primitive Culture."* § *Intro. by Paul Radin*  TB/33
EDWARD BURNETT TYLOR: Religion in Primitive Culture. *Part II of "Primitive Culture."* § *Intro. by Paul Radin*                                                                                                        TB/34
W. LLOYD WARNER: A Black Civilization: *A Study of an Australian Tribe.* ‖ *Illus.*                   TB/3056

## Art and Art History

WALTER LOWRIE: Art in the Early Church. *Revised Edition. 452 illus.*                                 TB/124
EMILE MÂLE: The Gothic Image: *Religious Art in France of the Thirteenth Century.* § *190 illus.*    TB/44
MILLARD MEISS: Painting in Florence and Siena after the Black Death: *The Arts, Religion and Society in the Mid-Fourteenth Century. 169 illus.*      TB/1148
ERICH NEUMANN: The Archetypal World of Henry Moore. *107 illus.*                                      TB/2020
DORA & ERWIN PANOFSKY: Pandora's Box: *The Changing Aspects of a Mythical Symbol. Revised Edition. Illus.*                                                                                                           TB/2021
ERWIN PANOFSKY: Studies in Iconology: *Humanistic Themes in the Art of the Renaissance. 180 illustrations*                                                                                                            TB/1077
ALEXANDRE PIANKOFF: The Shrines of Tut-Ankh-Amon. *Edited by N. Rambova. 117 illus.*                  TB/2011
JEAN SEZNEC: The Survival of the Pagan Gods: *The Mythological Tradition and Its Place in Renaissance Humanism and Art. 108 illustrations*            TB/2004
OTTO VON SIMSON: The Gothic Cathedral: *Origins of Gothic Architecture and the Medieval Concept of Order. 58 illus.*                                  TB/2018
HEINRICH ZIMMER: Myths and Symbols in Indian Art and Civilization. *70 illustrations*                TB/2005

## Business, Economics & Economic History

REINHARD BENDIX: Work and Authority in Industry: *Ideologies of Management in the Course of Industrialization* TB/3035
GILBERT BURCK & EDITORS OF FORTUNE: The Computer Age: *And Its Potential for Management* TB/1179
THOMAS C. COCHRAN: The American Business System: *A Historical Perspective, 1900-1955* TB/1080
THOMAS C. COCHRAN: The Inner Revolution: *Essays on the Social Sciences in History* TB/1140
THOMAS C. COCHRAN & WILLIAM MILLER: The Age of Enterprise: *A Social History of Industrial America* TB/1054
ROBERT DAHL & CHARLES E. LINDBLOM: Politics, Economics, and Welfare: *Planning & Politico-Economic Systems Resolved into Basic Social Processes* TB/3037
PETER F. DRUCKER: The New Society: *The Anatomy of Industrial Order* TB/1082
EDITORS OF FORTUNE: America in the Sixties: *The Economy and the Society* TB/1015
ROBERT L. HEILBRONER: The Great Ascent: *The Struggle for Economic Development in Our Time* TB/3030
FRANK H. KNIGHT: The Economic Organization TB/1214
FRANK H. KNIGHT: Risk, Uncertainty and Profit TB/1215
ABBA P. LERNER: Everybody's Business: *Current Assumptions in Economics and Public Policy* TB/3051
ROBERT GREEN MC CLOSKEY: American Conservatism in the Age of Enterprise, 1865-1910 TB/1137
PAUL MANTOUX: The Industrial Revolution in the Eighteenth Century: *The Beginnings of the Modern Factory System in England* ⁰ TB/1079
WILLIAM MILLER, Ed.: Men in Business: *Essays on the Historical Role of the Entrepreneur* TB/1081
RICHARD B. MORRIS: Government and Labor in Early America TB/1244
HERBERT SIMON: The Shape of Automation: *For Men and Management* TB/1245
PERRIN STRYKER: The Character of the Executive: *Eleven Studies in Managerial Qualities* TB/1041
PIERRE URI: Partnership for Progress: *A Program for Transatlantic Action* TB/3036

## Contemporary Culture

JACQUES BARZUN: The House of Intellect TB/1051
JOHN U. NEF: Cultural Foundations of Industrial Civilization TB/1024
NATHAN M. PUSEY: The Age of the Scholar: *Observations on Education in a Troubled Decade* TB/1157
PAUL VALÉRY: The Outlook for Intelligence TB/2016

## Historiography & Philosophy of History

JACOB BURCKHARDT: On History and Historians. *Intro. by H. R. Trevor-Roper* TB/1216
WILHELM DILTHEY: Pattern and Meaning in History: *Thoughts on History and Society.* ⁰ *Edited with an Introduction by H. P. Rickman* TB/1075
J. H. HEXTER: Reappraisals in History: *New Views on History & Society in Early Modern Europe* TB/1100
H. STUART HUGHES: History as Art and as Science: *Twin Vistas on the Past* TB/1207
RAYMOND KLIBANSKY & H. J. PATON, Eds.: Philosophy and History: *The Ernst Cassirer Festschrift. Illus.* TB/1115
GEORGE H. NADEL, Ed.: Studies in the Philosophy of History: *Selected Essays from History and Theory* TB/1208
JOSE ORTEGA Y GASSET: The Modern Theme. *Introduction by Jose Ferrater Mora* TB/1038
KARL R. POPPER: The Open Society and Its Enemies
*Vol. I: The Spell of Plato* TB/1101
*Vol. II: The High Tide of Prophecy: Hegel, Marx and the Aftermath* TB/1102
KARL R. POPPER: The Poverty of Historicism ⁰ TB/1126

G. J. RENIER: History: Its Purpose and Method TB/1209
W. H. WALSH: Philosophy of History: *An Introduction* TB/1020

## History: General

L. CARRINGTON GOODRICH: A Short History of the Chinese People. *Illus.* TB/3015
DAN N. JACOBS & HANS H. BAERWALD: Chinese Communism: *Selected Documents* TB/3031
BERNARD LEWIS: The Arabs in History TB/1029

## History: Ancient

A. ANDREWES: The Greek Tyrants TB/1103
ADOLF ERMAN, Ed.: The Ancient Egyptians: *A Sourcebook of Their Writings. New material and Introduction by William Kelly Simpson* TB/1233
MICHAEL GRANT: Ancient History ⁰ TB/1190
SAMUEL NOAH KRAMER: Sumerian Mythology TB/1055
NAPHTALI LEWIS & MEYER REINHOLD, Eds.: Roman Civilization. *Sourcebook I: The Republic* TB/1231
NAPHTALI LEWIS & MEYER REINHOLD, Eds.: Roman Civilization. *Sourcebook II: The Empire* TB/1232

## History: Medieval

P. BOISSONNADE: Life and Work in Medieval Europe: *The Evolution of the Medieval Economy, the 5th to the 15th Century.* ⁰ *Preface by Lynn White, Jr.* TB/1141
HELEN CAM: England before Elizabeth TB/1026
NORMAN COHN: The Pursuit of the Millennium: *Revolutionary Messianism in Medieval and Reformation Europe* TB/1037
G. G. COULTON: Medieval Village, Manor, and Monastery TB/1022
HEINRICH FICHTENAU: The Carolingian Empire: *The Age of Charlemagne* TB/1142
F. L. GANSHOF: Feudalism TB/1058
EDWARD GIBBON: The Triumph of Christendom in the Roman Empire (*Chaps. XV-XX of "Decline and Fall," J. B. Bury edition*). § *Illus.* TB/46
W. O. HASSALL, Ed.: Medieval England: *As Viewed by Contemporaries* TB/1205
DENYS HAY: The Medieval Centuries ⁰ TB/1192
J. M. HUSSEY: The Byzantine World TB/1057
FERDINAND LOT: The End of the Ancient World and the Beginnings of the Middle Ages. *Introduction by Glanville Downey* TB/1044
G. MOLLAT: The Popes at Avignon: 1305-1378 TB/308
CHARLES PETIT-DUTAILLIS: The Feudal Monarchy in France and England: *From the Tenth to the Thirteenth Century* ⁰ TB/1165
HENRI PIRENNE: Early Democracies in the Low Countries: *Urban Society and Political Conflict in the Middle Ages and the Renaissance. Introduction by John H. Mundy* TB/1110
STEVEN RUNCIMAN: A History of the Crusades.
*Volume I: The First Crusade and the Foundation of the Kingdom of Jerusalem. Illus.* TB/1143
*Volume II: The Kingdom of Jerusalem and the Frankish East, 1100-1187. Illus.* TB/1243
FERDINAND SCHEVILL: Siena: *The History of a Medieval Commune. Intro. by William M. Bowsky* TB/1164
SULPICIUS SEVERUS et al.: The Western Fathers: *Being the Lives of Martin of Tours, Ambrose, Augustine of Hippo, Honoratus of Arles and Germanus of Auxerre. Edited and translated by F. R. Hoare* TB/309
HENRY OSBORN TAYLOR: The Classical Heritage of the Middle Ages. *Foreword and Biblio. by Kenneth M. Setton* TB/1117
F. VAN DER MEER: Augustine the Bishop: *Church and Society at the Dawn of the Middle Ages* TB/304
J. M. WALLACE-HADRILL: The Barbarian West: *The Early Middle Ages, A.D. 400-1000* TB/1061

3

*History: Modern European*

ERWIN PANOFSKY: Studies in Iconology: *Humanistic Themes in the Art of the Renaissance. 180 illustrations* TB/1077

JEAN SEZNEC: The Survival of the Pagan Gods: *The Mythological Tradition and its Place in Renaissance Humanism and Art. 108 illustrations* TB/2004

HELLMUT WILHELM: Change: *Eight Lectures on the I Ching* TB/2019

HEINRICH ZIMMER: Myths and Symbols in Indian Art and Civilization. *70 illustrations* TB/2005

## Philosophy

G. E. M. ANSCOMBE: An Introduction to Wittgenstein's Tractatus. *Second edition, Revised.* ° TB/1210

HENRI BERGSON: Time and Free Will: *An Essay on the Immediate Data of Consciousness* ° TB/1021

H. J. BLACKHAM: Six Existentialist Thinkers: *Kierkegaard, Nietzsche, Jaspers, Marcel, Heidegger, Sartre* ° TB/1002

CRANE BRINTON: Nietzsche. *New Preface, Bibliography and Epilogue by the Author* TB/1197

ERNST CASSIRER: The Individual and the Cosmos in Renaissance Philosophy. *Translated with an Introduction by Mario Domandi* TB/1097

ERNST CASSIRER: Rousseau, Kant and Goethe. *Introduction by Peter Gay* TB/1092

FREDERICK COPLESTON: Medieval Philosophy ° TB/376

F. M. CORNFORD: Principium Sapientiae: *A Study of the Origins of Greek Philosophical Thought. Edited by W. K. C. Guthrie* TB/1213

F. M. CORNFORD: From Religion to Philosophy: *A Study in the Origins of Western Speculation* § TB/20

WILFRID DESAN: The Tragic Finale: *An Essay on the Philosophy of Jean-Paul Sartre* TB/1030

A. P. D'ENTRÈVES: Natural Law: *An Historical Survey* TB/1223

HERBERT FINGARETTE: The Self in Transformation: *Psychoanalysis, Philosophy and the Life of the Spirit* ‖ TB/1177

PAUL FRIEDLÄNDER: Plato: *An Introduction* TB/2017

ÉTIENNE GILSON: Dante and Philosophy TB/1089

WILLIAM CHASE GREENE: Moira: *Fate, Good, and Evil in Greek Thought* TB/1104

W. K. C. GUTHRIE: The Greek Philosophers: *From Thales to Aristotle* ° TB/1008

F. H. HEINEMANN: Existentialism and the Modern Predicament TB/28

ISAAC HUSIK: A History of Medieval Jewish Philosophy JP/3

EDMUND HUSSERL: Phenomenology and the Crisis of Philosophy. *Translated with an Introduction by Quentin Lauer* TB/1170

IMMANUEL KANT: The Doctrine of Virtue, *being Part II of The Metaphysic of Morals. Trans. with Notes & Intro. by Mary J. Gregor. Foreword by H. J. Paton* TB/110

IMMANUEL KANT: Groundwork of the Metaphysic of Morals. *Trans. & analyzed by H. J. Paton* TB/1159

IMMANUEL KANT: Lectures on Ethics. § *Introduction by Lewis W. Beck* TB/105

IMMANUEL KANT: Religion Within the Limits of Reason Alone. § *Intro. by T. M. Greene & J. Silber* TB/67

QUENTIN LAUER: Phenomenology: *Its Genesis and Prospect* TB/1169

GABRIEL MARCEL: Being and Having: *An Existential Diary. Intro. by James Collins* TB/310

GEORGE A. MORGAN: What Nietzsche Means TB/1198

PHILO, SAADYA GAON, & JEHUDA HALEVI: Three Jewish Philosophers. *Ed. by Hans Lewy, Alexander Altmann, & Isaak Heinemann* TB/813

MICHAEL POLANYI: Personal Knowledge: *Towards a Post-Critical Philosophy* TB/1158

WILLARD VAN ORMAN QUINE: Elementary Logic: *Revised Edition* TB/577

WILLARD VAN ORMAN QUINE: From a Logical Point of View: *Logico-Philosophical Essays* TB/566

BERTRAND RUSSELL et al.: The Philosophy of Bertrand Russell. *Edited by Paul Arthur Schilpp*
Vol. I TB/1095; Vol. II TB/1096

L. S. STEBBING: A Modern Introduction to Logic TB/538

ALFRED NORTH WHITEHEAD: Process and Reality: *An Essay in Cosmology* TB/1033

PHILIP P. WIENER: Evolution and the Founders of Pragmatism. *Foreword by John Dewey* TB/1212

WILHELM WINDELBAND: A History of Philosophy
Vol. I: *Greek, Roman, Medieval* TB/38
Vol. II: *Renaissance, Enlightenment, Modern* TB/39

LUDWIG WITTGENSTEIN: The Blue and Brown Books ° TB/1211

## Political Science & Government

JEREMY BENTHAM: The Handbook of Political Fallacies. *Introduction by Crane Brinton* TB/1069

KENNETH E. BOULDING: Conflict and Defense: *A General Theory* TB/3024

CRANE BRINTON: English Political Thought in the Nineteenth Century TB/1071

EDWARD S. CORWIN: American Constitutional History: *Essays edited by Alpheus T. Mason and Gerald Garvey* TB/1136

ROBERT DAHL & CHARLES E. LINDBLOM: Politics, Economics, and Welfare: *Planning and Politico-Economic Systems Resolved into Basic Social Processes* TB/3037

JOHN NEVILLE FIGGIS: The Divine Right of Kings. *Introduction by G. R. Elton* TB/1191

JOHN NEVILLE FIGGIS: Political Thought from Gerson to Grotius: *1414-1625: Seven Studies. Introduction by Garrett Mattingly* TB/1032

F. L. GANSHOF: Feudalism TB/1058

G. P. GOOCH: English Democratic Ideas in Seventeenth Century TB/1006

J. H. HEXTER: More's Utopia: *The Biography of an Idea. New Epilogue by the Author* TB/1195

SIDNEY HOOK: Reason, Social Myths and Democracy TB/1237

ROBERT H. JACKSON: The Supreme Court in the American System of Government TB/1106

DAN N. JACOBS, Ed.: The New Communist Manifesto & *Related Documents. Third edition, Revised* TB/1078

DAN N. JACOBS & HANS BAERWALD, Eds.: Chinese Communism: *Selected Documents* TB/3031

ROBERT GREEN MCCLOSKEY: American Conservatism in the Age of Enterprise, 1865-1910 TB/1137

KINGSLEY MARTIN: French Liberal Thought in the Eighteenth Century: *Political Ideas from Bayle to Condorcet* TB/1114

ROBERTO MICHELS: First Lectures in Political Sociology. *Edited by Alfred De Grazia* ‖ ° TB/1224

JOHN STUART MILL: On Bentham and Coleridge. *Introduction by F. R. Leavis* TB/1070

BARRINGTON MOORE, JR.: Political Power and Social Theory: *Seven Studies* ‖ TB/1221

BARRINGTON MOORE, JR.: Soviet Politics—The Dilemma of Power: *The Role of Ideas in Social Change* ‖ TB/1222

JOHN B. MORRALL: Political Thought in Medieval Times TB/1076

JOHN PLAMENATZ: German Marxism and Russian Communism. ° *New Preface by the Author* TB/1189

KARL R. POPPER: The Open Society and Its Enemies
Vol. I: *The Spell of Plato* TB/1101
Vol. II: *The High Tide of Prophecy: Hegel, Marx, and the Aftermath* TB/1102

HENRI DE SAINT-SIMON: Social Organization, The Science of Man, and Other Writings. *Edited and Translated by Felix Markham* TB/1152

JOSEPH A. SCHUMPETER: Capitalism, Socialism and Democracy TB/3008

CHARLES H. SHINN: Mining Camps: *A Study in American Frontier Government.* ‡ *Edited by Rodman W. Paul* TB/3062

## Psychology

ALFRED ADLER: The Individual Psychology of Alfred Adler. *Edited by Heinz L. and Rowena R. Ansbacher* TB/1154
ALFRED ADLER: Problems of Neurosis. *Introduction by Heinz L. Ansbacher* TB/1145
ANTON T. BOISEN: The Exploration of the Inner World: *A Study of Mental Disorder and Religious Experience* TB/87
HERBERT FINGARETTE: The Self in Transformation: *Psychoanalysis, Philosophy and the Life of the Spirit* ‖ TB/1177
SIGMUND FREUD: On Creativity and the Unconscious: *Papers on the Psychology of Art, Literature, Love, Religion.* § *Intro. by Benjamin Nelson* TB/45
C. JUDSON HERRICK: The Evolution of Human Nature TB/545
WILLIAM JAMES: Psychology: *The Briefer Course. Edited with an Intro. by Gordon Allport* TB/1034
C. G. JUNG: Psychological Reflections TB/2001
C. G. JUNG: Symbols of Transformation: *An Analysis of the Prelude to a Case of Schizophrenia. Illus.*
Vol. I: TB/2009; Vol. II TB/2010
C. G. JUNG & C. KERÉNYI: Essays on a Science of Mythology: *The Myths of the Divine Child and the Divine Maiden* TB/2014
JOHN T. MC NEILL: A History of the Cure of Souls TB/126
KARL MENNINGER: Theory of Psychoanalytic Technique TB/1144
ERICH NEUMANN: Amor and Psyche: *The Psychic Development of the Feminine* TB/2012
ERICH NEUMANN: The Archetypal World of Henry Moore. *107 illus.* TB/2020
ERICH NEUMANN: The Origins and History of Consciousness Vol. I *Illus.* TB/2007; Vol. II TB/2008
C. P. OBERNDORF: A History of Psychoanalysis in America TB/1147
RALPH BARTON PERRY: The Thought and Character of William James: *Briefer Version* TB/1156
JEAN PIAGET, BÄRBEL INHELDER, & ALINA SZEMIŅSKA: The Child's Conception of Geometry ° TB/1146
JOHN H. SCHAAR: Escape from Authority: *The Perspectives of Erich Fromm* TB/1155

## Sociology

JACQUES BARZUN: Race: *A Study in Superstition. Revised Edition* TB/1172
BERNARD BERELSON, Ed.: The Behavioral Sciences Today TB/1127
ABRAHAM CAHAN: The Rise of David Levinsky: *A documentary novel of social mobility in early twentieth century America. Intro. by John Higham* TB/1028
THOMAS C. COCHRAN: The Inner Revolution: *Essays on the Social Sciences in History* TB/1140
ALLISON DAVIS & JOHN DOLLARD: Children of Bondage: *The Personality Development of Negro Youth in the Urban South* ‖ TB/3049
ST. CLAIR DRAKE & HORACE R. CAYTON: Black Metropolis: *A Study of Negro Life in a Northern City. Revised and Enlarged. Intro. by Everett C. Hughes*
Vol. I TB/1086; Vol. II TB/1087
EMILE DURKHEIM et al.: Essays on Sociology and Philosophy: *With Analyses of Durkheim's Life and Work.* ‖ *Edited by Kurt H. Wolff* TB/1151
LEON FESTINGER, HENRY W. RIECKEN & STANLEY SCHACHTER: When Prophecy Fails: *A Social and Psychological Account of a Modern Group that Predicted the Destruction of the World* ‖ TB/1132

ALVIN W. GOULDNER: Wildcat Strike: *A Study in Worker-Management Relationships* ‖ TB/1176
FRANCIS J. GRUND: Aristocracy in America: *Social Class in the Formative Years of the New Nation* TB/1001
KURT LEWIN: Field Theory in Social Science: *Selected Theoretical Papers.* ‖ *Edited with a Foreword by Dorwin Cartwright* TB/1135
R. M. MACIVER: Social Causation TB/1153
ROBERT K. MERTON, LEONARD BROOM, LEONARD S. COTTRELL, JR., Editors: Sociology Today: *Problems and Prospects* ‖ Vol. I TB/1173; Vol. II TB/1174
ROBERTO MICHELS: First Lectures in Political Sociology. *Edited by Alfred De Grazia* ‖ ° TB/1224
BARRINGTON MOORE, JR.: Political Power and Social Theory: *Seven Studies* ‖ TB/1221
BARRINGTON MOORE, JR.: Soviet Politics—The Dilemma of Power: *The Role of Ideas in Social Change* ‖ TB/1222
TALCOTT PARSONS & EDWARD A. SHILS, Editors: Toward a General Theory of Action: *Theoretical Foundations for the Social Sciences* TB/1083
JOHN H. ROHRER & MUNRO S. EDMONSON, Eds.: The Eighth Generation Grows Up: *Cultures and Personalities of New Orleans Negroes* ‖ TB/3050
ARNOLD ROSE: The Negro in America: *The Condensed Version of Gunnar Myrdal's An American Dilemma* TB/3048
KURT SAMUELSSON: Religion and Economic Action: *A Critique of Max Weber's The Protestant Ethic and the Spirit of Capitalism.* ‖ ° *Trans. by E. G. French. Ed. with Intro. by D. C. Coleman* TB/1131
PHILIP SELZNICK: TVA and the Grass Roots: *A Study in the Sociology of Formal Organization* TB/1230
GEORG SIMMEL et al.: Essays on Sociology, Philosophy, and Aesthetics. | *Edited by Kurt H. Wolff* TB/1234
HERBERT SIMON: The Shape of Automation: *For Men and Management* TB/1245
PITIRIM A. SOROKIN: Contemporary Sociological Theories. *Through the First Quarter of the 20th Century* TB/3046
MAURICE R. STEIN: The Eclipse of Community: *An Interpretation of American Studies* TB/1128
FERDINAND TÖNNIES: Community and Society: *Gemeinschaft und Gesellschaft. Translated and edited by Charles P. Loomis* TB/1116
W. LLOYD WARNER & Associates: Democracy in Jonesville: *A Study in Quality and Inequality* TB/1129
W. LLOYD WARNER: Social Class in America: *The Evaluation of Status* TB/1013

# RELIGION

## Ancient & Classical

J. H. BREASTED: Development of Religion and Thought in Ancient Egypt. *Introduction by John A. Wilson* TB/57
HENRI FRANKFORT: Ancient Egyptian Religion: *An Interpretation* TB/77
G. RACHEL LEVY: Religious Conceptions of the Stone Age and their Influence upon European Thought. *Illus. Introduction by Henri Frankfort* TB/106
MARTIN P. NILSSON: Greek Folk Religion. *Foreword by Arthur Darby Nock* TB/78
ALEXANDRE PIANKOFF: The Shrines of Tut-Ankh-Amon. *Edited by N. Rambova. 117 illus.* TB/2011
H. J. ROSE: Religion in Greece and Rome TB/55

## Biblical Thought & Literature

W. F. ALBRIGHT: The Biblical Period from Abraham to Ezra TB/102
C. K. BARRETT, Ed.: The New Testament Background: *Selected Documents* TB/86
C. H. DODD: The Authority of the Bible TB/43
M. S. ENSLIN: Christian Beginnings TB/5
M. S. ENSLIN: The Literature of the Christian Movement TB/6

## Christianity: The Roman and Eastern Traditions

## Oriental Religions: Far Eastern, Near Eastern

## Philosophy of Religion

## Religion, Culture & Society

# NATURAL SCIENCES AND MATHEMATICS

## Biological Sciences

BOSTON PUBLIC LIBRARY

3 9999 00300 962 6

# WITHDRAWN

No longer the property of the
Boston Public Library.
Sale of this material benefited the Library

---

**Boston Public Library**

Copley Square

General Library

D16
.8
.H625

0651265277

The Date Due Card in the pocket indicates the date on or before which this
book should be returned to the Library.

Please do not remove cards from this
pocket.